THE PRENUPTIAL INVESTIGATION

A HISTORICAL SYNOPSIS AND A CANONICAL COMMENTARY

The Catholic University of America
Canon Law Studies
No. 274

THE PRENUPTIAL INVESTIGATION

A Historical Synopsis and Commentary

BY
REV. THOMAS B. FULTON, J.C.L.
Priest of the Archdiocese of Toronto

A DISSERTATION

SUBMITTED TO THE FACULTY OF THE SCHOOL OF CANON LAW OF THE CATHOLIC UNIVERSITY OF AMERICA IN PARTIAL FULFILLMENT OF THE REQUIREMENTS FOR THE DEGREE OF DOCTOR IN CANON LAW

The Catholic University of America Press
Washington, D.C.
1948

NIHIL OBSTAT:

JOANNES ROGG SCHMIDT, A.B. J.C.D.
Censor Deputatus,
Washingtonii, die I iunii, 1948.

IMPRIMATUR:

✠JACOBUS C. CARDINAL MCGUIGAN, D.D.,
Archiepiscopus Torontinus,
Toronto, die 5 iunii, 1948.

PRINTED BY
THE MISSION PRESS,
67 BOND STREET,
TORONTO, CANADA

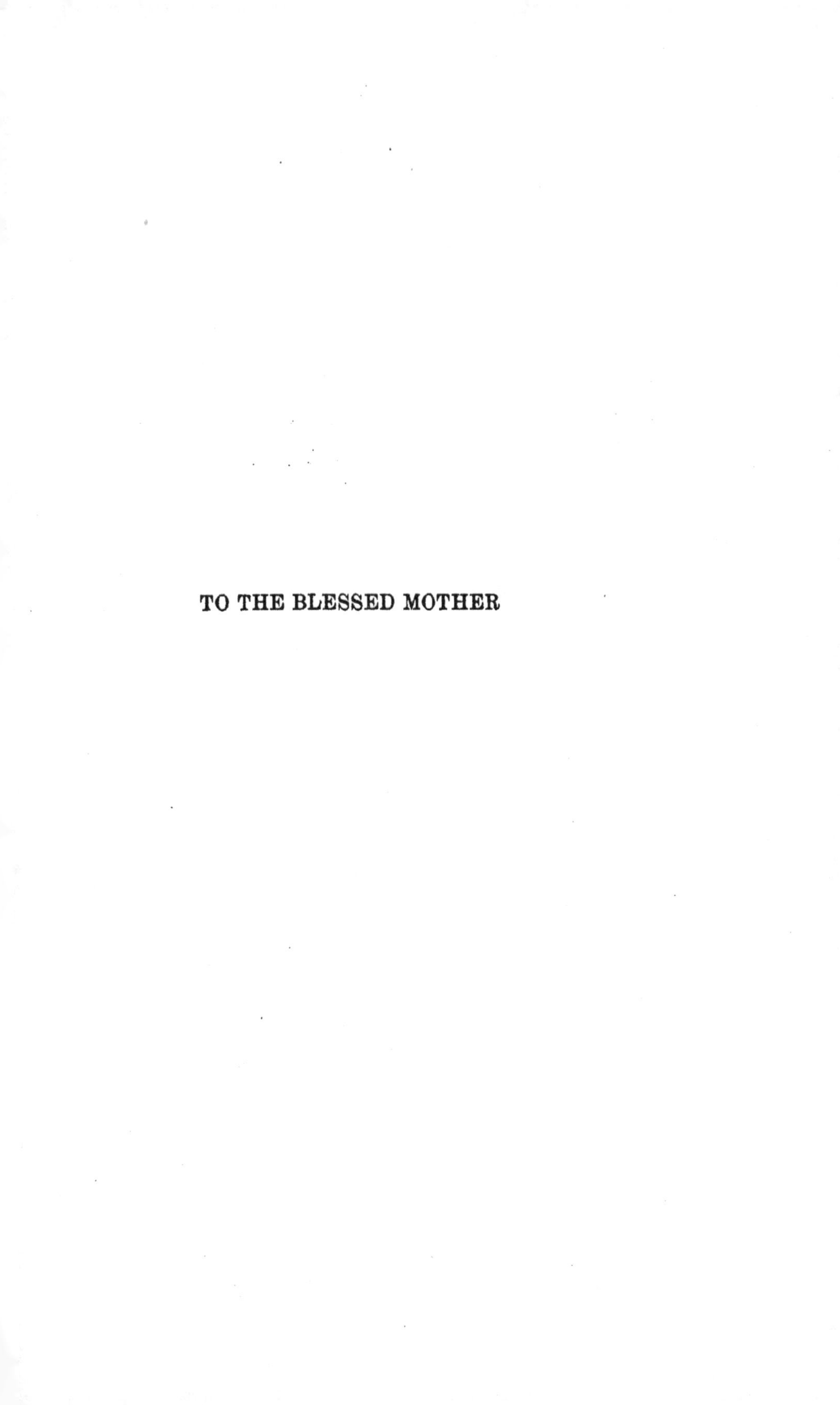

TO THE BLESSED MOTHER

TABLE OF CONTENTS

CHAPTER IX

PAGE

CHAPTER X

FOREWORD

The Catholic Church is the divinely appointed dispenser and custodian of the Sacraments of the New Law. Its constant solicitude in fulfilling this sacred duty is nowhere more strikingly demonstrated than in the manner in which it has consistently defended the sanctity and dignity of the eminently social sacrament of matrimony, upon which depends to so great an extent the welfare of human society and the happiness of countless individuals in that society. In every age the voice of Christ's Church has been raised in condemnation of false and evil theories, which have threatened to dishonor and disrespect this sacred institution. More important, however, is the systematic matrimonial legislation which it has established in harmony with the Divine Law and augmented with centuries of wise experience. This legislation is both theoretical and practical; it considers the fundamental elements essential to a valid marriage, and determines their application in practice.

In the category of practical regulations, the prenuptial investigation holds fundamentally an important position, for it safeguards directly the approach and the entrance to the married state. A well conducted investigation gives assurance of a valid marriage, for it determines that the elements essential to a proper union are present in a particular case, and on the other hand that there is nothing present which can detract from a valid and licit celebration. Its importance in the modern era can hardly be over-emphasized. Large and populous cities with parishes unprecedented in size, along with the easy and frequent modes of travel, bring before the pastor of today prospective candidates for marriage of whom he knows little or nothing. Yet in these difficult circumstances the pastor must decide whether or not they are fit subjects for a valid and lawful union; whether or not the marriage is being contracted with a knowledge and realization of the true Christan nature of the contract. These questions upon which depend so largely the future success and happiness of the marriage can be answered only by means of a diligent and conclusive investigation.

The obligation of conducting this investigation was placed upon pastors by the Code of Canon Law, which became effective in the year 1918. The precise norms by which the pastor is to be guided in the actual prosecution of this duty were recently outlined in an Instruction which the Sacred Congregation of the Sacraments issued on June 29, 1941.

It is the purpose of this dissertation to discuss these various regulations in order that a clear and exact understanding may be had of them. The first section of the work will attempt to outline the historical background and development of this legal institution of prenuptial investigation from the time of its original appearance to the promulgation of the Code of Canon Law. The second section will consider in detail the various elements of the current legislation.

The writer wishes to take this occasion to express his gratitude to His Eminence, James C. Cardinal McGuigan, Archbishop of Toronto, for the opportunity of pursuing graduate studies in Canon Law at The Catholic University of America; to the members of the Faculty of the School of Canon Law for their kind assistance and helpful direction during his course at the University; and to all others who contributed by their interest and aid towards the completion of this work.

PART ONE

HISTORICAL SYNOPSIS

CHAPTER I

PROVISIONS ASSURING THE VALIDITY OF THE MATRIMONIAL CONTRACT PRIOR TO THE FOURTH LATERAN COUNCIL (1215)

No universal legislation regarding the prenuptial investigation appeared before the Fourth Lateran Council (1215). In the preceding years, salutary customs, consonant with the Christian ideals of the sacredness of the institute of marriage, served to safeguard the dignity bestowed on it by Christ. When evils arose, threatening to infringe upon this sanctity, definite local pronouncements were enacted with a view to fortifying the sacrament and to preserving it safe from these influences. Although these enactments were often isolated items of legislation, their efficacy was such that, through gradual diffusion, they formed the basis for later general developments and the final statutes for the Universal Church. These influences, relative to the prenuptial investigation, will be considered in the first chapter.

Article I. Influence of Roman Law

The marriage of the early Christians was greatly influenced by the law and customs of the Empire into which the Church was born. It seems that Christian marriage was simply that of the Roman law, and especially of Roman custom, with a prayer of Christian blessing added somewhere in the ceremony[1]. But in the highly organized legal system of Rome with its wealth of matrimonial legislation, there was nevertheless

[1] Oscar D. Watkins, *Holy Matrimony* (New York, 1895), p. 90; Franciscus X. Wernz, *Ius Decretalium*, Vol. IV, *Ius Matrimoniale Ecclesiae Catholicae* (Romae, I, 1904), n. 153, p. 213; Dodwell, *The Time and Place for the Celebration of Marriage*, The Catholic University of America Canon Law Studies, n. 154 (Washington, D.C.: The Catholic University of America Press, 1942), p. 3.

no indication of any prescribed prenuptial investigation. A slight suggestion thereof could possibly be construed from the seventy-fourth Novel of Justinian (527-565)[2]. Therein it was stated that those of noble rank who desired to enter marriage without the customary dotal contract which was required of such persons were compelled to approach the Defender of the Most Holy Church and declare their intention. A statement to this effect was drawn up by the Defender and signed by three or four clerics who acted as witnesses. This document was to be preserved in the Church archives. This practice, however, seems to have been required not as a form of prenuptial investigation but as a necessary documentary proof of such marriages.

Nevertheless the free status of the contracting parties and the consequent validity of the marriage was assured by the existing institutions. The *sponsalia* or bethrothal which preceded marriage, through the knowledge it occasioned regarding the contracting parties, served to uncover any existing impediments.[3] Furthermore, the consent of the *paterfamilias* was indispensable for a lawful union, and it was not likely that this consent would be given to a marriage which was contrary to the law, or which would bring disgrace and dishonor upon the family name.[4] Finally, the severe penalties imposed upon delinquents dissuaded both the head of the family and the contracting parties from permitting or entering unlawful unions.[5]

Article 2. Influence of the Early Religious Ceremony

From the earliest days the Church began to accompany the contract of marriage with a religious ceremony befitting the reception of a divinely instituted sacrament. Apparently the essential ceremony consisted in the reception of a special nuptial

[2] N. (74.4) 2.

[3] D. (23.1) 1-18; C. (5.12); Corbett, *The Roman Law of Marriage* (Oxford: Clarendon Press, 1930), p. 23.

[4] I. (1.10); D. (23.2) 18; C. (5.40) 3; R. W. Leage, *Roman Private Law* (2. ed., edited by C. H. Ziegler, London: MacMillan, 1932), p. 99.

[5] I. (1.10) 12; D. (3.2) 1; D. (23.2) 51; C. (5.5) 2, 3, 4, 6; C. (5.8) 2; C. (5.9) 1, 2.

blessing, and later also in the spouses' attendance at the Holy Sacrifice of the Mass.[6] Although it is certain that the observance of this religious ceremony was in no way required for the validity of the marriage, nevertheless it brought the majority of contemplated unions directly to the attention of the clergy. It is not rash to assume that the zealous clergy of those early centuries made a substantial effort to ascertain whether or not the parties who approached them were both worthy and capable of receiving this sacrament. As evidence to support these assertions a few excerpts from early Christian writers are cited below.

St. Ignatius of Antioch (107) in his letter to St. Polycarp (155/156) bore testimony to the interest of the bishops of the Church in the marriage of their subjects. He wrote: "For those of both sexes who contemplate marriage it is proper to enter the union with the sanction of the bishop."[7] No definite juridical obligation can be deduced from this statement, since it is phrased in the language of counsel rather than of command, but it is noteworthy as an indication that marriages were referred to the clergy for their ratification.

Tertullian (ca. 230) condemned those marriages which Christians contracted outside the Church, while on the other hand he praised those marriages as ideal in which the Christians received all the blessings amid the accompanying ceremonies.[8] Pope Siricius (384-399) referred specifically to the blessing to be imposed by the priest on the woman about to be married.[9] Simi-

[6] Ludovicus A. Muratori, *Liturgia Romana Vetus* (2 Vols., Venetiis: 1748), I, 244, 245; 446, 447; 721-723. In these passages the author discusses the religious ceremonial of marriage as incorporated in the Leonine and Gelasian sacramentaries.

[7] C. 5, F.X. Funk, *Patres Apostolici* (2 ed., 2 vols., Tubingae, 1901), I, 291; Translation from J. Kleist, *The Epistles of St. Clement of Rome and St. Ignatius of Antioch, Ancient Christian Writers*, n. 1 (ed. J. Quasten and J. C. Plumpe, Washington: Newman Bookshop, 1946), p. 98.

[8] *De Pudicitia*, c. 4—*Corpus Scriptorum Ecclesiasticorum Latinorum*, XX (ed. Augustus Reifferscheid et Georgius Wissowa, Vindobonae: 1890), p. 225.

[9] *Epistola ad Himerium*, c. 4—J. P. Migne, *Patrologiae Cursus Completus, Series Latina* (221 vols., Parisiis: 1844-1864), XIII, 1136 (hereafter cited MPL); Philippus Jaffe, *Regesta Pontificium Romanorum ab Condita Ecclesia ad annum post Christum natum MCXCVIII* (2. ed., correctum et auctam auspiciis Gulielmi Wattenbach curaverunt F. Kaltenbrunner, P. Ewald, S. Lowenfeld, 2 tomes in 1 vol., Lipsiae; 1885-1888; cited as JK, JE, and JL), JK, n. 255.

larly Pope Innocent I (407-417) was quite emphatic in speaking of this nuptial blessing inasmuch as he termed it a divine institution.[10] St. Ambrose (397) spoke of the sanctification of marriage by means of the priest's blessing as obligatory.[11] Pope Hormisdas (514-523) likewise spoke of the essential blessing of the priest, according to a letter cited by Gratian.[12] St. Isidore of Seville (560-636) bore witness to similar observances in Spain.[13]

The *Statuta Ecclesiae Antiqua,* for a long time falsely attributed to the IV Council of Carthage (398), but now recognized as originating towards the middle of the fifth century,[14] indicated the customary ceremony which was observed: "When the bridegroom and the bride are to receive the blessing of the priest, let them be conducted by their parents or by the bridesmaids, and when they have received the benediction, let them out of respect for the blessing remain the same night in virginity."[15]

Article 3. Introduction of an Actual Prenuptial Investigation and its Immediate Causes.

Two evils in particular accelerated the development and introduction of the prenuptial investigation as a necessary prelude to marriage: the prevalence of marriages between blood-relatives and the equally prevalent clandestine marriages. The social and economic background of the early middle ages was largely responsible for the increasing number of marriages contracted by those who were related by ties of blood. Communities lived a rather segregated existence, social and commercial intercourse between the scattered localities was infrequent, travel was of a restricted nature. As a result of these conditions very

[10] Epistola ad Victricium, c. 6—MPL, XX, 475; JK, n. 286.

[11] *Epistalo XIX ad Vigilium,* c. 7—MPL, XV, 984.

[12] C. 2, C. XXX, q.5: this letter, however, is considered apocryphal, and is not found in any of the collections of letters of the early Popes. Cf. A. Thiel, *Epistolae Romanorum Pontificum Genuinae a S. Hilario usque ad Pelagium II,* I (Brunsbergae, 1868), p. 1006.

[13] *De Ecclesiasticis Officis,* lib. II, c.20— *MPL,* LXXXIII, 810.

[14] A. Van Hove, *Prolegomena ad Codicem Iuris Canonici* (editio altera auctior et emendatior, Mechliniae: Romae H. Dessain, 1945), pp. 152-153.

[15] C. 13—H. T. Bruns, *Canones Apostolorum et Consiliorum Saeculorum IV, V, VI, VII* (2 vols., Berolini: 1839), I, 143.

often marriage partners were sought from among one's kinfolk.[16]

The Church had originally accepted the prescriptions of Roman Law concerning the impediment of blood-relationship without adding any determinations of a distinctly ecclesiastical character.[17] From the sixth century forward, however, the impediment was considered in many councils. There were enactments which condemned these incestuous unions and defined the exact degrees of blood-relationship within which marriages were forbidden.[18] The Council of Friuli (791) gave quite definite directions in this regard. It prescribed that during the time of the espousal the priest should ascertain from neighbours and the older people of the locality who were acquainted with the families of the espoused, whether or not there existed between the parties any ties of blood which would prevent a valid and lawful union.[19]

In the Capitulary of Charlemagne (802) there was a further specific indication of a definitely required prenuptial investigation. The enactment was occasioned by the prevalent evil of incestuous unions.[20] The Emperor decreed that a diligent inquiry be conducted by the bishops and priests for the purpose of determining the existence of the impediment of blood-relationship in those parties in whom it was suspected.

---

[16] Francis X. Wahl, *The Matrimonial Impediments of Consanguinity and Affinity*, The Catholic University of America Canon Law Studies, n. 90 (Washington, D.C.: The Catholic University of America, 1934), pp. 18, 19.

[17] F. Wernz-P. Vidal, *Ius Canonicum*, V, *Ius Matrimoniale* (e. ed., a P. Aguirre recognita, Romae: Apud Aedes Universitatis Gregoriana, 1946), n. 346, pp. 431-435 (hereafter cited *Ius Matrimoniale*). Herein is discussed the controverted question as to the exact extent of the impediment in Roman law, and its consequent acceptance by the Church.

[18] Council of Epaon (517), c. 30—*Monumenta Germaniae Historica*, Legum Sectio III, *Concilia Aevi Merowingici*, Tomus I (ed. a Werminghoff, Hannoverae: 1893), p. 26 (hereafter cited as *MGH Concilia)*; Council of Auvergne (535), c. 12—*MGH, Concilia*, I, 68: III Council of Orleans (538), c. 11—*MGH, Concilia*, I. 76; Council of Tours (567), c. 22—*MGH, Concilia*, I, 131; Council of Paris (614), c. 16—*MGH, Concilia*, I, 190; Council of Rome (721), cc. 8, 9—Jean Hardouin, *Acta Conciliorum et Epistolae Decretales ac Constitutiones Summorum Pontificum* (12 vols., Parisiis: 1714-1715, III, 1885).

[19] Ioannes Mansi, *Sacrorum Conciliorum Nova et Amplissima Collectio* (53 vols. in 60, Parisiis-Arnhem-Lipsiae, 1901-1927. XIII, 848 hereafter cited as Mansi.)

[20] *Capitulare Missorum Generale*, c. 35—*MGH*, Legum Sectio II, *Capitularia Regum Francorum*, Tomus I (edd. a A Boretius et Victor Krause, Hannoverae, 1883), p. 98.

Similarly Benedict the Levite (middle of the 9th century) mentioned that a prenuptial investigation was to be instituted in the church. The examination was to center, not only upon the impediment of blood-relationship, but also upon that of a possible previous valid marriage or espousal.[21]

Likewise the problem of clandestine marriages occasioned numerous pronouncements and gave further impetus to the development of the investigation. It was made clear that the desired type of marriage was that which was contracted before the ministers of the Church, and in which the parties received the blessing of the priest amid all the accompanying ceremonies, as detailed in the preceding article. Marriages contracted contrary to these regulations were consistently discouraged, and the approved marriage was repeatedly recommended.

Numerous councils insisted that marriage be celebrated at the doors of the church, or *in facie ecclesiae,* in the presence of the priest and witnesses with the giving of the nuptial blessing and the attendance at the nuptial Mass.[22]

Pope Nicholas I (858-867), in reaffirming the traditional Christian form of marriage, insisted that marriage should be contracted publicly with the blessing of the priest, although he denied that secret unions were invalid.[23]

Among the pseudo-Isidorian decretals is contained a letter supposedly written by Pope Evaristus (97-105) to the Bishops

---

[21] *Collectio Capitularium,* lib. III, 179—MPL, XCVII, 820.

[22] Council of Friuli (791), c. 8—Mansi, XIII, 848; Council of Rouen (1072), c. 14—Mansi, XX, 38; Council of London (1102), c. 32—Mansi, XX, 1152; Council of London (1174), c. 18—Mansi, XXII, 151; Council of London (1200), c. 11—Mansi, XXII, 719.

The celebration of marriage *in facie ecclesiae,* or at the doors of the church, originated among the Germanic peoples. Many of the solemnities with which they celebrated marriage were of such a nature that they could not be conveniently observed within the church itself, and hence it became necessary and customary to complete these at the doors of the church. Thereafter the spouses entered the church to assist at Mass and to receive Holy Communion. Consequently the custom of exchanging the matrimonial consent at the doors of the church became quite prevalent throughout the Church, and endured until the sixteenth century, especially in France and England. Cf. Wernz-Vidal, *Ius Matrimoniale,* n. 529, p. 668.

[23] *Ad consulta vestra,* n. 99, cap. 3—*MGH, Epistolarum Tomus VI, Epistolae Karolini Aevi,* Tomus IV (ed. Ernestus Perels, Berolini apud Weidmannos, 1925), p. 569; c. 3, C. XXX, q. 5; JL, n. 2812.

of Africa. The letter stated that marriages were not legitimate unless the customary formalities were observed and the blessing of the priest was received.[24]

The Council of Rouen (1072) imposed on the priest a serious obligation of diligently investigating nupturients, and repeated the prohibition of clandestine marriages. The severe penalty of deposition was to be inflicted upon any priest who was negligent in this matter. The Council also testified to the extent of the impediment of consanguinity in those days. In consequence of the influence of the Germanic law, the method of computation then in force was adopted. Marriage was prohibited to the seventh degree of blood-relationship inclusively.[25]

From these developments it is evident that it was the mind of the Church that all marriages be contracted in the presence of the priest, and that it was his duty to see to it that there existed no cause which might detract from the sanctity and validity of the sacrament.

In addition to the legislation which sought to counteract the two major evils which have been considered in the foregoing pages, there are indications, especially in the legislation of the later middle ages, of a further danger which demanded the making of a special inquiry on the part of those who were to assist at marriages. It concerned the question of freedom of consent on the part of those who entered marriage. Alexander III (1159-1181), in a letter written to the Bishop of Pavia, stated that true consent was lacking whenever force or fear intervened for effecting an expression of consent, and consequently the marriage was invalid. Wherefore, if doubt arose as to the possession of freedom by one who entered marriage, the bishop was to conduct a diligent investigation to clarify the matter. If he found that force or fear was actually present, he was not to permit the marriage until this evil had been eliminated.[26]

A similar pronouncement is contained in a letter of Lucius III (1181-1185). In response to a question concerning the pen-

---

[25] C. 14—Mansi, XX. 38.
[26] C. 14, X, *de sponsalibus et matrimoniis*, IV, 1; JL., n. 13774.

alty to be imposed on a certain woman who had failed to fulfill her promise of contracting marriage with a certain man, the Pope replied that marriage must be entered freely, and accordingly in the presented case the woman could and should be urged to abide by her promise, but was not to be forced to fulfill her oath.[27]

Article 4. Introduction of the Banns.

In his decree *Cum in Tua* Innocent III (1198-1216), writing to the Bishop of Beauvais, referred to the custom prevalent in the Church in France of announcing the forthcoming marriages by means of a proclamation of the banns.[28] The Pope stated that this custom was to aid the priest in conducting his investigation of the parties about to enter marriage.

It is generally agreed that this practice of publicly proclaiming the names of the parties to a marriage was introduced by Bishop Odo of Paris (1196-1209),[29] He ruled that before assisting at any marriage the priest was to inquire among the people of the locality regarding the legality of the contract in this fashion. The violation of this law on his part implied excommunication. In any case of doubt the bishop was to be consulted concerning the questionable impediment.[30]

The same ruling obtained force at about the same time in England, as is evident from a decree of the Council of London (1200), which established that marriage was not to be celebrated

[26] C. 1, C. XXX, q. 5; *Decretales Pseudo-Isidorianae et Capituli Angilramni* (ed. Paulus Hinschius, Lipsiae: 1863), p. 87.

[27] C. 17, X, *de sponsalibus et matrimoniis*, IV, 1; JL, n. 15165.

[28] " . . . bannis, ut tuis verbis utamur, in ecclesiis editis secundum consuetudinem ecclesiae Gallicanae".—c. 27, X, *de sponsalibus et matrimoniis*, IV, 1; A Potthast, *Regesta Pontificum Romanorum inde ab anno post Christum MCXCVIII ad annum MCCCIV* (2 vols., Berolini, 1874-1875), n. 4614.

[29] Petrus Gasparri, *Tractatus Canonicus de Matrimonio* (2 vols., Romae: Typis Polyglottis Vaticanis, 1932), I, n. 147 (hereafter the pre-Code edition (1904 will be cited *De Matrimonio;* the post code edition (1932) *Tractatus Canonicus de Matrimonio);* Wernz-Vidal, *Ius Matrimoniale*, n. 121; James Brendan Roberts, *The Banns of Marriage*, The Catholic University of America Canon Law Studies, n. 64 (Washington, D.C.: The Catholic University of America, 1931), pp. 10-11; A. Esmein, *Le Mariage en Droit Canonique* (2 ed. 2 vols., ed. a R. Genestal-J. Dauvillier, Paris: Recueil Sirey, 1929,-1935), I, 203.

[30] *Constitutiones Synodales Udonis Parisiensis*, c. 7—Mansi, XXII, 679.

until a threefold proclamation of it had been made in the church.[31]

Within the next few years this practice spread throughout France and Italy, and thereupon was enacted as a law for the Universal Church in the IV General Council of the Lateran (1215).[32]

Although the proclamation of the banns was to become an obligation distinct from the investigation to be conducted by the priest, its origin at that particular time is worthy of note, for it demonstrates the increasing realization of the Church that the free status of the parties who proposed to contract marriage had to be established most effectively.

---

[31] C. 11—Mansi, XXII, 719.

[32] C. 51—Mansi, XX, 1038; c. 3, X, *de sponsalibus et matrimoniis*, IV, 1.

CHAPTER II

PROVISIONS OF THE FOURTH LATERAN COUNCIL (1215)

The IV Lateran Council, the twelfth general council of the Church, was solemnly convened in the presence of Pope Innocent III on November 11, 1215. Since it aimed at a general reform for the Universal Church, the vexing problems of consanguineous and clandestine marriages were discussed, and remedial measures were enacted. Due to the purely local character of the previous legislation on this subject, effective means were lacking for combatting the spread of these evils. The general legislation of the Council provided a uniform safeguard for the validity and the sanctity of the sacrament of matrimony, especially through its introduction of the proclamation of the banns as also of the making of the prenuptial investigation a necessary preliminary to all marriages.

The details of this legislation are found in canon 51 of the decrees of the Council. Confirmation of its character as general law was had through its inclusion in the Decretals of Gregory IX, promulgated in 1234.[1] The text of this important canon is as follows:

> Since the prohibition of the conjugal union in the three last degrees has been revoked, we wish that it be strictly observed in the other degrees. Whence, following in the footsteps of our predecessors, we absolutely forbid clandestine marriages; and we forbid also that a priest presume to witness such. Wherefore, extending to other localities generally the particular custom that prevails in some, we decree that when marriages are to be contracted they must be announced publicly in the churches by the priests during a suitable and fixed time, so that if legitimate impediments exist, they may be made known. *Let the priests nevertheless investigate whether any impediments exist.* But when there is ground for doubt concerning the contemplated union, let the marriage be ex-

[1] C. 3, X, *de clandestina desponsatione,* IV, 3; IV General Council of the Lateran (1215), c. 51—Mansi, XX, 1038.

> pressly forbidden until it is evident from reliable sources what ought to be done in regard to it. But if anyone should presume to contract a clandestine or forbidden marriage of this kind within a prohibited degree, even through ignorance, the children from such a union shall be considered illegitimate, nor shall the ignorance of the parents be pleaded as an extenuating circumstance in their behalf, since they by contracting such marriages appear not as wanting in knowledge but rather as affecting ignorance. In like manner the children shall be considered illegitimate if both parents knowing that a legitimate impediment exists, presume to contract such a marriage *in conspectu ecclesiae* (not clandestinely) in disregard of every prohibition. The parochial priest who deliberately neglects to forbid such unions, or any regular priest who presumes to witness them, let them be suspended from office for a period of three years, and, if the nature of their offense demands it, let them be punished more severely. On those also who presume to contract such marriages in a lawful degree, a condign punishment is to be imposed. If anyone maliciously presents an impediment for the purpose of frustrating a legitimate marriage, let him not escape ecclesiastical punishment.[2]

The various determinations of this important canon will be considered in the following articles, special reference being made to the writing of the glossators and commentators on the Decretals.

Article 1. Determination of the Impediments of Consanguinity and Clandestinity.

By the decrees of this Council there was revoked the former extent of the impediment of consanguinity.[3] Previously blood-relationship had constituted an impediment to marriage to the seventh degree inclusively, as references to the legislation of the time reveal.[4] By this pronouncement, however, the impediment was revoked in the last three degrees, and thus the law stood as

[2] IV General Council of the Lateran, 1215), c. 51—Mansi, XX, 1038; Translation by J. H. Schroeder, *Disciplinary Decrees of the General Councils* (St. Louis: Herder Book Co., 1937), p. 280. Italics for the sentence were supplied by the writer.

[3] *Glossa ordinaria*, ad c. 3, X, *de clandestina desponsatione*, IV, 3, s. v. *revocata*. .

[4] III Council of Orleans (538), c. 11—*MGH*, Legum Sectio III, *Concilia* I, 76; c. 16, c. XXXV, qq. 2, 3; JE, n. 2239; c. 17, c. XXXV, qq. 2, 3; JL, n. 4399; Council of Rome (1059), c. 11—Mansi, XIX, 898.

prohibiting marriage to the fourth degree of blood-relationship.[5]

Concerning the impediment of clandestinity, it was determined that thenceforth a marriage would be considered as clandestine if it were contracted without the required witnesses, or without the customary solemnities, that is, especially without the nuptial blessing, or finally if it were contracted contrary to the prescriptions of canon 51 of this council, that is, without the proclamation of the banns.[6]

Boich (ca. 1350) in his commentary considered as equally clandestine those marriages which were contracted without the permission of the bishop whenever this was required, and also the marriages of those who had not attained the age of puberty, or any marriages contracted contrary to a special prohibition of the Church.[7]

Having defined and condemned the evils which in particular were to be overcome, the canon proceeded to determine the means to be employed by pastors in combatting these evils.

Article 2. The Prenuptial Investigation.

The custom of publishing the banns of marriage, which was discussed in the preceding chapter,[8] was approved of as a salutary means of preventing forbidden unions, and became transformed into a general law of the Church.[9]

This announcement of marriage was to be made not only in the church which the parties were accustomed to attend, but also in the other churches of the locality in which they lived. It was also to be proclaimed in churches beyond this locality, if this were necessary for the satisfactory establishment of the free

---

[5] Hostiensis (Henricus de Segusio), *Commentaria in Quinque Decretalium Libros* (5 vols. in 3, Venetiis, 1581), in c. 3, X, *de clandestina desponsatione*, IV, 3, s. v. *in ultimis tribus gradibus* (hereafter cited *Commentaria).*

[6] *Glossa Ordinaria*, ad c. 3, X, *de clandestina desponsatione*, IV, 3, s. v. *clandestina;* Hostiensis, *Commentaria*, ad c. 3, X, *de clandestina desponsatione*, IV, 3, s. v. *huiusmodi clandestina.*

[7] *Commentaria in Quinque Libros Decretalium* (Venetiis, 1576), lib. IV, tit. 3, c. 3; cf. Panormitanus, *Glossa*, ad c. 3, X, *de clandestina desponsatione*, IV, 3.

[8] Cf. *supra*, p. 8.

[9] IV General Council of the Lateran, (1215), c. 51—Mansi, XX, 1038; c. 3, X, *de clandestina desponsatione*, IV, 3.

status of the parties. Especially was this to be observed if the one or the other of them had belonged to a different parish, or had lived in another place for a sufficient length of time to contract an impediment.[10]

Although the number of publications was left undecided in the canon itself, Hostiensis (1271) indicated that three proclamations seemed to constitute the ideal and standard number, but that the bishop could decide this matter in synod. Once, however, it had been determined in this way, a prelate inferior to the bishop could not dispense from the stated number of banns.[11]

This obligation of proclaiming the banns was incumbent upon the parish priests.[12] Further it was held that the word "*presbyteri*" of canon 51 of this Council denoted both the secular and the religious clergy, since in the enactment of penal sanctions against the violation of this rule mention was made not only of the parochial clergy but of regulars as well.[13]

The obligations of the priest were not completely fulfilled through the simple publication of the banns. The Council indicated that he was to augment this precaution with his own investigation. This latter was to take the form of an examination of the parties with a view to the discovery of any possible impediments, special attention being directed to the prevalent impediment of consanguinity and to the averting of clandestine marriage. It was likewise his duty to investigate marriages already contracted.[14]

From a study of related decretals, as has been indicated in the previous chapter, it is learned that the priest was to seek out any cause which might render the union unlawful or invalid. Inquiry was to be made regarding the possible presence of an extant matrimonial bond, and it was indicated that, if one of the parties had contracted a previous marriage, a definite proof

[10] Hostiensis, *Commentaria*, ad c. 3, X, *de clandestina desponsatione*, IV, 3, s. v. *in ecclesiis*.

[11] Ibid., s. v. *competenti;* c. 16, X, *de maioritate et obedientia*, I, 33.

[12] Ibid., s. v. *per presbyteros*.

[13] Donovan, *The Pastor's Obligation in Prenuptial Investigation*. The Catholic University of America Canon Law Studies, n. 115 (Washington: The Catholic University of America, 1938), p. 27.

[14] Hostiensis, *Commentaria*, ad. c. 3, X *de clandestina desponsatione*, IV, 3, s. v. *investiget*.

of the death of the former spouse was required before a second marriage was allowed.[15]

Similarly, the freedom of the parties was always to be evident; any cause which impeded this freedom of consent, as required for a valid contract, was to be removed.[16]

Just as the priest was bound to publish the banns and examine the parties, so also were the faithful bound to reveal any cause that jeopardized the validity of the union.[17] Hostiensis indicated that the blood-relatives of the parties should be heard before all others. He precluded excommunicates from the right of denouncing the threat of invalidity for the proposed marriage.[18]

If after the proclamations or the investigation the probable existence of an impediment was revealed, or if doubt remained regarding its non-existence, the priest was to enjoin the parties concerned not to enter the marriage. This prohibition was to be referred by the priest to the bishop.[19]

Meanwhile the priest was to continue his investigation in order to determine more clearly the nature of the objection raised. If the person who denounced the marriage was honest and upright, and declared that a forbidden degree of consanguinity was present, or that some grave danger would result from the union, the priest was to prohibit the parties from marrying. If the person was not known to be honest and upright, or if the raised objections could not be established by proof, so that as a result a doubt still remained, the priest was to advise against the marriage, but he could not prohibit it.[20]

Hostiensis further indicated that if in a case a special prohibition was invoked it was to be issued publicly. As a con-

---

[15] C. 19, X, *de sponsalibus et matrimoniis*, IV, 1; JL, n. 16370.

[16] C. 17, X, *de sponsalibus et matrimoniis*, IV, 1; JL, n. 15165; c. 14, X, *de sponsalibus et matrimoniis*, IV, 1.

[17] Bernardus Parmensis, *Glossa ordinaria*, ad c. 3, X, *de clandestina desponsatione*, IV, 3.

[18] Hostiensis, *Commentaria*, ad c. 3, X, *de clandestina desponsatione*, IV, 3, s. v. *valuerit*.

[19] Bernardus Parmensis, *Glossa ordinaria*, ad c. 3, X, *de clandestina desponsatione*, IV, 3, s. v. *probabilis coniectura;* Hostiensis, *Commentaria*, ad loc. cit., s. v. *interdicatur*.

[20] C. 27, X, *de sponsalibus et matrimoniis*, IV, 1.

sequence any marriage contracted in defiance of this prohibition was to be regarded as clandestine.[21]

The glossators likewise discussed the question of the possible denunciation of a marriage already contracted. Those who had failed to reveal an impediment of whose existence they claimed to have knowledge the while they assisted at the celebration or witnessed the ceremony were not to be allowed to impugn the validity of the contracted union. Their earlier display of bad faith made their later testimony suspect in character. Others who appeared to offer legitimate objections, inasmuch as they could point to a sufficient cause in excuse for their lack of denouncing the marriage at an earlier date, were to be allowed to raise a question regarding the status of that union.[22]

Article 3. Penalties Imposed for Neglect of the Law

The first effect consequent upon a disregard of the regulations of this Council concerned the offspring of the marriage. Parties who presumed to enter marriage which was clandestine or prohibited, as also the parties between whom there was a degree of blood-relationship that barred the contracting of marriage, brought upon the children born of the union the mark of illegitimacy. The plea of ignorance was dismissed in such cases, such ignorance being considered as culpable. These dangers could readily be forestalled through the use of proper diligence in the observance of the required formalities.[23]

If both parties were aware of an existing impediment and yet presumed to contract marriage, the children of the union were certainly illegitimate. For the case in which one of the parties of the marriage was ignorant of the existing impediment, and thus entered the marriage in good faith, Hostiensis stated that the subsequent offspring was legitimate.[24]. He

---

[21] *Commentaria*, ad c. 3, X, *de clandestina desponsatione*, IV, 3, s. v. *expressa*.

[22] Bernardus Parmensis, *Glossa ordinaria*, ad c. 3, X, *de clandestina desponsatione*, IV, 3, s. v. *valuerit*.

[23] *Glossa ordinaria*, ad c. 3, X, *de clandestina desponsatione*, IV, 3, s. v. *ignoranter*.

[24] *Commentaria*, ad c. 3, X, *de clandestina desponsatione*, IV 3, s. v. *in conspectu Ecclesiae*.

discounted as untenable the contrary opinion which held for partial legitimacy and partial illegitimacy.[25]

Persons who maliciously reported a non-existing impediment in order to impede a legitimate marriage were to be punished with ecclesiastical penalties for their crime, even by being excommunicated, according to the discretion of the judge. A cleric who calumniously denounced a legitimate marriage was to be suspended from office and benefice.[26].

The penalties to be imposed upon priests who were negligent in this matter were more severe, and were to be inflicted upon both the secular and the religious clergy, even though the latter were exempt. Priests who neglected to prohibit forbidden unions or who took any part in their celebration, were punished with suspension from office for three years. A more serious penalty could be inflicted if the gravity of the neglect warranted it.[27]

In some places, in accordance with the statutes of the Roman Pontiff, absolution from these penalties were reserved to the Holy See. In such cases neither the bishop nor any prelate inferior to the Pope could dispense the priest thus suspended. To him no permission to celebrate Mass could be given. Even though he was not excommunicated, yet according to the current customary practice he was to be shunned as an excommunicate.[28]

---

[25] *Glossa ordinaria*, ad *loc cit.*, s. v. *si ambo parentes*.

[26] *Glossa ordinaria*, ad *loc. cit.*, s. v. *malitiose;* Hostiensis, *Commentaria*, ad *loc. cit.*, s. v. *canonicam*.

[27] C. 3, X, *de clandestina desponsatione*, IV, 3.

[28] Hostiensis, *Commentaria*, ad *loc. cit.*, s. v. *per triennium*.

CHAPTER III

LOCAL ENACTMENTS RELATIVE TO THE PRENUPTIAL INVESTIGATION FROM THE FOURTH LATERAN COUNCIL TO THE COUNCIL OF TRENT (1545-1563)

Within a few years of the IV Lateran Council the general directions of its decrees spread throughout the Universal Church. Among its reformatory decrees this Council had ordered that provincial councils be held annually for the reformation of morals.[1] In such local councils, convened in France, Italy, Germany, England, Scotland, Ireland, and indeed, in all parts of the Church, the matrimonial enactments of the general council were reaffirmed and adapted to the particular problems of each locality. Consequently the legislation on the previous investigation to be conducted by the priest, and on the safeguards to be observed prior to marriage, entered a new stage of development. Just as local legislation in the centuries which preceded the IV Lateran Council had prepared the way for its definite enactments, so also the decrees of the particular councils of the thirteenth and fourteenth centuries, in determining and defining the general norms to be observed, served as a prelude to the still more definite determinations later to be enacted by the Council of Trent.

In general, the bulk of this local legislation can be reduced to three main contributions.

1. The regulations regarding the banns and the investigation to be made by the priest were more clearly specified.
2. Some directive norms were given with reference to the celebration of marriage by travellers and strangers.
3. Further consideration was given to the persistent problem of clandestine marriages.

The following articles will consider these main developments.

[1] IV General Council of the Lateran (1215), c. 6—Mansi, XX, 991.

Article 1. The Banns and the Investigation by the Priest

A study of the councils which were convened in various localities from the IV Lateran Council to the Council of Trent reveals that there was practical unanimity in the decision that the proclamations should be announced publicly in the church *three times.* The Lateran Council had left undetermined the number of times the banns should be called. Most of the local legislation decreed that the intention to marry was to be published on three Sundays or feast days, and that a certain interval was to elapse between the completion of these publications and the actual marriage ceremony.[2] A few councils were more definite still, stating that the proclamations were to be made after the Gospel at the sacrifice of the Mass.[3]

In all the above mentioned councils and synods, in harmony with the general legislation of the Lateran Council, there was placed on the priest the additional obligation of personally examining the parties who proposed to contract marriage. This investigation was to cover all the impediments to marriage, and in this regard the Synod of Würzburg (1298) mentioned thirteen.[4]

More specific instructions were given regarding the procedure to be followed by the priest when he discovered it as possible that an impediment existed. The marriage was to be prohibited until further investigation was made by the priest, and a report of the prohibition as enjoined by the priest was to be sent to the bishop or the *officialis,* either of whom possessed an acknowledged competence to render a decision in

---

[2] Council of Oxford (1222)—Mansi, XXII, 1177; Council of Scotland (1225), c. 45—Mansi, XXII, 1242; Provincial Council of Trier (1227), c. 5—Mansi, XXIII, 29; The *Praecepta Antiqua* of the Diocese of Rouen (1235), c. 69—Mansi, XXIII, 384; Synodal Statutes of the Church of Le Mans (1247)—Mansi, XXIII, 748; Council of Trier (1277), c. 5—Mansi, XXIV, 196; Council of Cologne (1280), c. 10—Mansi, XXIV, 356; Synod of Nîmes (1287), c. 9—Mansi, XXIV, 904; Synod of Würzburg (1298), c. 18—Mansi, XXIV, 1194; Council of Prague (1355), c. 50—Mansi, XXVI, 401; Council of York (1367), c. 9—Mansi, XXVI, 471; Council of Magdeburg (1370), c. 32—Mansi, XXVI, 583.

[3] E. g., the Council of Cologne (1280), c. 10—Mansi, XXIV, 356; the Synod of Nîmes (1287), c. 9—Mansi, XXIV, 904.

[4] C. 18—Mansi, XXIV, 1194.

the matter should the doubt persist.[5] The Synod of Nîmes indicated a quasi-judicial procedure for such cases; the priest was to report the case to the bishop, the *officialis* or the archdeacon; the parties in question together with the person who had denounced the proposed union were to be cited; and thereupon the case was considered in conjunction with the reasons for which the priest had ordered the marriage to be delayed.[6]

Article 2. Marriages of Travellers and Strangers

The IV Lateran Council made no provision regarding the nature and the extent of the priest's investigation in the case of the marriages of *peregrini,* of *ignoti,* or of *vagi.* The class of *peregrini,* rendered in English as travellers, included those who were domiciled in a parish other than that in which they now sought to contract marriage; the *ignoti* and the *vagi,* herein referred to as strangers, were those who had no permanent abode. Pastors were frequently faced with the problem of marrying such persons of whom they knew little or nothing, or of uniting a man and a woman who came from towns separated by a considerable distance. This type of marriage became increasingly more frequent in the centuries following the Lateran Council, in view of the influx of students to the universities, and in consequence of the travel occasioned by new commercial activity.

Local councils considered this problem. They indicated what precautions were to be observed for the ascertainment of the free status of such classes of persons.[7] The Synod of Dublin (ca. 1217) demanded that the priest institute a diligent inquiry in the case of a party who belonged to another parish. A report

[5] Council of Scotland (1225), c., 45—Mansi, XXII, 1242; Synodal Statutes of the Church of Le Mans (1247)—Mansi, XXIII, 748; Council of Cologne (1280), c. 10—Mansi, XXIV, 356.

[6] C. 9—Mansi, XXIV, 904.

[7] Constitutions of the Synod of Dublin (ca. 1217)—Mansi, XIII, 1127; Provincial Council of Trier (1277), c. 5—Mansi, XXIV, 196; Constitutions of Richard of Sarum (1217), c. 56—Mansi, XXII, 1125; Council of Cologne (1536), c. 45—Mansi, XXXII, 1268; Council of Mainz (1549) c. 58—Mansi, XXXII, 1413.

of this inquiry was to be sent to his bishop.[8] The Provincial Council of Trier (1227) represented the general trend of the legislation of these centuries in this regard.[9] Strangers had to present testimonial letters from their bishop, their *officialis* or some other prelate empowered to issue them, for otherwise no priest could rightly witness their marriages. The testimonial letter had to contain a statement of freedom for the contracting of marriage on the part of all strangers.[10]

The later councils demanded authentic testimonial letters from the pastor of the former abode of the travellers or strangers. These letters had to state that the parties were not bound by any previous marriage, and had moreover to furnish the permission of the proper pastor for the witnessing of the marriage.[11]

Article 3. Clandestine Marriages

Despite the prohibition enacted by the IV Lateran Council, clandestine marriages continued to present a problem to pastors. The secret nature of these marriages and the consequent impossibility of conducting the prescribed investigations rendered the legislation quite ineffective with regard to these unions. In the centuries following the Lateran Council, there was a consistent enactment of local legislation which condemned and reprobated this type of marriage, and moreover severely punished those who contracted such unions.[12]

Many councils enacted positive legislation which demanded that matrimonial consent be exchanged *at the doors of the*

---

[8] Mansi, XXII, 1127.

[9] C. 5—Mansi, XXIII, 29.

[10] Constitutions of Richard of Sarum (1217), c. 56—Mansi, XXII, 1125. The same canon required that the banns of marriage be announced in the parish of the stranger.

[11] Council of Cologne (1536), c. 45—Mansi, XXXII, 1268; Council of Mainz (1549), c. 58—Mansi, XXXII, 1413.

[12] Council of Scotland (1225), c. 45—Mansi, XXII, 1242; the *Praecepta Antiqua* of the Diocese of Rouen (1235), c. 69—Mansi, XXIII, 384; Synod of Bayeux, c. 69—Mansi, XXV, 74; Synod of Oxford (1237), c. 7—Mansi, XXIV, 793; Council of Cologne (1536), c. 45—Mansi, XXXII, 1268; Council of Mainz (1549), c. 58—Mansi, XXXII, 1413.

church and that the nuptial blessing be received.[13] Marriage was not to take place in private houses,[14] in taverns,[15] or in private oratories.[16] Reverence and decency was to be observed in connection with the celebration of marriage; undue levity and riotous festivities were to be avoided.[17]

The form to be observed in the contracting of marriage was quite generally indicated by the councils which treated of this question. The properly observed form consisted in the presence of a priest and also of three or four witnesses who had been summoned for this purpose.[18]

These various regulations helped in some degree to reduce the number of clandestine marriages, and to inculcate in the minds of the faithful the sacred character of the sacrament of matrimony. They did not and could not, however, eradicate the dangers consequent upon the contracting of clandestine marriages, for such marriages were considered and recognized as valid until the pronouncements of the Council of Trent, which called for the contracting of marriage through the use of a public form if the marriage was to enjoy the acknowledged status of a valid celebration.

---

[13] Synodal Statutes of the Church of Le Mans (1247)—Mansi, XXIII, 748; Council of Langesis (1278), c. 3—Mansi, XXIV, 213; Council of Lyons (1449), c. 14—Mansi, XXXII, 97.

[14] Council of Madgeburg (1370), c. 32—Mansi, XXVI, 583.

[15] Constitutions of Richard of Sarum (1217), c. 55—Mansi, XXII, 1124.

[16] Council of Paris (1429), c. 32—Mansi, XXVIII, 1111.

[17] Constitutions of Richard of Sarum (1217), c. 55—Mansi, XXII, 1124; Council of Scotland (1225), c. 45—Mansi, XXII, 1242; Provincial Council of Trier (1227), c. 5—Mansi, XXIII, 29; Synod of Oxford (1287), c. 7—Masi, XXIV, 793; Council of Salzburg (1420), c. 12—Mansi, XXVIII, 1014.

[18] Constitutions of the Synod of Dublin (ca. 1217)—Mansi, XXII, 1127; Constitutions of Richard of Sarum (1217), c. 55—Mansi, XXII, 1124; Synod of Oxford (1287), c. 7—Mansi, XXIV, 793.

CHAPTER IV

LEGISLATION OF THE COUNCIL OF TRENT AND RELATED DETERMINATIONS OF PARTICULAR COUNCILS

Article 1. The Council of Trent.

The marriage legislation of the Council of Trent (1545-1564) played a most important part in the development of the prenuptial investigation. This followed with a view to regulating the contracting of marriage.

By determining a definite form as required for the validity of all marriages the Council put an end to the previous evil of clandestine unions. The celebrated decree *Tametsi* declared null and void any marriage which was not celebrated before the ordinary, the pastor, or a delegate of either of them, and also before two or three witnesses.[1] Thenceforth all those who contemplated the contracting of marriage had to approach the bishop or the priest, and thereby all were subjected to the investigation required by the Church. Secret unions which abstracted from the presence and assistance of the ordinary or of the pastor, or of someone duly delegated by either of these, could no longer be contracted as valid matrimonial unions.

Furthermore, the obligation of investigating the status of those about to be married fell to a definite priest, as indicated by the phrase *"praesente Parocho"* of the decree. Since he alone could validly assist at the marriage, the burden of examining the parties in order to determine their free status necessarily had to be his. For which pastor did it remain to assume this obligation? Both the tenor of the decree and the understanding of the canonists who commented on this phrase indicated that it was the *parochus proprius* that is, the pastor

---

[1] Conc. Trident., sess. XXIV, *de ref. matrim.*, c. 1.

of the place where either party had a domicile.[2] This teaching was confirmed by the Holy See in a constitution of Pope Urban VIII, in 1627.[3] After two centuries of dispute, the interpretation was extended to include also the pastor of quasi-domicile.[4] Since, therefore, the investigation was to be conducted by a definite priest, and necessarily by one who had some knowledge of the parties, it thereby could become much more effective than it had been formerly.

Upon this proper pastor was also placed the obligation of publishing the banns of the forthcoming marriages. The local legislation of the preceding centuries influenced the Tridentine Council in its determination that the banns were to be proclaimed on three successive feast days, during Mass. If no impediment was revealed, the priest was to proceed with the celebration of the marriage in the presence of the people.[5]

The provision which commanded the pastor to register the marriages contracted within his parish was to prove of great assistance in the future investigation of those who contemplated the contracting of marriage. The names of the parties and of the witnesses, as well as the date and place of the marriage, were to be inscribed in a book especially designated for this purpose.[6] Through this means there was provided a legal proof of the marriage, which could, if needed, be produced as evidence when any question arose as to the existence of the impediment of a previous bond of marriage.

Another question which has evoked consideration in numerous local councils of the preceding centuries was given decisive treatment in the Council of Trent, namely, the prob-

---

[2] Thomas Sanchez, *De Sancto Matrimonii Sacramento Disputationum Libri Tres* (Venetiis, 1607), Tom. I, lib. III, disp. 23 (hereafter cited *De Matrimonio)*; Emmanuel Gonzales-Tellez, *Commentaria perpetua in Singulos Textos Quinque Librorum Decretalium Gregorii IX* (5 vols. in 4, Lugduni, 1715), Tomus IV, tit. 3, c. 3, nn. 8, 9.

[3] Urbanus VIII, const. *Exponi vobis*, 14 aug. 1627—*Bullarum Diplomatum et Privilegiorum Sanctorum Romanorum Pontificum Taurinensis Editio* (25 vols., Augustae Taurinorum, 1857-1872), XIII, 537.

[4] S. C. S. Off., litt. encycl., 7 iun. 1867—*Collectanea S. Congregationis de Ppopaganda Fide* (2 vols., Romae: Typographis Polyglotta S. C. de Propaganda Fide, 1907), n. 1407 (hereafter cited *Collectanea)*.

[5] Conc. Trident., sess. XXIV, *de ref. matrim.*, c. 1.

[6] Conc. Trident., sess. XXIV, *de ref. matrim.*, c. 1.

lem of the marriages of the *vagi*, or the strangers. Because of the actions of unprincipled persons who abandoned their legitimate consorts and sought to enter marriage with others in places where they were unknown, and because of the consequent danger of bigamous unions, the Fathers of the Council enacted certain precautions which pastors were to observe in dealing with the marriages of strangers. Pastors were to conduct a diligent investigation regarding the status of such persons, and to forward a complete report of this examination to the bishop, who alone could give permission for the celebration of the marriage. Civil magistrates were also exhorted to restrain such persons from easy access to marriage.[7]

The command of the Fathers of the Council that all ordinaries publish and promulgate these decrees as soon as possible was not realized, and thereby their efficacy was weakened. There remained many parishes, dioceses and countries where these decrees gained no force for the simple reason that they were not promulgated.

Article 2. Related Local Legislation

Many particular councils of the century subsequent to the Council of Trent repeated its legislation and ordered that pastors publicize its enactments on marriage.[8] They clarified and amplified the decrees of the Council of Trent, and thus rendered them more effective in their respective dioceses.

The legislation regarding the investigation of those who contemplated the contracting of marriage, which investigation was to be conducted by the pastor in addition to his fulfillment of the obligation of proclaiming the banns, affords a

---

[7] Conc. Trident., sess. XXIV, *de ref. matrim.*, c. 7.

[8] Council of Ravenna (1568), *de matrimonio*—Mansi, XXXV A, 624; II Provincial Council of Milan (1569), c. 26—Mansi, XXXIV A, 113; Council of Urbino (1569), *de matrimonio*—Mansi, XXXV A, 667; Council of Malines (1570), *de spons. et matrim.*—Mansi, XXXIV A, 583; Council of Florence (1573), *de sacr. matrim.*—Mansi, XXXV A, 767; Council of Rouen (1581), c. 13—Mansi, XXXIV A, 626; Council of Bourges (1584), tit. 27—Mansi, XXXIV A, 909; Council of Aachen (1585), *de matrim.*—Mansi, XXXIV bis, 957; Council of Bordeaux (1624), cap. VII, *de matrim.*—Mansi, XXXIV bis, 1564.

good example of the supplementary action called for in consequence of particular enactments. The IV Provincial Council of Milan (1576) decreed in this regard that the parties were to be questioned separately.[9] In the questioning of a woman the priest was to conduct the investigation in a decent place, where she was still in the sight of others, and yet distant enough that they could not hear her, so that she would be afforded complete freedom in answering the questions of the priest.[10] Moreover, the priest was to question the person judiciously, so that the party would be prompted to answer truthfully, and not be given an occasion through shame to seek evading the truth.[11]

The investigation was to be concerned with ascertaining the freedom of the parties in entering the marriage; with discovering whether either party was hindered from entering a new contract because of an existing valid marriage; whether either party was bound to abstain from marriage by the vow of chastity or the vow to embrace the religious state; whether there was present a prohibitive degree of consanguinity or of affinity, or whether the impediment of spiritual relationship attended the case under investigation.[12] If through the investigation it was discovered that one of the parties was entering the marriage through force or fear, or that any other hindrance was present, the parties were to be forbidden to enter the union.[13] If doubt arose as to the existence of an impediment, the matter was to be referred to the bishop, who could decide whether or not the marriage could be contracted.[14] In some places the vicar general or the *officialis* was empowered to make this decision.[15]

---

[9] IV Provincial Council of Milan (1576), c. 9—Mansi, XXXIV A, 315, 316.

[10] IV Provincial Council of Milan (1576), c. 9—Mansi, XXXIV A, 315, 316; Council of Sienna (1599), c. 2—Mansi, XXXVI bis, 539.

[11] Council of Sienna (1599), c. 2—Mansi, XXXVI bis, 539.

[12] VI Provincial Council of Milan (1582), c. 27—Mansi, XXXIV A, 527; Council of Besancon (1571), c. 10—Mansi, XXXVI bis, 60.

[13] Council of Malines (1570), c. 2—Mansi, XXXIV A, 583.

[14] Synodal Statutes of the Church of Nevers, c. 34—Mansi, XXXII, 294.

[15] Council of Besançon (1571), c. 8—Mansi, XCVI bis, 60.

Specific instructions regarding the testimonial letters, which were required of those who were not domiciled in the place in which the marriage was to be contracted, are frequently found in the legislation of these particular councils. If one party had a domicile in another diocese, he had to present to the priest who was to assist at the marriage testimonial letters from his proper pastor stating that the banns had been announced and that the person in question was free to enter marriage.[16] Furthermore, the testimony of the pastor alone was not sufficient: the letters had to bear the seal and signature of the proper bishop or his delegate.[17] If the party was domiciled within the same diocese but in a different parish, testimonial letters were likewise required. In this case the testimony of the proper pastor could be attested to by the vicar forane.[18]

In these particular regulations can be seen the origin of the requirements contained in the Instruction of the Sacred Congregation of the Sacraments of the year 1941, wherein it is stated that in the marriages of persons from different dioceses the documents and forms required by the Instruction must pass through the diocesan curia.[19]

The Council of Cambria (1631) indicates the beginnings of another modern requirement in the prenuptial investigation, namely, the determination of the knowledge of Christian doctrine in the parties contemplating marriage, as that demand is now contained in the Code of Canon Law.[20] In this Council it was decreed that the parties were to have received the sacrament of confirmation and that they were to know the Commandments of the Decalogue and the Precepts of the Church, as also the prayers, namely, the *Our Father*, the *Hail Mary*, and the *Apostle's Creed*.[21]

---

[16] II provincial Council of Milan (1569), c. 26—Mansi XXXIV A, 113.

[17] II Provincial Council of Milan (1569), c. 26—Mansi, XXXIV A, 113; Council of Malines (1570), c. 3—Mansi, XXXIV A, 583; Council of Besançon (1571), cc. 13-14—Mansi, XXXVI bis, 60.

[18] Council of Aachen (1585), *de matrim.*—Mansi, XXXIV bis, 957.

[19] S. C. de Sacramentis, 29 iun. 1941—*AAS*, XXXIII (1941).

[20] Can. 1020, 2.

[21] C. 3—Mansi, XXXVI ter, 180.

These various local determinations contributed to the efficiency of the prenuptial investigation, but the lack of uniformity in the Universal Church impaired the desired effectiveness of such legislation. The Constitutions of the Roman Pontiffs relative to this matter, to be treated in the following chapter, sought to introduce a general standard of observance in this matter.

CHAPTER V

THE JURIDICAL INTERROGATION OF WITNESSES ACCORDING TO THE DECREE *CUM ALIAS* (1670)

During the pontificate of Pope Clement X (1670-1676) a new precaution was added to the prenuptial investigation, calculated especially to detect and prevent intended bigamous and polygamous unions. This latest addition in the law was promulgated particularly by means of the decree *Cum alias* of the Sacred Congregation of the Holy Office, in which it was legislated that a definite juridical examination of witnesses was to be instituted prior to the celebration of every marriage, with a view to establishing the free status of the parties who were contemplating the union.[1] It was in fact a summary juridical process, in which reliable witnesses for each party to the marriage were interrogated as to their knowledge of the party and of the circumstances relative to the marriage. No marriage was to be celebrated until the freedom of the contracting parties was established in this fashion to the satisfaction of the episcopal curia.[2]

It is evident that this was not altogether a novel procedure, for in the preface to this decree reference was made to two previous instructions of the Sacred Congregation of the Holy Office, of the years 1658 and 1665, which apparently called for a similar interrogation of witnesses.[3] In consequence of the improper observance of these earlier instructions in some provinces, and as a result of the absolute neglect in others, the Holy Office issued the decree *Cum alias* to reiterate its

[1] S. C. S. Off., decr., *Cum alias*, 21 aug. 1670—*Codicis Iuris Canonici Fontes*, cura Emi Petri Card. Gasparri editi, 9 vols., Romae (postea Civitate Vaticana): Typis Polyglottis Vaticanis, 1923-1939 (vols. VII-IX ed. cura et studio Emi Iustiniani Card. Seredi), n. 742 (hereafter cited *Fontes)*.

[2] Esmein, *Le Mariage en Droit Canonique*, II, 223, 224.

[3] S. C. S. Off., decr., *Cum Alias*, 21 aug. 1670—Fontes, n. 742; Feije, *De Impedimentis et Dispensationibus Matrimonialibus* (3. ed., 2 vols., Lovanii, 1885), n. 254.

insistence that the freedom of the parties be established in this manner.[4] These earlier instructions of the years 1658 and 1665 are not found in the usual collections of the documents of the Holy See.

This legislation was duly promulgated and made obligatory for the universal Church. Throughout the following centuries the observance of its regulations was insisted upon by many local councils,[5] and many responses, to which reference will be made in this chapter, were issued by the Holy See to clarify its requirements.

The consideration of this important document may be divided into three sections. The discussion will accordingly turn on:

I. The witnesses who were to testify;

II. The officials who were to preside over and conduct the interrogation;

III. The actual matter and form of the examination.

Article 1. The Witnesses

Blood-relatives were to be preferred to others as witnesses, since it was naturally presumed that they were better informed in matters pertaining to the parties. Even members of the immediate family of the person who was to be married were allowed to testify.[6] Similarly, citizens or residents of the locality were generally considered as more reliable witnesses than outsiders or those who came from distant localities. As a rule *vagi* and soldiers were not admitted as suitable witnesses. In a particular case, however, they could be accepted, if in the prudent consideration of the judge the circumstances warranted it.

---

[4] *Fontes*, n. 742.

[5] Council of Naples (1699), c. 2—Mansi, XXXVI ter, 757; I Provincial Council of Westminster (1852), cap. 22—Mansi, XLIV, 742; Council of Ravenna (1855), c. 8—Mansi, XLVII, 220; I Council of Smyrna (1869), appendix I—*Acta et Decreta Sacrorum Conciliorum Recentiorum, Collectio Lacensis* (7 vols., Friburgi Brisgoviae, 1870-1890), VI, 579-585 (hereafter cited *Coll. Lac.);* Council of New Granada (1868), c. 11—Coll. Lac., VI, 521; Council of Urbino (1859), c. 66—*Coll. Lac.*, VI, 25.

[6] S. C. S. Off., resp. 24 febr. 1847—*Fontes*, n. 900.

The notary, who was to be present at the interrogation, was to declare in writing that the witness was known to him. For this he was to use the formula, "*persona mihi bene cognita.*" If the witness happened to be a person unknown to him, the interrogation was to be suspended until some other person who was known to the notary identified the witness by name and testified to his or her reliability.

It seems that there were to be two witnesses for each party to the marriage, that is, two for the man, and two for the woman. The same two witnesses, however, could testify for both. Further, either men or women were allowed to fulfill this office.[7] A later response of the Holy See allowed also non-Catholics to act as witnesses, especially when Catholics could not be had. The customary oath *de veritate dicenda,* which was administered to the Catholic witness previous to the interrogation, was as a general rule not to be demanded of non-Catholics.[8]

Article 2. The Presiding Officials

In Rome the witnesses were to be examined before a notary and an *officialis* specially appointed for this purpose by the Cardinal Vicar. Outside of Rome the examination was to be conducted before a notary and the vicar general, or some other outstanding priest designated by the bishop.[9]

A later response of the Holy See permitted bishops to choose their vicars forane and the chancellors of the latter as suitable officials for the prosecution of the examination, on the condition that the completed depositions be transmitted to the episcopal curia, where the value of the testimony as establishing the free status of the parties was to be adjudicated.[10]

---

[7] F. Santi, *Praelectiones Iuris Canonici* (4 ed., 5 vols., a M. Leitner recognita, Ratisbonae: Pustet, 1903-1905), Lib. IV, tit. 21, n. 33.

[8] S. C. S. Off., resp. 2 apr. 1873, ad I—*Fontes,* n. 1025.

[9] S. C. S. Off., decr. *Cum alias,* 21 aug. 1670—*Fontes,* n. 742; D. Bouix, *Tractatus de Judiciis Ecclesiasticis* (2. ed., 2 vols., Parisiis, 1855), II 463.

[10] S. C. S. Off., resp. 24 febr. 1847—*Fontes,* n. 900; Monacelli, *Formularium Legale Practicum Fori Ecclesiastici* (4 vols. in 3, Romae: 1844), Vol. I, tit. viii, form. 1, n. 1; Bouix, *Tractatus de Judiciis Ecclesiasticis,* II, 463.

The Instruction of the Holy Office to the Oriental Ordinaries in 1890 stated that the examination, if conducted in the episcopal city, was to be presided over by the vicar general; if in other parts of the diocese, then by the pastor. In the latter case the completed documents were to be forwarded to the episcopal curia.[11]

The delegation of a particular priest for conducting this examination could be granted for a single case, or habitually for all cases.[12]

Article 3. The Interrogation of the Witnesses

1. The witness was to be instructed on the gravity of taking an oath, and warned of the penalty for perjury.

2. The witness was interrogated as to his Christian name, surname, country, age, occupation and place of residence.

3. He was asked whether he was an inhabitant of the locality in which the examination was taking place, or whether he came from elsewhere. If he was an outsider, he was questioned as to the length of time he had been in the place where he was testifying.

4. The witness was asked whether in putting in his appearance he gave testimony of his own accord, or upon request. If the former, he was dismissed on the presumption that his testimony was unreliable. If the latter, he was asked upon whose request he appeared; where, when, how often and in whose presence the request was made. Did he know of any impediment that existed between the parties?

5. Had the witness been given, promised or offered anything by way of compensation for his testimony either by the parties or by anyone else in their name?

6. The witness was asked how long and how well he had known the party in whose behalf he was testifying.

7. Were the parties residents of the community in which

[11] S. C. S. Off., instr. (ad Ep. Orient.), 33 aug. 1890, ad 3—*Fontes*, n. 1128.

[12] Santi, *Prelectiones Iuris Canonici*, Lib. IV, tit. 21, n. 33.

the examination was taking place, or were they from elsewhere? If the latter, permission to contract marriage was withheld until testimonial letters asserting their freedom to marry were obtained from the proper ordinary.

8. If the party was an inhabitant of the locality, in what parish or parishes had he lived prior to the time, and in what parish was he living at the time of the deposition? The witness was asked if the party had a wife or husband living in any of these parishes, or whether the party was barred from marriage by religious profession, sacred orders or any other impediment.

9. If he replied in the negative to the foregoing questions, he was asked how he was able to substantiate his statement; if in the affirmative, what proofs could he produce to confirm his assertions?

10. If the witness stated that the party had been previously married, but that the wife or husband was deceased, he was questioned as to the time and the place of death, and the source of his knowledge of these facts. The information thus obtained was to be confirmed by authentic documents, such as certificates of death and burial procured by the curia from hospital or from military authorities.

11. The witness was further questioned in this case as to whether the party, after the death of the consort, had entered a second union, or whether this could have taken place, even though it was unknown to the witness.

12. In all these matters the *officialis* was to ascertain the source of the knowledge, and to procure proofs to confirm the statements of the witness.

The depositions of the witnesses were to be put in writing by the notary and certified by the signatures of witnesses, of the official who was delegated by the bishop to preside at the interrogation, and of the notary.[13] If the testimony established the free status to the satisfaction of the episcopal curia, then

[13] P. Gasparri, *De Matrimonio* (3. ed., 2 vols., Parisiis, 1904), I, n. 176.

permission to proceed with the publication of the banns for the marriage was to be granted.

The marriages of *vagi* and of others who came from outside the diocese (referred to as *exteri* in the decree) produced special difficulties which demanded special precautions. The decree *Cum alias* repeated the legislation of the Council of Trent regarding the investigation of *vagi* who presented themselves for marriage.[14] In the case of those who were domiciled in a diocese other than that in which the marriage was to take place, testimonial letters had to be obtained from their proper ordinary. These letters had to assert the parties' freedom to marry, before they were permitted to contract marriage.[15] If a party, although now actually domiciled in the diocese of the proposed marriage, had formerly resided in a different diocese or dioceses, similar testimonial letters of the ordinary of the diocese of origin and of the ordinaries of the other dioceses in which the party had residence needed to be produced.[16] If the person had before the age of puberty or shortly afterwards taken up residence in the ultimate diocese where he currently had his domicile, the testimonial letters were not demanded.[17]

In the above mentioned cases of *vagi* and *exteri,* when it was impossible to obtain these required testimonial letters, or to determine the free status of the parties through the interrogation of suitable witnesses a suppletory oath taken by the parties, fortifying their assertions of their freedom to marry, was to be considered as acceptable, according to a response given by the Holy Office. This departure from the customary requirements was permitted in order that the native right of marriage be not rendered impossible because of the inability of the parties to fulfill the ordinary requisites of the law in such unusual cases.[18] Nevertheless, in cases which presented

[14] S. C. S. Off., decr. *Cum alias*, 21 aug. 1670—*Fontes*, n. 742; Conc. Trident., sess. XXIV, *de ref. matrim.*, c. 7; cf. supra, Chapter IV, p.

[15] S. C. S. Off., decr., *Cum alias*, 21 aug. 1670, n. 7—*Fontes*, n. 742.

[16] Gasparri, *De Matrimonio*, I, nn. 178-181.

[17] Gasparri, *op. cit.*, I. n. 117.

[18] S. C. S. Off., resp. 1 febr. 1865, ad II—*Collectanea*, n. 1267; *Fontes*, n. 980.

extraordinary problems the bishop was to refer the difficulty to the Holy Office.[19]

To what extent the regulations of the decree *Cum alias* were followed in practice is not clearly evident. It seems that only in Rome and in the Papal States did they receive faithful and consistent observance. Gasparri (1852-1934), writing in the year 1904, stated that outside Italy the decree was not observed; in other parts of the Church it either had never been received or it had fallen into desuetude. Among these places of non-observance he mentioned France in particular, stating that in that country the freedom to marry was determined solely through the proclamation of the banns and through the actual investigation of the parties.[20] Wernz (1842-1914), in his *Ius Matrimoniale* which appeared in the same year, observed that the execution of the decree was confined to the Papal States.[21] Bouix (1808-1870) at an earlier time (1855) had also testified to the non-observance of the decree. He felt that this non-observance simply resulted from the impossibility of following all the prescriptions in practice.[22]

These authors discussed also the possibility of the abrogation of these prescriptions in consequence of the prolonged disregard concerning them. Bouix was of the opinion that the decree had not been abrogated, since Pope Leo XII (1823-1829) had renewed and confirmed it, thus interrupting the time necessary for the prescription against the law.[23] Gasparri likewise dismised the possibility of its abrogation. He argued that the Holy See, although certainly aware of the contrary custom, had repudiated it by continuing to insist on the observance of the interrogation of witnesses.[24]

With the advent of the present Code of Canon Law the question became definitely settled. Since the present law is

[19] *Ibid.*, ad V—*Collectanea*, n. 1267; *Fontes*, n. 980.
[20] *De Matrimonio*, I, n. 185.
[21] N. 133, p. 189.
[22] *Tractatus de Judiciis Ecclesiasticis*, II, 465; cf. etiam Esmein, *Le Mariage en Droit Canonique*, II, 225.
[23] *Op. cit.*, II, 465.
[24] *De Matrimonio*, I, n. 185.

silent regarding the juridical examination of witnesses prior to every marriage, the prescripts of the decree *Cum alias* are to be considered as abrogated. According to the present legislation, the testimony of witnesses is to be obtained only in cases in which doubt arises as to the existence of an impediment.[25]

---

[25] Can. 1031, 1, 1°.

CHAPTER VI

THE DEVELOPMENT OF THE PRENUPTIAL INVESTIGATION IN THE DOCUMENTS OF POPE BENEDICT XIV (1740-1758)

The pontificate of Pope Benedict XIV (1740-1758) is singularly noteworthy for the development which it occasioned in the field of Canon Law as a whole. The question of the prenuptial investigation was not excluded from the consideration of this celebrated canonist. In various encylical letters, in papal constitutions and in his monumental work *De Synodo Dioecesana,* the Pontiff reaffirmed the requirements of the law as established by the IV General Council of the Lateran and by the Council of Trent, and proceeded to define in clearer concepts the manner in which bishops and pastors were to determine the free status and the worthy character of those who contemplate the contracting of marriage.

Article 1. Confirmation and Clarification of Proceeding Legislation

Unquestionably the most important document regarding the prenuptial investigation which came from the pen of Pope Benedict XIV was his encyclical letter *Nimiam licentiam* of May 18, 1743.[1] A consideration of this letter reveals that its determinations were embodied almost entirely in the present code of Canon Law, and thus it may be considered as the immediate basis for the present law.[2] The issuance of the letter was prompted by the abuses which had arisen in the contracting of the sacrament of matrimony, especially in the Kingdom of Poland, and hence it was directed as a corrective norm to the archbishops and bishops of that country.[3]

Therein it was declared that, before the banns of a pros-

---

[1] *Fontes*, n. 337.
[2] Cf. can. 1020.
[3] Gasparri, *De Matrimonio*, I, n. 186.

pective marriage were publicly proclaimed in the church, the proper pastor was to conduct personally a diligent examination of the contracting parties. As had been determined in certain particular councils after the enactment of the Tridentine legislation,[4] they were to be questioned separately, so that they would be prompted to reveal freely, truthfully and frankly the information requested of them by the pastor.[5]

The investigation was to concern first of all the consent to the marriage, to ascertain whether or not both parties were entering the union freely, willingly and with true marital consent. Subsequently the pastor was to determine the possible existence and the precise nature of any impediment, the presence of which would prohibit the marriage between the persons concerned. He was further to discover whether or not either party had entered a contract of betrothal with a third person. Likewise he was to ascertain whether parental consent had been obtained for the marriage. Finally, the pastor was permitted to supplement this inquiry with any other similar points which he deemed advisable in a particular case.

If, as a result of the inquisition, some impediment or condition which could vitiate the contemplated marriage was discovered, the proclamation of the banns was to be delayed and the matter was to be reported to the bishop. The latter, after mature consideration, was to decide on the course to be followed, granting if necessary the required dispensations.[6]

The necessity and importance of this prenuptial investigation was similarly emphasized in the Papal Constitution *Firmandis,* which was issued the following year.[7] In this document the Pope instructed the bishops that they were to make a special inquiry into the legislation and into the observance of the legislation regarding the examination of the parties prior to marriage. The bishops were to conduct this investi-

---

[4] IV Provincial Council of Milan (1576), c. 9—Mansi, XXXIV A, 315, 316; Council of Sienna (1599), c. 16—Mansi, XXXVI bis, 539, 542.

[5] Benedictus XIV, ep. encycl. *Nimiam licentiam,* 18 maii 1743, 10—*Fontes,* n. 337.

[6] *Loc. cit.*

[7] Benedictus XIV, const. *Firmandis,* 6 nov. 1744, 9—*Fontes,* n. 349.

gation especially at the time of their episcopal visitation. To this end the bishops were to interrogate the parish priests on the inquiries which the latter customarily conducted before the proclamation of the banns to determine whether no impediments existed, whether freedom of consent was guaranteed, and whether there was assurance of the knowledge of Christian doctrine,as required on the part of the contracting parties.[8] It may be noted here that it is precisely on these three points that the pastor under the present law must interrogate the prospective bride and groom.[9]

Article 2. Investigation Regarding the Knowledge of Christian Doctrine

The directive that the pastor include in the prenuptial investigation an inquisition regarding the knowledge of Christian doctrine on the side of the parties was not originally introduced by Pope Benedict XIV; it had already been considered in previous legislation. It was this Pontiff, however, who defined it more clearly, and who insisted upon its observance more emphatically.

In his encylical letter, *Etsi minime,* he declared that if through the required investigation of the priest it was determined that the prospective bride and groom were ignorant of the truths which must necessarily be known for salvation, they were not to be united in matrimony.[10]

The question, however, had been treated more comprehensively in his canonical treatise *De Synodo Dioecesana.* Therein the latter pope had discussed at some length the previous statements on the necessity of this particular phase of the antenuptial investigation. The opinion which regarded it as unlawful to forbid the celebration of marriage in consequence of the parties' ignorance of Christian doctrine had there been duly refuted,

---

[8] *Loc. cit.*

[9] Can. 1020, c. 2; S. C. de Sacramentis, instr. 29 iun. 1941, n. 2—*AAS*, XXXIII (1941), 298.

[10] Benedictus XIV, ep encycl *Etsi minime*, 7 febr. 1742, c. 11—*Fontes*. n. 324.

and the correct norm to be followed in the future had there been clearly set down.[11]

A Synod of Bologna (1634) had indeed stated that a man and a woman could not be prohibited from marriage simply because they were ignorant of Christian doctrine, although the pastor could threaten to delay the union in order to induce them to learn more readily the rudiments of the faith.[12] Similarly it had been the contention of Sanchez (1550-1610) that, since the lack of religious knowledge was not found in the common lists of matrimonial impediments, it should not be regarded as a prohibition to marriage.[13]

Pope Benedict XIV, however, discarded these opinions as erroneously contrary to the teaching of the Church in the Roman Ritual, in various synods and in many edicts of the Roman Pontiffs.[14] The Ritual required that both parties know the rudiments of their religion in order that they be fitted to teach their children these salutary truths.[15] The V Provincial Council of Milan (1570), convoked by St. Charles Borromeo (1538-1584), had decreed that parish priests who found the parties to a marriage insufficiently instructed in their religion were to refrain from assisting at such a union.[16] At a meeting of the Sacred Congregation of the Inquisition, held in the presence of Pope Innocent XII (1691-1700) in the year 1697, it had been established that pastors should not proclaim the banns of marriage without previously ascertaining that the intending parties were sufficiently instructed in the rudiments of their faith.[17] And this decree had been confirmed by Pope Clement XI (1700-1721).[18]

---

[11] Benedictus XIV, *De Synodo Dioecesana* (2 vols., Romae, 1805), Lib. VIII, c. 14, nn. 1-6.

[12] Benedictus XIV, *op. cit.*, Lib. VIII, c. 14, n. 1.

[13] *De Matrimonio*, Lib. III, disp. 15, n. 18; Benedictus XIV, *op. cit.*, Lib. VIII, c. 14, n. 2.

[14] *De Synodo Dioecesana*, Lib. VIII, c. 14, n. 3.

[15] Tit. VII, c. 1, *de sacramento matrimonii*, nn. 1, 10.

[16] C. 17—Mansi, XXXIV A, 480; Benedictus XIV, *De Synodo Dioecesana*, Lib. VIII, c. 14, n. 3.

[17] Benedictus XIV, *loc. cit.*; cf. De Smet, *De Sponsalibus et Matrimonio*, (Brugus, 1909), n. 331.

[18] *Bullarium Clementis XI* (Romae: Typographia Rev. Camerae Apostolicae 1723), n. 11, p. 376; Benedictus XIV, *loc. cit.*

After citing various other similar examples of the traditional teaching of the Church which manifested the emphasis with which a knowledge of Christian doctrine was required in the nupturients, Pope Benedict XIV stated that in the future no parties who were insufficiently instructed in their religion should be admitted to marriage.[19] He placed such persons in the category of unworthy Catholics by arguing that one who remained culpably ignorant of the rudiments of the faith, which he was bound by precept to know, thereby reflected a perseverance in a state of mortal sin and was therefore deservedly forbidden to contract marriage.[20]

Due consideration was to be accorded, however, to those of dull understanding who, although they had made an effort to learn the principal mysteries of faith, were incapable of learning them by heart or of repeating them. With reference to such it was the pastor's duty frequently to repeat his instructions regarding these necessary mysteries, so that what they had learned in a rudimentary fashion would not be entirely forgotten. The rudiments of the faith were considered to comprise the following: a knowledge of the mysteries of the Unity and Trinity of God, of God as Remunerator, of the Incarnation and Redemption of Christ; a knowledge of the sacraments necessary for salvation; and a knowledge of the Commandments of God and of the Precepts of the Church.[21]

Although such ignorance of the faith did not constitute an impediment in the strict sense, nevertheless it had a dilatory effect on the proposed contracting of marriage; it delayed the union until the ignorance was dispelled. In order to arrive at a decision in this regard it was necessary for the pastor to submit the parties to this further special investigation.[22]

In a later encyclical letter, *Cum religioso*, the same Pontiff repeated his insistence on the necessity of religious knowledge

---

[19] *Op. cit.*, Lib. VIII, c. 14, n. 3.

[20] *Op. cit.*, Lib. VIII, c. 14, n. 6; cf. etiam, De Smet, *De Sponsalibus et Matrimonio*, n. 331.

[21] *Op. cit.*, Lib. VIII, c. 14, n. 6.

[22] De Becker, *De Sponsalibus et Matrimonio Praelectiones Canonicae* (Lovanii, 1903), p. 376; Wernz, *Ius Matrimoniale*, n. 131; Gasparri, *De Matrimonio*, I, n. 537.

on the part of the nupturients, and once more emphasized the pastors' obligation of instructing the persons at whose marriages they had the right to assist.[23]

Article 3. The Special Investigation in Cases of Marriages of Conscience

In the second year of his Pontificate Benedict XIV issued his encyclical letter *Satis Vobis*, which had as its purpose the instruction of bishops concerning marriages of conscience.[24] This type of marriage was secret. It was celebrated, without the previous proclamation of the banns, before the pastor or a priest designated by the pastor and two witnesses sworn to secrecy regarding the ceremony. The encylical sought to offset the evils which had arisen because of improper secret marriages by establishing the marriage of conscience as an approved canonical institute.[25]

Thenceforth competent superiors could permit this type of secret marriage whenever a cause sufficiently grave and reasonable to justify this extraordinary remedy presented itself.[26] Since in view of the extraordinary manner in the celebration of the marriage the customary means of establishing the free status of the parties, that is, the proclamation of the banns, were foregone, it was extremely important that the pastor conduct a diligent examination of the persons concerned.

This particular investigation had a twofold purpose: it

---

[23] Benedictus XIV, litt. encycl. *Cum religiosi*, 26 iun, 1754, c. 4—*Fontes*, n. 429.

[24] 17 nov. 1741—*Fontes*, n. 319; cf. *De Synodo Dioecesana*, Lib. XIII, c. 23, n. 12; Pallottini *Collectio omnium conclusionum quae in causis propositis apud Sacram Congregationem Cardinalium S. Concilii Tridentini interpretum prodierunt ab eius institutione anno MCLIV ad annum MDCCCLX, distinctis titulis alphabetico ordine per materias digesta* (18 vols., Romae: 1868-1895), s. v. *Matrimonium*, XXVI, n. 9 (hereafter cited Pallottini); Ferraris, *Prompta Bibliotheca, Canonica. Iuridica, Moralis, Theologica necnon Ascetica, Polemica, Rubricistica, Historica* (9 vols., Romae: 1885-1899) s. v. *Matrimonium*, art. IX, n. 63 (hereafter cited as Ferraris).

[25] Coburn, *Marriages of Conscience*, The Catholic University of America Canon Law Studies, n. 191 (Washington, D.C., The Catholic University of America Press, 1944), p. 40.

[26] Benedictus XIV, litt. encycl., *Satis Vobis*, 17 nov. 1741, c. 5—*Fontes*, n. 319.

sought to establish not only the seriousness of the cause which arranged the marriage of conscience, but also the capacity of the parties to enter the marriage. To this end the character, the qualities and the condition of the applicants were to be duly appraised. If the parents were opposed to the marriage, their opinion was to be considered for the sake of determining whether the celebration of the marriage was nevertheless justified. Because of current abuses arising from the retention of ecclesiastical benefices by clerics in minor orders who had entered the married state, the investigation of such possibilities was to be included. Most important, however, was the need of producing in documentary form a clear statement of the free status of the parties, in order to avert all danger of polygamous unions.[27]

Bishops were to command pastors, as also all others whom they delegated to assist at such marriages, to instruct the parties relative to their obligation of seeing to the baptism and education in Christian doctrine and morals of the children born of the union.[28]

This encyclical contains the classical text of the law on marriages of conscience. In substance that text became eventually incorporated in the present Code of Canon Law.[29]

---

[27] Benedictus XIV, ep. encycl., *Satis Vobis*, 17 nov. 1741, c. 7—*Fontes*, n. 319.

[28] *Ibid.*, c. 9—*Fontes*, n. 319.

[29] Cf. cans. 1104-1108.

CHAPTER VII

PRENUPTIAL INVESTIGATION FROM THE PONTIFICATE OF BENEDICT XIV TO THE CODE OF CANON LAW (1918)

Article 1. Local Councils and Papal Responses

By the close of the Pontificate of Benedict XIV the basic requirements of the prenuptial investigation had been established. Actually no major development occurred after that time. Much confirmatory legislation, however, was enacted. This legislation emphasized the utility and the necessity of a previous examination of the nupturients to establish their freedom to marry, and repeated the statement of the pastors' obligation in this regard. Virtually all the Councils of the nineteenth century considered among their decrees at least one or the other aspect of the prenuptial investigation.

The Benedictine legislation concerning the obligation of pastors to ascertain the knowledge of Christian doctrine on the part of those intending marriage was frequently insisted upon in particular councils.[1] In these councils the pastors were commanded to investigate the actual status of the religious knowledge of the contracting parties, and to refrain from admitting to marriage those who were found to be ignorant of the rudiments of the faith, until they had diligently instructed such persons in the principal mysteries of religion.

Much consideration was also given to the procedure to be followed when *vagi* or *peregrini* presented themselves for mar-

[1] Council of Rouen (1830), c. 20, n. 3—Mansi, LXIV, 47; I Provincial Council of Australia (1844), decr. XIII—*Coll. Lac.*, III, 1053; Council of Pisa (1850), sess. IX, c. 1—*Coll. Lac.*, VI, 237; Council of Thurles (1850), tit. XVI, n. 53—*Coll. Lac.*, III, 783; Council of Ravenna (1855), cap. VIII, n. 3—*Coll. Lac.*, VI, 167; Council of Urbino (1859), c. 69—*Coll. Lac.*, VI, 26; Council of Venice (1859), pars III, c. 2—*Coll. Lac.*, VI, 337; Council of Quito (1863), decr. III, n. 4—*Coll. Lac.*, VI, 402; Council of New Granada (1868), tit. IV, c. 11—*Coll. Lac..*, VI, 520.

riage.[2] In regard to these the pastor was to conduct a diligent examination in order to determine their freedom to marry. The required testimonial letters were to be obtained from the proper pastor. These letters were to bear the seal and signature of the bishop of the diocese in question whenever that procedure could be followed. All cases of this type were to be referred to the ordinary of the diocese in which the marriage was to take place, for he alone could give the permission required for its celebration.

The decree *Cum alias,* although it remained disregarded in many sections, was confirmed in several local councils, which insisted upon the interrogation of witnesses as a necessary means for establishing the free status to contract marriage.[3]

The requirements of the law concerning the prenuptial investigation were applied to the territories of the United States and Canada by the Councils of Baltimore and the II Provincial Council of Quebec respectively.[4] In these councils the observance of the three principal elements of the examination as determined by Benedict XIV was enjoined on pastors as a means to guide them in their inquisitions. Pastors had to be able to determine that the consent to the marriage was being given freely, that there existed no impediments, and that the parties were instructed in Christian doctrine.

---

[2] Council of the Ruthenians (1720), tit. III, n. 8—Mansi, XXX bis, 1504; Council of Tuam (1817), c. 9—*Coll. Lac.*, III, 764; Council of Rouen (1830), c. 20—Mansi, XLIV, 47; Council of Sens (1850), c. 8—Mansi, XLIV, 235; Council of Toulouse (1850), c. 76—Mansi, XLIV, 392; Council of Thurles (1850), tit. XVI, n. 55—*Coll. Lac.*, III, 783; I Provincial Council of Westminster (1852), decr. XXI, n. 7—*Coll. Lac.*, III, 937; II Provincial Council of Quebec (1854), tit. XIII, n. 55—*Coll. Lac.*, III, 648; Council of the Port of Spain (1854), art. VI, n. 2—*Coll. Lac.*, III, 1099; Council of Ravenna (1855), cap. VIII, nn. 4-6—*Coll. Lac.*, VI, 167; Council of Urbino (1859), n. 68—*Coll. Lac.*, VI, 25; Council of New Granada (1868), tit. IV, c. 11—*Coll. Lac.*, VI, 521.

[3] Council of the Ruthenians (1720), tit. III, n. 8—Mansi, XXX bis, 1504; I Provincial Council of Westminster (1852), decr. XXI, n. 7—*Coll. Lac.*, III, 937; Council of Urbino (1859), c. 66—*Coll. Lac.*, VI, 25; Council of Ravenna (1855), cap. VIII, n. 6—*Coll. Lac.*, VI, 168; Council of New Granada (1866), tit. IV, c. 11—*Coll. Lac.*, VI, 521; I Council of Smyrna (1869), cap. V, n. 6—*Coll. Lac.*, VI, 572.

[4] Diocesan Synod of Baltimore (1791), sess. IV, c. 8—*Coll. Lac.*, III, 4, 5; *Concilii Plenarii Baltimorensis II Acta et Decreta,* tit. V, cap. 9, nn. 328, 329—Coll. Lac., III, 487; II Provincial Council of Quebec (1854), c. XIII, nn. 3, 5—*Coll. Lac.*, III, 647, 648.

A response of the Sacred Congregation of the Holy Office to the Bishop of Bardstown, Kentucky, issued May 9, 1821, urged pastors to see to it that nupturients were instructed in the faith, and that they approached the sacrament of penance and received Holy Communion at the time of their marriage.[5]

The reply of the Sacred Congregation for the Propagation of the Faith to the Bishop of Quebec on April 17, 1820, stated that public sinners were not, except for very serious reasons, to be admitted to the contracting of marriage if they refused to confess their sins. Occult sinners could not be excluded from the contracting of marriage, but they were to be admonished by the pastors of their religious duties.[6]

Article 2. Investigation in Cases of the Alleged Death of a Former Spouse

The decree *Cum alias,* concerning the interrogation of witnesses, had demanded that a special investigation be conducted in cases in which it was alleged that a former spouse had died.[7] It was especially required that authentic documentary evidence be produced in substantiation of the assertions of the fact of death.

Subsequent to the decree *Cum alias* the Holy See issued various responses to clarify its norms and to give directives for specific cases.[8] The legislation on this point culminated in two Instructions of the Sacred Congregation of the Holy Office, the *Ingentes bellorum clades* of June 22, 1822, and the *Matrimonii vinculo* of May 13, 1868.

The first of these Instructions, the *Ingentes bellorum clades,*[9] followed closely the order and arrangement in the de-

---

[5] *Fontes,* n. 861.

[6] *Fontes,* n. 4716.

[7] S. C. S. Off., decr. 21 aug. 1670, n. 11—*Fontes,* n. 742; cf. Chapter V. p.

[8] S. C. S. Off., resp. (ad Vic. Apost. Transvaal), 23 iun. 1671—*Fontes,* n. 745; S. C. de Prop. Fide, instr. (ad Pro-Vic. Apos. Tunkin. Occident.), 1792—*Fontes,* n. 4632; S. C. C., in Papiensi Matrimonii, 12 dec. 1733—*Thesaurus Resolutionum Sacrae Congregationis Concilii,* VI, 210.

[9] *Concilii Plenarii Baltimorensis II Acta et Decreta* (ed. altera, Baltimorae: John Murphy, 1894), Appendix IV, pp. 284-286.

cree *Cum alias.*[10] In addition it considered those difficult cases in which it was impossible to obtain direct testimony to substantiate the claim that the former spouse had died. Admitting that often proofs considered individually were in themselves insufficient, it asserted that a consideration of a number of such minor proofs when taken together could suffice to induce the necessary moral certitude. Therefore no means of proof was to be disregarded; even conjectures, presumptions and public opinion would have their effect in confirming the testimony of witnesses.[11] This instruction was reissued on two later occasions.[12]

Finally, however, because of the increasing number of petitions sent to the Holy See concerning this matter, the more complete Instruction, *Matrimonii vinculo,* was issued in the year 1868.[13] It outlined definite norms to guide bishops and pastors in the attaining of moral certainty regarding the alleged death. Long absence, it was stated, was in itself no proof. Either authentic documents or the testimonies of two reliable witnesses were required to provide a basis for conclusive certainty. In extraordinary cases, when but one witness was obtainable, the testimony of this single witness could suffice, provided that he was trustworthy and that his assertions were not improbable in what they alleged. In default of both documents and the testimony of reliable witnesses the subsidiary adminicular proofs permitted by the earlier Instruction, *Ingentes bellorum clades,* were to be considered. Should doubt still persist, then the only course remaining was the reference of the case to the Holy See.[14] The Instruction *Matrimonii vinculo* remained and still

---

[10] S. C. S. Off. decr., 21 aug. 1670—*Fontes*, n. 742; cf. *supra*, Chapter V. p.

[11] S. C. S. Off., instr. *Ingentes bellorum clades*, 12 iun. 1822—*Coll. Lac.*, III, 557-558; *Concilii Plenarii Baltimorensis II Acta et Decreta*, Appendix IV, pp. 284-286.

[12] S. C. S. Off., 28 iun. 1865—*Fontes*, n. 984; S. C. S. Off., 21 nov. 1866 —*Fontes*, n. 997.

[13] S. C. S. Off., 13 maii 1868, n. 2—*Fontes*, n. 1002.

[14] *Loc. cit.* Cf. Rice, *Proof of Death in Prenuptial Investigation*, The Catholic University of America Canon Law Studies, 123 (Washington, The Catholic University of America Press, 1940), pp. 30-36.

remains the norm for the settlement of cases involving the question of the alleged death of one of the consorts.

Article 3. Influences of Civil Law Marriages on the Investigation

As a result of the French Revolution (1791), the State usurped the exclusive rights of the Church over marriage and established the civil ceremony as obligatory. This secularist notion spread rapidly from France to other nations with the consequent adoption by them of the newly formed Napoleonic Code.[15]

With this introduction new problems faced pastors in the preparation of parties for marriage. Lax Catholics were prone to disregard the authority of the Church over marriage by entering unions solely before the civil Magistrate. In such regions where the decree *Tametsi* of the Council of Trent concerning the form of marriage had never been promulgated, such unions were considered valid in the eyes of the Church, provided that no diriment impediment was present. Consequent civil divorce with a view to future marriage did not remove the impediment of previous bond arising from the first marriage. The result was that pastors were obliged to investigate more assiduously the possible existence of the impediment to which any extant valid matrimonial union gave rise.

Since the State, too, conducted an investigation previous to the concession of permission to marry, the question arose whether the priest could accept this investigation as sufficient proof of the free state of the parties, and thus refrain from instituting the customary ecclesiastical examination when the latter approached him for the religious ceremony. The majority of the canonists insisted that the previous investigation conducted according to the law of the State in no way abrogated the duty of the priest, since the civil authorities took no cogniz-

---

[15] McSorley, *Outline History of the Church by Centuries* (St. Louis: Herder, 1945), p. 742.

ance of many of the diriment impediments established by the Church.[16]

Nevertheless, in the light of the Church's recognition of the competency of the State concerning the civil effects of marriage, many councils urged pastors to take care that the civil formalities and regulations were observed by the contracting parties.[17]

Article 4. The Decree *Ne temere*[18]

The celebrated decree *Ne temere,* by establishing a definite obligatory form for the contracting of marriage throughout the universal Church, healed a basic defect which had hampered its efforts to ensure the sanctity and lawfulness of Christian wedlock. The prenuptial investigation, although instituted for that purpose, was minimized if not also nullified in its desired effect in many sections of the world, inasmuch as the faithful in these regions were able to enter a valid marriage without submitting to the requirement of the preliminary inquisition conducted by the priest. Thenceforth, however, such an evasion of the demand made by ecclesiastical authority became impossible, for all Catholics who throughout the Church universal contemplated the contracting of marriage had to appear before either the local ordinary, or the pastor in his parish, or a priest delegated by either, and before two witnesses, for the valid contracting of the proposed matrimonial union.[19] Consequently all marriages had to be subjected to the previous investigation

[16] Feije, *De Impedimentis et Dispensationibus Matrimonialibus,* n. 258; Bouix, *Tractatus de Judiciis Ecclesiasticis,* II, 485; Esmein, *Le Mariage en Droit Canonique,* II, 225; Gasparri, *De Matrimonio,* II, Allegatum III, n. V, ad dub. 5, p. 489; Gasparri, *op. cit.,* I, n. 185.

[17] Council of Rouen (1830), c. XX, n. 6—Mansi, XLIV, 47; Council of Rheims (1849), tit. XI, cap. 2—*Coll. Lac.,* IV, 126; Council of Bordeaux (1850), cap. VIII, n. 2—Mansi, XLIV, 88; Council of Clermont (1850), tit. V—Mansi, XLIV, 483; Council of Port of Spain (1854), art. VI, n. 5—*Coll. Lac.,* III, 1099; Convention of the Bishops of Austria (1856), tit. I, n. 69—*Coll. Lac.,* V, 1295; Council of Kalocsa (1863), tit. III, c. 12—*Coll. Lac.,* V., 858; Council of Utrecht (1865), tit. IV, c. 12—*Coll. Lac.,* V. 840.

[18] S. C. C., 2 aug. 1907—*Fontes,* n. 4340.

[19] S. C. C., decr. *Ne temere,* 2 aug. 1907, V, nn. 1, 4—Fontes, n. 4340.

of the priest, for the decree forbade him to assist at any marriage until he was certain of the free status of the contracting parties.[20]

The Sacred Congregation of the Sacraments a few years later issued a further Instruction with a view to correcting pastors with regard to the making of the prenuptial investigation.[21] Ordinaries were urged to see to it that pastors of their jurisdiction observed the regulations of the decree *Ne temere.* Furthermore, a new requisite called for fulfillment. Whenever a party to the marriage had been baptized in a parish other than that in which the marriage was to be celebrated, a certificate of his or her baptism was to be obtained. The efficacy of this regulation depended on the observance of the direction of the decree *Ne temere,* which required pastors to have each marriage recorded not only in the marriage register of the parish in which it had been celebrated, but also in the baptismal register of the parish in which each party had been baptized.[22] This salutary innovation, whose object was the discovery of any possible previous unions contracted by either of the parties, greatly facilitated the investigation of the priest. To enforce these regulations ordinaries were empowered to punish priests who were delinquent in this regard.[23]

These were the final developments prior to the promulgation of the present Code of Canon Law on Pentecost Sunday, May 27, 1917. The present law, as built upon the various developments discussed in this and the foregoing chapters, is contained particularly in canon 1020.

Summary of the Historical Development

The first traces of the prenuptial investigation are found in the writings of St. Ignatius of Antioch, in which mention was made of the practice of seeking the consent of the bishop prior to marriage. It is unlikely that bishops gave this appro-

---

[20] *Loc. cit.*

[21] 6 mart. 1911—*Acta Apostolicae Sedis, Commentarium Officiale,* (Romae, 1909-1929; Civitate Vaticana, 1929—), III (1911), 102, 103.

[22] S. C. C., 2 aug. 1007, IX, nn. 1, 2—*Fontes,* n. 4340.

[23] S. C. de Sacramentis, instr. 6 mart. 1911—*AAS,* III (1911), 103.

bation without having obtained some assurance of the free state of the parties. Furthermore, it is probable that, when the Faith was being spread among the population that lived outside of the episcopal cities, the consent was sought of those priests who began to share the duties of the pastoral office of the bishop. During the ninth century, when marriages between blood-relatives had become a prevalent evil, a more definite and legal investigation was instituted in certain localities, evidence of which can be found in the Capitularies of Charlemagne and in the collection of capitularies made by Benedict the Levite. Due to the influence of this localized legislation, the prenuptial investigation was introduced into the general law of the Church by the IV General Council of the Lateran (1215). Additional prescripts, especially concerning the marriages of *vagi,* were issued in the Council of Trent. A more exacting investigation became the law with the appearance of the decree *Cum alias* in the year 1670, which decreed a juridical interrogation of witnesses with a view to establishing the freedom of the parties to marry. However, the law as it exists today was substantially formed by Benedict XIV, who determined that the investigation should concern itself with the establishment of the freedom of consent, of the freedom from impediments, and of the existence of a knowledge regarding the rudiments of the Faith. The legislation appearing after that time was directed mainly at providing norms for the investigation of particular types of marriages, or for the settlement of specific problems that had arisen. The prenuptial investigation entered the modern era with the issuance of the decree *Ne temere* in 1907.

PART TWO — CANONICAL COMMENTARY

CHAPTER VIII

INTRODUCTORY REMARKS CONCERNING THE OBLIGATION AND THE NATURE OF THE PRENUPTIAL INVESTIGATION

The previous legislation concerning the prenuptial investigation which has been traced through its principal evolutions in the preceding chapters acquired its modern form with the promulgation of the Code of Canon Law in the year 1917. It is contained in Chapter I of Title VII, "*De matrimonio,*" of the Third Book of the Code, and especially in canon 1020, which reads as follows:

Section 1. Parochus cui ius est assistendi matrimonio, opportuno antea tempore, deligenter investiget num matrimonio contrahendo aliquid obstet.

Section 2. Tum sponsum tum sponsam etiam seorsum et caute interroget num aliquo detineantur impedimento, an consensum liber, praesertim mulier, praestent, et an in doctrina christiana sufficienter instructi sint, nisi ob personarum qualitatem haec ultima interrogatio inutilis appareat.

Section 3. Ordinarii loci est peculiares normas pro huiusmodi parochi investigatione dare.

Herein the obligation and the essential elements of the investigation are clearly determined. The Holy See, however, solicitous that the requirements of the law be thoroughly understood in this important matter and that carelessness in observing its precepts be corrected, issued through the Sacred Congregation of the Sacraments two Instructions concerning this legislation.[1] These documents, in keeping with the purpose of such instructions as determined by Pope

[1] 26 iun. 1921—*AAS*, VIII (1921), 348-349; 29 iun. 1941—*AAS*, XXXIII (1941), 297-318.

Benedict XV (1914-1922) in his *Motu Proprio, "Cum iuris canonici,"*[2] seek to throw greater light upon the requirements of the law, and thus attribute greater efficiency to the matter of investigating persons about to be married. They are to be looked upon as explaining and complementing the legislation of the Code.

The first of these two Instructions, that of the year 1921, was prompted by the complaints of many ordinaries that pastors were failing to observe the regulations of the Code concerning the investigation regarding the canonical freedom to marry, and were neglecting to send notification of marriages contracted to the parishes of baptism. The Instruction had special reference to the marriages of emigrants from Europe. It reminded ordinaries and pastors that no marriage was to be witnessed until the free state of the parties had been investigated according to the law of the Code; that a certificate of baptism was to be obtained if the party had been baptized outside the parish of the investigating priest; that pastors were to send a notification of the marriage to the parish of baptism; and that the transmission of the required documents was to be made through the Chancery Office of the Episcopal Curia. Finally, ordinaries were to see to it that these prescriptions were faithfully observed, even to the extent of punishing violators with canonical sanctions.[3]

The second and far more comprehensive Instruction, that of the year 1941, demands with great insistence that the prenuptial investigation conducted by the pastor be so thorough that everything possible be done for preventing parties from entering invalid or unlawful unions. To assist priests in conducting this examination, the requirements of the Code, as contained especially in Canon 1020, are explained in detail, and a definite form of investigation to be used for all marriages is indicated. The Sacred Congregation is most

---

[2] 15 sept. 1917, n. II—*AAS*, IX (1917), 483.

[3] S. C. de Sacramentis, instr. 26 iun. 1921—*AAS*, XIII (1921), 348-349; T. Lincoln Bouscaren, *The Canon Law Digest* (2 vols., Milwaukee: Bruce Publishing Co., 1934, 1943), I, 497.

insistent that the regulations of the Instruction be diligently observed; it beseeches ordinaries to take the necessary steps to introduce in their respective dioceses the recommended mode of procedure, and to exercise every care that the details of the Instruction be put into effect.[4]

It is the intention of the writer to consider in detail the canonical legislation on the prenuptial investigation as contained fundamentally in canon 1020, with special emphasis being placed on the additional explanatory regulations of the Instruction of the Sacred Congregation of the Sacraments of the year 1941. This Instruction will hereafter be referred to as the Instruction *Sacrosanctum matrimonii.*

The present introductory chapter will concern itself with determining the pastor upon whom the obligation of investigating is to be placed, the extent of his obligation, the persons subject to it, and in a general way the manner of conducting the investigation.

Article 1. The Investigating Pastor

A. Scope of the Term "Pastor"

The term "pastor" may be accepted either in a strict sense or in a broad sense. A pastor in the strict sense is an individual priest or a moral person upon whom a parish is conferred in title with the care of souls, to be exercised under the authority of the local ordinary.[5] In the broad sense, the term "pastor" includes also those priests who are made equivalent to pastors in the law, in so far as they have certain pastoral rights and obligations, including the right to assist at marriages. This latter category comprises:

(a) *quasi-pastors,* or those who have charge of quasi-parishes.[6]

---

[4] S. C. de Sacramentis, instr. 29 iun. 1941, n. 12—*AAS*, XXXIII (1941), 306.

[5] Can. 451, c. 1.

[6] Can. 451, c. 2.

(b) *vicarii curati,* who exercise the actual care of souls in a parish entrusted to a moral person;[7]

(c) *vicarii oeconomii,* or administrators, who take charge of a parish during its vacancy;[8]

(d) *vicarii substituti,* who with the approval of the ordinary are entrusted with the care of the parish by the pastor during the time of the pastor's absence;[9]

(e) *vicarii adiutores,* who are assigned to aid a disabled pastor, if they enjoy full parochial rights, or if their letters of appointment grant them the authority to assist at marriages.[10]

With regard to *vicarii cooperatores,* or assistants, particular attention must be paid to diocesan statutes, wherein are determined their rights and obligations regarding assistance at marriages. Frequently they are given a general delegation to assist at all marriages in the parish to which they are attached, as is permissible by the law of the Code.[11]

B. Priests Who Have a Right to Assist at Marriages

Before a pastor may assist validly at any marriage, he must already have taken canonical possession of his parish according to the prescripts of canon 1444, § 1, or have legitimately entered into his office. Furthermore he must not be excommunicated, interdicted or suspended by a court sentence, or declared to be such by an ecclesiastical tribunal.[12]

Secondly, a pastor can assist validly only at marriages which take place within the limits of his parish; but in that territory he does so not only for the marriages of his subjects but for others as well.[13]

Finally, the pastor must freely ask and receive the con-

[7] Can. 471, c. 1.
[8] Can. 473, c. 1.
[9] Can. 465, cc. 4, 5; can. 474.
[10] Can. 475.
[11] Can. 1096, c. 1.
[12] Can. 1095, c. 1, n. 1.
[13] Can. 1095, c. 1, n. 2.

sent of the parties; he must not be compelled to do so by means of violence or through grave fear.[14]

The fact that a pastor has complied with these conditions necessary for a valid assistance does not, however, give him the right to assist lawfully at all marriages. Canon 1097 delineates certain added conditions as required for lawful assistance. It requires, first of all, that the pastor duly ascertain the freedom of the parties to intermarry in accordance with the prescriptions of the law. Secondly, he must have a title to assist at the marriage, arising from the fact that at least one of the parties has a domicile, a quasi-domicile or a month's residence in his parish or, in the case of a *vagus,* an actual residence in the parish at the time of marriage.

From the foregoing it is evident that several pastors may at one and the same time be equally competent to assist at a particular marriage. This plurality of competent pastors may arise from the fact that the prospective bride and groom have domiciles, or a month's residence in different parishes. In such cases the law attributes to the pastor of the bride a preferred right to assist at the marriage, ruling that the marriage is to be celebrated before the pastor of the bride, unless some just cause excuses.[15] This cause need not be a serious one, provided that it is reasonable.

There is a difference of opinion as to whether the words "*coram parocho sponsae*" refer to the pastor of a non-Catholic bride. The negative opinion holds that the non-Catholic is not a subject of the pastor in whose parish she lives.[16] Another opinion distinguishes between a non-Catholic who is baptized and one who is unbaptized, contending that in the first case the pastor of the bride has preference, and in the second he has not.[17] A third opinion interprets the phrase as applying equally to the

[14] Can. 1095, c. 1, n. 3.

[15] Can. 1097, c. 2.

[16] Ludovicus Fanfani, *De Iure Parochorum ad norman Codicis Iuris Canonici* (Taurini-Romae: Marietti, 1924), n. 309.

[17] G. Payen, *De Matrimonio in Missionibus ac potissimum in Sinis Tractatus Practicus et Casus* (2. ed., 3 vols., Zi-ka-wei: In Typographia T'ou-se-we, 1935-1936) II, n. 1805 (hereafter this work will be cited as Payen. *De Matrimonio.)*

pastor of a non-Catholic bride and to the pastor of a Catholic bride.[18] In the United States and Canada it is customary for the pastor of the groom to assist at a marriage in which the bride is a non-Catholic. Since the Holy See has made no definite pronouncement in this matter, this manner of acting is quite permissible.

A further plurality of pastors may result from the fact that the bride or the groom have several domiciles or quasi-domiciles, or have a domicile and quasi-domicile or a month's residence in different parishes at the same time. In such cases it seems that the bride may choose one of the competent pastors to assist at the marriage.[19]

Furthermore a pastor who has not the right to assist lawfully at a marriage inasmuch as neither of the parties to the marriage has a domicile, a quasi-domicile or a month's residence in his parish can receive permission to do so from a pastor who is thus legally competent.[20]

Finally, a competent pastor can delegate a particular priest to assist at a given marriage which is to take place in his parish.[21] This delegation, however, is not to be granted until the free status of the contracting parties has been established in accordance with the prescripts of the law.[22]

C. Pastors Who are to Conduct the Investigation

Canon 1020 states that the pastor who has the right to assist at the marriage ought to conduct a diligent investigation at a suitable time before the marriage. The Instruction *Sacrosanctum matrimonii* similarly states that the pastor to

[18] John J. Carberry, *The Juridical Form of Marriage*, The Catholic University of America Canon Law Studies, n. 84 (Washington: The Catholic University of America, 1930), p. 109; Francis J. Schenk, *The Matrimonial Impediments of Mixed Religion and Disparity of Cult*, The Catholic University of America Canon Law Studies, n. 51 (Washington: The Catholic University of America, 1929), p. 285 (hereafter cited as Schenk, *Mixed Religion and Disparity of Cult)*.

[19] Donovan, *The Pastor's Obligation in the Prenuptial Investigation*, p. 80.

[20] Can. 1097, c. 1, n. 3.

[21] Can. 1096, c. 1.

[22] Cf. can. 1096, c. 2.

whom it pertains to assist at the marriage has the right and duty of investigating and adds that, unless a good reason excuse, this will be the pastor of the bride.[23]

In view of what has been said in the preceding section of this article, by the pastor of the bride is meant the pastor of that parish in which the bride has a domicile, a quasi-domicile or a month's residence; by the pastor of the groom, the pastor of the parish in which the groom has a domicile, a quasi-domicile or a month's residence, or in the case of *vagi*, actual residence at the time of marriage. Therefore any pastor in whose parish the bride or groom has established one of these various types of residence is competent to assist at their marriage, and when he consents to exercise his right to do so, he assumes automatically the duty of investigating concerning the free status of the parties.

Recalling the preference given to the pastor of the bride in canon 1097, § 1, n. 3, the Instruction states that the right and duty of investigating will devolve upon the pastor of the bride, unless a good cause excuses. But the Instruction continues as follows, "the pastor of the groom, however, either on his own accord, or at the instance of the groom or of the bride's pastor shall institute an examination to make sure of the free state of the groom, and upon conclusion of this investigation shall send at once to the bride's pastor written proof thereof along with such other requisite documents as may be found in his parish archives."[24]

According to the wording of the Instruction, it is apparent that the primary obligation of conducting the investigation is placed upon the competent pastor before whom the parties appear for marriage, who normally will be the pastor of the bride. It is equally apparent, however, that the Holy See desires that whenever possible the groom is to be investigated by his own pastor, who naturally should be in a better position to ascertain the free status of his subject. Wherefore, when the parties appear before the pastor of the

[23] S. C. de Sacramentis, instr. 29 iun. 1941, n. 4—*AAS*, XXXIII (1941), 299.

[24] *Loc. cit.*

bride for marriage, he should send the groom to his own pastor for the prenuptial investigation, whenever this can be done conveniently. Frequently the groom will go to his own pastor on his own accord, either because he is living at some distance from the parish of the bride in which the marriage is to take place, or because he prefers to undergo the investigation before his own pastor. But even if he is not requested to conduct the prenuptial examination by the pastor of the bride or by the groom himself, the pastor of the groom on his own account should institute a diligent investigation to establish the freedom of his subject to marry. A written account of the examination, together with the pertinent documents he may have in his parish registers, must then be sent to the pastor who is to assist at the marriage.[25] In the transmission of these documents, the procedure outlined in Chapter XII of this work is to be followed.[26]. Similarly the pastor of the bride should institute a separate examination of the bride, whenever for some just cause the marriage is to take place before the pastor of the groom.

When the marriage is to take place before a pastor who assists thereat by virtue of permission granted by the pastor of the parish in which one of the parties has a domicile, a quasi-domicile or a month's residence, or before a priest who has been delegated to do so, the investigation is to be conducted by the pastor who grants the permission or the delegation, in accordance with the procedure discussed in the preceding paragraph, i.e., the pastor of the bride will personally investigate the freedom of the bride, and will refer the groom to his own pastor for a similar investigation. This manner of acting is deduced from the prescripts of canon 1096, § 2, which states that the pastor is not to grant permission to another priest to assist at the marriage unless he has fulfilled all the requisites of the law for the establishing

---

[25] P. Aguirre, "Brevis explanatio Instructionis"—*Periodica de Re Canonica, Morali, Liturgica* (Brugis, 1927-), XXX (1941), 370-385.

[26] Cf. *infra*, pp. 163-165, S. C. de Sacramentis, instr. 29 iun. 1941, n. 4 (a)—*AAS*, XXXIII (1941), 299.

of the free state of the parties.[27] An efficient and effective prenuptial investigation demands that such should be the case, for surely the pastor to whom has been committed the care of souls is in a much better position to examine those with whom he has had frequent contact, and of whom he consequently has greater knowledge, than one who has merely a limited interest in them.[28]

Article 2. Gravity of the Pastor's Obligation

The Instruction *Sacrosanctum matrimonii* states that the duty of investigating binds the pastor *sub gravi* as is evident from the gravity of the matter concerned. He is not dispensed from this task in simple consequence of being morally certain that nothing stands in the way of the licit and valid celebration of the marriage; the investigation must be made by the pastor personally, unless a good reason excuse him.[29]

The clear wording of the Instruction leaves no room for doubt as to the serious nature of the pastor's obligation of inquiring personally into the free status of those about to be married. Indeed this obligation, as has been seen in the previous legislation, has always been considered a grave one.[30]

Furthermore, moral theologians and canonists are in accord in pronouncing the seriousness of the pastor's obligation in this matter.[31] An added indication as to the gravity of this obligation is had in the concluding paragraph of the Instruc-

---

[27] Gasparri, *Tractatus Canonicus de Matrimonio*, I, n. 129.

[28] Gasparri, *loc. cit.;* T. Lincoln Bouscaren and Adam C. Ellis, *Canon Law, A Text and Commentary* (Milwaukee: Bruce, 1946), p. 410; (hereafter cited Bouscaren-Ellis, *Canon Law);* Carberry, *The Juridical Form of Marriage*, 81.

[29] S. C. de Sacramentis, instr., 29 iun. 1941, n. 4 (a)—*AAS*, XXXIII (1941), 299.

[30] IV General Council of the Lateran (1215), c. 51—Mansi, XX, 1038, Benedictus XIV, ep. encycl., *Etsi minime*, 7 febr. 1742, § 11—*Fontes*, n. 324; Benedictus XIV, ep. encycl., *Nimiam licentiam*, 18 maii 1743, § 10 —*Fontes*, n. 337.

[31] H. Noldin-A. Schmitt, *Summa Theologiae Moralis* (26 ed., 3 vols., Oeniponte, Lipsiae: Ratisbonae: Pustet, 1940), III, n. 546; Gasparri, *Tractatus Canonicus de Matrimonio*, I, n. 130; F. Cappello, *Tractatus Canonico-Moralis de Sacramentis*, vol. V, *De Matrimonio* (5 ed., Romae: Marietti, 1947), n. 146 (hereafter cited *De Matrimonio)*.

tion,[32] wherein the Sacred Congregation directs ordinaries, in accordance with canon 2222, § 1, to punish pastors who are negligent in this regard.

The gravity of this obligation arises from the nature and the importance of the prenuptial investigation, and from the purpose of the law, which is to safeguard the sanctity of the matrimonial contract by ensuring a valid and a lawful union. So important is the obligation that, even in cases in which the pastor is morally certain that nothing stands in the way of a valid and licit union, he must nevertheless make the required investigations. This principle is in keeping with the general norm enacted in Canon 21 of the Code, which states that laws enacted for the purpose of preventing a general danger bind even in particular cases in which it appears that the danger is nonexistent. Even in the extreme case of the danger of death, the investigation must not be entirely omitted, but rather some assurance of freedom to marry must be obtained.[33]

Finally, this obligation is incumbent upon the pastor personally. As has been indicated above,[34] the entire investigation as outlined in the Instruction *Sacrosanctum matrimonii* is to be carried out by the pastors of the bride and the groom, even when another priest is to be delegated or given permission to assist at the marriage.[35] A just cause, however, and not necessarily a grave one, will permit the pastor to commit the duty of investigating to another.[36] Certainly a reasonable cause exists for the pastors of large parishes in modern cities to commission their assistants to share this obligation of investigating. To insist that the pastor personally conduct the prenuptial examination for the numerous parties who present themselves for marriage in such parishes would not only place an unwarranted burden

---

[32] S. C. de Sacramentis, instr. 29 iun. 1941, n. 12—*AAS*, XXXIII (1941), 306, 307.

[33] Can. 1019, § 2.

[34] Cf. *supra*, p.

[35] Cans. 1096, § 2, 1097, § 1, n. 3; S. C. de Sacramentis, instr., 29 iun. 1941, n. 4 (a)—*AAS*, XXXIII (1941), 299; Coronata, *Tractatus Canonicus de Sacramentis* (3 vols., Romae: Marietti, 1943-1946), III, *De Matrimonio*, n. 75 (hereafter cited *De Matrimonio)*.

[36] Cappello, *De Matrimonio*, n. 151.

upon the pastor, but would also tend to lessen the effectiveness of the investigation.

In writing on this question, Bastnagel.[37] states that two pastoral duties are to be considered, viz., the duty of personally making the investigation, and the duty of imparting pastoral training to those priests who are associated with him in the care of souls. This latter duty will constitute a reasonable cause for prompting the pastor to depute his curates to assist him in investigating the persons about to be married.

In conclusion it may be said that circumstances will often justify the pastor in delegating others to conduct the prenuptial investigation; at times the welfare of souls will demand that he do so.

Article 3. The Subject of the Investigation

As has been considered in the two preceding articles, the obligation of investigating those persons at whose marriage he has a right to assist is placed directly upon the pastor by virtue of the fact that at least one of the contracting parties has a domicile, a quasi-domicile, or a month's residence in his parish. The question now arises: who are the persons who must appear before a Catholic pastor in order to contract validly the sacrament of matrimony, and thereby submit themselves to the investigation of the pastor?

In this regard it is necessary first of all to recall the prescripts of canon 1099, which indicates the persons who are bound by the canonical form of marriage. From a consideration of this canon, it may be concluded that the following are subject to the prenuptial investigation of the pastor in whose parish they have a domicile, a quasi-domicile, or a month's residence:

(1) all persons baptized in the Catholic Church, except

---

[37] "Parish Assistants and the Prenuptial Investigation"—*The Jurist*, VII (1947), 173.

the ones mentioned in canon 1099, § 2;[38] (2) all persons converted to the Catholic Church from heresy or schism, even though they have again lapsed into heresy or schism;[39] and (3) such other persons who wish to marry those who receive mention in numbers (1) and (2), even though such other persons are not bound to the Catholic form when they marry among themselves, viz., infidels, heretics, schismatics, Orientals.[40]

Likewise it may be deduced that the following persons are *not subject* to the prenuptial investigation of the Catholic pastor:

(1) unconverted non-Catholics, whether baptized, such as heretics and schismatics, or unbaptized, such as infidels or pagans, whenever such persons marry among themselves;[41] and (2) persons born of non-Catholic parentage who, although baptized in the Catholic Church, were nevertheless reared from infancy in heresy, in schism or without any religion, when they marry non-Catholics.[42] In this regard the decision of the Pontifical Commission for the Authentic Interpretation of the Code must be kept in mind; it declared that among the *ab acatholici nati* are included also those who were born of parents of whom only one was a non-Catholic, even if at the time of the marriage the cautions were given according to canons 1061 and 1071.[43] A later decision which contemplated the same set of circumstances included in this exception also the children born of apostate parents.[44] Apostate parents are those who have completely given up the Christian faith, or, in a wider sense, those who openly have rejected the Catholic faith and thereupon have become members of non-Catholic sects, or, without joining a sect, are generally known to have rejected the Catholic religion

[38] Can. 1099, § 1, n. 1. For a classification of those persons who are to be considered as baptized in the Catholic Church, cf. H. Ayrinhac-P. Lydon, *Marriage Legislation in the New Code of Canon Law* (New York: Benziger Brother, 1932), n. 133 (hereafter cited as Ayrinhac-Lydon, *Marriage Legislation);* William J. Doheny, *Canonical Procedure in Matrimonial Cases*, vol. II, *Informal Procedure* (Milwaukee; Bruce, 1944), 38-40 (hereafter cited as *Canonical Procedure*, II).

[39] Can. 1099, § 1, n. 1; Can. 1325, 2.

[40] Can. 1099, § 1, nn. 2, 3.

[41] Can. 1099, § 2.

[42] Can. 1099, § 2.

[43] 20 iul. 1929—*AAS*, XXI (1929), 573.

[44] 17 febr. 1930—*AAS*, XXII (1930), 195.

and to have become free-thinkers. Merely negligent Catholics who rarely attend Mass or rarely approach the sacraments are not apostates.[45]

The Latin Code expressly mentions Orientals in relation to the form of marriage, but merely states that they are bound by the canonical form of marriage if they contract with Latins who are bound by this form.[46] The Code does not consider Orientals who marry among themselves, since the question of their form of marriage belongs to their own discipline.[47] It seems, however, that a Latin pastor can assist at the marriage of two Orientals if a resonable cause is present, since according to canon 1095, § 1, n. 2, a pastor in his parish can validly assist at the marriage of non-subjects.[48] The fact that Orientals in a certain locality have no pastor of their own rite would constitute such a reasonable cause.

In this regard the Sacred Congregation for the Oriental Church in an Instruction of the year 1935, issued in reply to a question from the Apostolic Delegate to the United States, declared in part. "There is no difficulty in declaring that the Maronites, as all Orientals for that matter, in places where they have no diocese of their own can contract marriage in accordance with the prescripts of canon 1094, i.e., before the pastor or the ordinary of the place or a priest delegated by either and before two witnesses."[49] In such cases in which the Latin pastor would undertake to assist at the marriage of two Orientals, it is only natural that he should investigate their freedom to intermarry. Thus in certain instances Orientals are subject to the prenuptial investigation of the Latin pastor, even when they marry among themselves.

---

[45] *Periodica*—XX (1931), 77-81; Ayrinhac-Lydon, *Marriage Legislation*, n. 256.

[46] Can. 1099, § 1, n. 3.

[47] Joseph F. Marbach, *Marriage Legislation for the Catholics of the Oriental Rites in the United States and Canada*, The Catholic University of America Canon Law Studies, n. 243, (Washington: The Catholic University of America Press, 1946), 205.

[48] Marbach, *op. cit.*, 209.

[49] Stephen C. Gulovich, *Matrimonial Laws of the Catholic Eastern Churches*—*Jurist*, IV (1944), 235-236; Marbach, *op. cit.*, 209.

The extraordinary cases mentioned in canon 1098 present a further question. According to this canon, if it is impossible without grave inconvenience to send for or go to the pastors or ordinary, or to a priest delegated by either of these to assist at a marriage in accordance with the prescripts of canons 1095 and 1096, then 1) in case of danger of death, marriage will be contracted validly and licitly in the presence of the witnesses only; and it will be the same outside of the danger of death, provided it be prudently foreseen that this condition of things is to last for a month; 2) in both cases if another priest is at hand who can come, he should be called and should assist at the marriage together with the witnesses, but the marriage would be valid if contracted in the presence of the witnesses alone.

The question arises: If such a priest is called to assist at the marriage, are the contracting parties subject to the prenuptial investigation at his hands? True it is, he is not the pastor, and it is upon the pastor that the obligation of investigating is placed in canon 1020, § 1. But the natural law would demand that before any priest assist at the contracting of this important sacrament, he should be assured that there be nothing present which would hinder the contract, and this he could ascertain only by investigation.

Furthermore, the general law as contained in canon 1019 demands that before any marriage be celebrated it must be ascertained that there is no obstacle to its valid and licit celebration. Even in danger of death the freedom to marry must be established, at least through the sworn statements of the parties, if more complete proofs are unobtainable, as is evident from the second paragraph of the canon. Thus it is the opinion of the writer that in these extraordinary circumstances these persons, though not bound to the canonical form of marriage, are subject to the investigation of the priest who is called upon to witness the marriage.

Article 4. The Time and Place for the Investigation

The Instruction *Sacrosanctum matrimonii*, as well as canon 1020, states that the investigation is to be made at an opportune time before the marriage. The Instruction goes on to say that this should be prior to the proclamation of the banns, or at least during the course thereof.[50] Herein is enunciated the general rule which is to be followed in all *ordinary* cases.

As to the connotation of the phrase *"at an opportune time,"* no precise mathematical space of time is determined but indications thereof are not lacking. Both the law of the Code and the interpretation of the Instruction specify that the investigation should take place preferably before or at least during the proclamation of the banns. This is not stated directly in the Code, but it is to be inferred from the law.

First of all, it may be pointed out that the order of Chapter I of Title VII in Book III, which concerns itself with the preliminaries to marriage, is such that the legislation on the prenuptial investigation precedes that of the proclamation of the banns.[51] Likewise, the tenor of canon 1031, which concerns the detection of impediments in relation to the proclamation of the banns, presupposes that the investigation precedes the publications, although it does admit that the existence of an impediment may be revealed after the proclamations and possibly as a result thereof. But ordinarily the publication is not to begin until a dispensation is had from an existing public impediment, and this naturally presupposes some previous examination for the detection of such impediments.

With this in mind, Payen (1941)[52] suggested that the investigation take place four or at least three weeks prior to the marriage. This determination is well chosen in view of the fact that the proclamation of the banns must usually begin at least three weeks before the marriage, and at least a week may be necessary to obtain through the mail the required dispensation from an impediment if one is revealed through the investigation. In practice it is safe to say that in all ordinary cases the pre-

[50] S. C. de Sacramentis, instr., 29 iun. 1941, n. 4 (a)—*AAS*, XXXIII (1941), 299.

[51] Canons 1019-1021 deal with the investigation; canons 1022-1031, with the banns.

[52] *De Matrimonio*, III, n. 377.

nuptial investigation should take place one month before the proposed date of marriage.

It is not possible at all times, however, to adhere to this determination of time; frequently extraordinary cases arise which demand a departure from this ruling. The most evident case is that of the danger of death. In this extreme circumstance, marriage cannot be postponed until a certain space of time has elapsed after the investigation of the priest, for such would be neither reasonable nor is it required by the law. In such cases the law exempts the priest from the detailed investigation; if other proofs are unobtainable the priest may accept solely the sworn affirmation of the parties that they are baptized and are not prohibited from marrying by any impediment, unless contrary indications are present.[53] The extensive faculties granted for these cases may be employed should any impediments be discovered which come within the scope of the faculties granted in Canons 1043 and 1044, and the matrimonial consent can be immediately asked for and received by the priest.

There are numerous other circumstances which point to the category of extraordinary cases and which thereby demand a shortening of the time between the investigation and the celebration of the marriage. Notable among these are the following urgencies: the convalidation of an invalid marriage, the rectifying of a union of concubinage, the consideration which must be given to a pregnant bride to safeguard the reputation of the parties, the necessity of an immediate departure of one or the other of the parties for distant places, such as the embarkation of a soldier for overseas service. But it must always be borne in mind that no particular urgency will excuse the pastor from making that investigation which is necessary and sufficient to establish the free status of the contracting parties.[54]

As to the *place* for the conducting of the prenuptial investigation, both the Code and the Instruction are silent. It must be asserted, however, that the place chosen should be a respectable one that is in keeping with the seriousness and the sacred-

[53] Can. 1019 § 2.

[54] S. C. de Sacramentis, instr., 4 iul, 1921, n. 1—*AAS*, XIII (1921), 348.

ness of the investigation. The parlor or reception room of the rectory, the pastor's office, and the sacristy can be considered as places suitable for this task. Only in cases of absolute necessity should the interrogation take place in private homes.[55]

Article 5. The Manner of Conducting the Investigation

Since the pastor must strive most diligently to establish the freedom of the parties for their intermarriage, he will be particularly attentive to the means set down in the Instruction *Sacrosanctum matrimonii* for the efficient attainment of that end. He will seek to verify their free status through appropriate documents, through the testimony of reliable witnesses whenever necessary, and especially through direct interrogation of the parties themselves. These various means are discussed at length in the succeeding chapters, but a few remarks concerning the manner in which the pastor is to interrogate the parties will be included in this introductory chapter.

According to canon 1020, § 2, the pastor is to interrogate both the groom and the bride, separately and carefully. Similarly the Instruction states that the pastor interrogate the spouses separately and carefully, that is, according to learned authors, distinctly and with due prudence, modesty and circumspection, particularly when asking about impediments and other circumstances which could suggest infamy or shame.[56]

First of all, it is to be noted that each party to the marriage must be examined separately. Because of the importance of the investigation, the law wishes to afford the party concerned every opportunity of speaking openly and frankly to the queries of the priest, and this can best be accomplished by means of a private interview. Furthermore, when the bride and groom are interrogated separately, one immediately after the other, the danger of collusion is considerably lessened.[57]

---

[55] Donovan, *The Pastor's Obligation in the Prenuptial Investigation* p. 98.

[56] S. C. de Sacramentis, instr., 29 iun. 1941, n. (d)—*AAS*, XXXIII (1941), 301.

[57] Donovan, *The Pastor's Obligation in the Prenuptial Investigation*, p. 101.

The second important quality of the priest's interrogation is that it must be careful. The Instruction, as cited above, explains that the pastor is to question the parties distinctly and with due modesty, prudence and circumspection. In other words he will take into consideration the disposition, the character and the learning of the party under question. His questions should be made understandable and clear; they should be phrased in language that will not injure the rightful sensibilities of the parties; they should be plain-spoken if necessary. Throughout the examination the pastor must so conduct himself that he will inspire the parties with confidence and with an appreciation for the sacredness of the sacrament of matrimony.

CHAPTER IX

PRELIMINARY QUESTIONS IN THE INTERROGATION OF THE PARTIES

The emphasis which the Instruction *Sacrosanctum matrimonii* places upon the actual interrogation of the parties by the pastor serves to indicate the important role it is intended to play in the prenuptial investigation. By far the greater part of the Instruction is devoted to a consideration of this phase of the investigation. The Code, in canon 1020, § 2, mentions the general lines which the interrogation is to follow; the Instruction denotes a definite form of interrogation to be observed in all cases.[1]

The importance of this interrogation arises primarily from the fact that it affords perhaps the most effective means whereby the pastor can establish the free status of those about to be married. Further, since the responses of the nupturients to the qustions of the pastor must be committed to a written statement, sworn to and attested by means of their signatures, a permanent record is constituted in which the parties have declared themselves free to marry and to be aware of their consequent obligations. This signed questionnaire is to be kept on file as evidence of the parties' responsibility, to be produced as a valuable document in the event that the validity of the marriage is attacked in the future.[2]

The prenuptial investigation taken in its entirety is clearly an administrative process, by means of which the pastor seeks to establish the free status of the parties to a marriage.[3] Since its object is to afford the pastor sufficient

[1] S. C. de Sacramentis, instr., 29 iun. 1941, Allegatum I—*AAS*, XXXIII (1941), 309.

[2] Ibid., Allegatum I, n. 19—*AAS*, XXXIII (1941), 313; Francis B. Donnelly, "Fraud and the Estoppel of Canon 1971, § 1, n. 1"—*The Jurist*, VI (1946), 381.

[3] Doheny, *Canonical Procedure*, II, 9.

evidence to pass judgment on the right of the parties to enter the married state, its general formalities are not unlike those which are observed in the judicial procedure of the Fourth Book of the Code. True it is, there is no summons, for the parties appear of their own accord. But their appearance before the pastor constitutes a quasi-petition whereby they seek to vindicate their right to enter the married state. Once they have subjected themselves to his scrutiny, the pastor employs many of the methods of proof common to actual judicial procedure to establish their freedom, such as documents, the testimony of witnesses, suppletory oaths and the statements of the parties themselves. The primary importance attached to this latter means of proof, however, is in contrast to the minimum importance of the depositions of the parties in judicial cases, wherein they are not of probatory value.

In the discussion of the interrogation of the parties which is had in the following pages, although the masculine gender singular is used when referring to the "party," whatever is stated applies equally to the bride and the groom, unless a distinction is otherwise noted.

Article 1. The Preliminary Oath "*de veritate dicenda*"

Because of the extreme importance of ascertaining the truth in this matter, the actual interrogation is preceded by the administration of the oath to the party. The law of the Code required the oath of the parties only in those extraordinary cases in which the pastor was unable to establish proof with the aid of the customary means;[4] The Instruction requires it in all cases. There is a similarity between this oath and the one required prior to the deposition of the parties in the judicial procedure.[5]

Before administering the oath to the party, the pastor is to remind him of the sacred character of the oath and of the severity of the punishments to which perjurers are subject. The pastor then asks the party if, in touching the book of

---

[4] Canons 1031, § 1, n. 1; 779; 800; 1019, § 2.

[5] Cf. can. 1744.

the Holy Gospels, he is willing to invoke the name of God in witness of the truth.[6]

The oath administered is that "*de tota et sola veritate dicenda,*" i.e., of telling the truth and nothing but the truth. It is usually formulated in this fashion: "Do you swear to tell the whole truth, and nothing but the truth as regards everything concerning which you are to be questioned?" The first part of the oath, *de tota veritate dicenda,* implies that the party has the obligation of telling all the truth of the matter about which he is being questioned, and excludes the possibility of restricting the truth to certain articles only.[7] The second part of the oath, *de sola veritate dicenda,* explicitly excludes the insertion of any falsehood in the testimony.[8]

The oath is to be asked of all spouses who present themselves to the pastor and subject themselves to his investigation. In the earlier legislation of the decree *Cum alias,* which dealt with the interrogation of witnesses, it was not required that the oath be tendered to non-Catholics.[9] There does not seem to be any good reason, however, why the oath should not be asked of non-Catholics today, especially of those who profess belief in God. For the most part they are aware of the confirmatory value, since it is a common implement of the civil courts. Nevertheless it is particularly important in these cases to stress the sacred and serious character of this act. If either a Catholic or a non-Catholic should refuse to be questioned under oath, the pastor should not insist upon it, but should make note in the questionnaire of the refusal of the oath and of the reason for its refusal.

Actually there is no reference in the Instruction *Sacrosanctum matrimonii* to the refusal of the party to take the oath. The parallel ruling of the Instruction *Provida Mater*

---

[6] S. C. de Sacramentis, instr., 29 iun. 1941, Allegatum I, n. 1—*AAS,* XXXIII (1941), 309. Cf. can. 2323 concerning the penalty for extrajudicial perjury.

[7] Coronata, *Institutiones Iuris Canonici* (2 ed. 5 vols., Taurini-Romae: Marietti, 1939-1947), III, n. 1295.

[8] Coronata, *loc. cit.*

[9] S. C. S. Off., decr., *Cum alias,* 21 aug., 1670—*Fontes,* n. 742.

Ecclesia, although given for judicial procedure, can serve to indicate the course to be followed by the pastor. Therein it is stated that if the party summoned to court refuses to give testimony under oath, and the judge deems that the testimony would be useful in the ascertaining of the truth, he may receive the testimony, making note in the records of the refusal and the reason thereof.[10]

In view of the insistence of the Instruction *Sacrosanctum matrimonii* on the importance of the interrogating the parties, it is to be concluded that the statement of the party, even if not attested to under oath, is to be preferred to the complete absence of any indication whatsoever of the party's freedom and attitude towards the marriage, which would perhaps be the result if the pastor refrained from questioning the party in consequence of the latter's refusal to take the oath. The refusal of the party, however, may forewarn the pastor that he is dealing with a careless or unworthy Catholic.

Article 2. The Identification of the Party

The preliminary questions of the pastor are calculated to identify the party in whose freedom to marry he is interested. Such general information as the full name and surname of the party, the names of his parents including the maiden name of his mother, his place of birth, his age, his religion and that of his bride, and his profession or occupation, is sought.[11]

It is important that the precise family name be had correctly. To this end it is advisable to have the party spell the name, especially in the case of a name which has several renderings. Similarity of names, whether of the parties themselves or of their parents, may suggest the possible existence of the impediments of consanguinity or affinity.

If the party is unknown to the pastor personally, the Instruction requires the production of some document bearing

[10] S. C. de Sacramentis, instr., 15 aug. 1936, art. 96, § 1—*AAS*, XXXIII (1936), 333.

[11] S. C. de Sacramentis, instr., 29 iun. 1941, Allegatum I, n. 1—*AAS*, XXXIII (1941), 309.

the party's photograph as a means of identification, i.e., a passport, a driver's license or a registration card.[12]

The ascertainment of the place of birth of the party is essential for several reasons. First of all, it may indicate the place of baptism. Then, again, it may suggest a certain racial origin and the consequent possibility that the party is the subject of a definite national parish. It may even at times reveal the fact that the person belongs to one or another of the various Oriental rites in the Church, thereby opening the way for the solution of possible jurisdictional problems.

Naturally the preliminary question concerning the religion of the party being interrogated, as well as his knowledge of the religious affiliation of the other party, is significant. It establishes at the outset the possible presence of the impediment of mixed religion or of disparity of worship. Furthermore, this knowledge will guide the pastor in accommodating his questions to the divergent mentality of a person of a different creed.

Likewise the knowledge of the occupation or profession of the party will provide a norm which can serve to direct the pastor in conducting the examination intelligibly and effectively. The station in life usually indicates the educational standard and intellectual capacity to which he must accommodate his questions.

Finally, it is evidently important to ascertain the exact age of the party, in as much as it is a direct indication as to the existence of the impediment of nonage, or as to lack of age required by the civil law for marriage, or lastly as to the necessity of obtaining the permission of the parents of the party before assisting at the marriage.[13]

Article 3. The Residence of the Party

The interrogation of the parties concerning their place of residence is directed primarily at determining whether or not the pastor is competent lawfully to assist at the marriage.

[12] S. C. de Sacramentis, instr., 29 iun. 1941, Allegatum I, n. 1—*AAS*, XXXIII (1941), 309.

[13] Can. 1067; 1016; 1034.

Therefore he must be assured that the parties have a domicile or a quasi-domicile, or have lived at least a month in his parish prior to the date of marriage.[14]

The pastor must keep in mind the principles regarding both the acquisition of and the loss of domicile or quasi-domicile. He will recall that a domicile is acquired either by residence in the parish with the intention of remaining there perpetually, or by actual residence there for ten complete years.[15] Similarly he will remember that a quasi-domicile is obtained either by residence in the parish with the intention of remaining there for the greater part of the year, that is, for over six months, or by actual residence for the greater part of the year.[16]. Both domicile and quasi-domicile are lost when one has departed from the place of his residence with the intention of not returning.[17] The questions of the pastor, then, should be of such a nature that they will establish clearly whether the party being questioned has acquired a domicile or a quasi-domicile, and whether, when once acquired, it has not been lost.

With this in mind the pastor will question the party as to his complete address (place, street and number), together with the name of the parish in which the residence is situated. Furthermore, he will question him as to the length of time he has lived in the place indicated, asking whether the residence is temporary or permanent. If it is learned that the present residence is of recent origin, the party is to be asked the names of any other parish or parishes in which he has lived, and whether or not he has departed therefrom permanently.

In practice the pastor encounters no difficulty if the party is well known to him or has been a parishioner of long standing. But the question of determining domicile or quasi-domicile in the case of one who has recently arrived in the parish often occasions a problem. If such a person does not

---

[14] Can. 1097, § 1, n. 2: S. C. de Sacramentis, instr., 29 iun. 1941, Allegatum I, n. 3—*AAS*, XXXIII (1941), 310.

[15] Can. 92, § 1.

[16] Can. 92, § 2.

[17] Can. 95.

intend to remain in the parish for at least six months, the only remaining method of establishing competence is the possibility of a month's residence in the parish prior to the date of marriage, unless the person is actually a *vagus*. In this latter case, the pastor may not assist at the marriage, except in a case of necessity, without obtaining permission from the ordinary or from a priest delegated by the ordinary.[18]

The Instruction *Sacrosanctum matrimonii*[19] also directs the pastor to ascertain precisely in what dioceses the party has lived for at least six months after having attained the age of puberty, i.e., for the groom, after the completion of his fourteenth year, for the bride, after the completion of her twelfth year.[20] He is to inquire as to the reasons for residence in these different dioceses, as to the duration of residence in each particular diocese, and he is to obtain the names of the different parishes in which the party lived in each diocese. This information is to be obtained, for it is obviously the mind of the Sacred Congregation that proofs of the free state of the party are to be sought in these various places.

The question arises as to the extent of the pastor's obligation in this regard. Is it necessary for him to seek these additional proofs in every case in which a party has lived in other parishes for the required period of six months after the age of puberty? Or are such proofs required only in cases in which there is positive doubt or suspicion as to the free state of the party?

In attempting to answer this question one must keep in mind the legislation enacted by the Code concerning the proclamation of the banns and other investigations regarding the freedom of status.[21] Therein it is stated that, when the parties have lived in several parishes for periods of six months or more after puberty, the pastor is to refer the matter to

[18] Can. 1032.

[19] S. C. de Sacramentis, instr., 29 iun. 1941, Allegatum I, n. 4—*AAS*, XXXIII (1941), 310.

[20] Can. 88, § 2.

[21] Can. 1023, § 2, 3.

the ordinary, who in turn is to decide whether the banns should be called in each parish, or whether other proofs or even conjectures will suffice to confirm the free state of the parties. Wherefore the pastor's obligation is to report the case to the ordinary, who then judges from the circumstances what course is to be followed. The pastor, however, may not on his own initiative proceed with the marriage without this reference to the ordinary. The latter may demand that the banns be published in these various parishes, or he may be satisfied with other indications of freedom to marry, such as the testimonial letters of the various pastors or the sworn statements of witnesses.[22]

These particular regulations are repeated in the Instruction in the special animadversions concerning the impediment of previous existing marriage bond, and pastors are warned of the danger of its existence especially among *vagi* or those who have come from distant places.[23]

In conclusion it may be said that it seems more consistent with the law and more salutary in practice for the pastor to refer all cases of multiple successive residence in different parishes to the ordinary.

Article 4. Consent of Parents in Marriages of Minors

In instances wherein a party to a marriage is a minor, that is, has not as yet completed his twenty-first year of age, the pastor must keep in mind the prescripts of canon 1034. Therein he is directed to admonish minors not to contract marriage without the knowledge of or against the reasonable opposition of their parents, and if they do not heed his advice he is not to assist at the marriage until he has consulted the ordinary.

Although normally the consent of the parents is required in the case of the marriage of minors, there is no question of validity in this regard. Minors who have attained the age required

---

[22] Coronata, *De Matrimonio*, n. 90.

[23] S. C. de Sacramentis, instr., 29 iun. 1941, n. 6—*AAS, XXXIII* (1941), 303.

by the law for a valid marriage, i.e., for males, sixteen years complete, and for females, fourteen years complete,[24] contract a valid union, even though they neglect to inform their parents of their intention to marry, or refuse to respect the wishes of their parents who are reasonably opposed to the marriage. Yet to disregard this ruling would be unlawful. Furthermore, filial love and parental reverence as well as prudence, dictates that young people should disclose their intention of marrying to the more prudent and experienced judgment of their parents.[25] Their freedom, however, must at all times be safeguarded.[26] They are not bound to enter the married state, or unwillingly to marry the candidate of their parents' choice.

The law in canon 1034 distinguishes between the reasonable and unreasonable opposition of parents. To determine the reasonableness or unreasonableness of the parents' opposition, i. e., refusal of consent, it is necessary to consider the reasons for their opposition in relation to those reasons which the minor has in wishing to enter marriage. The cause for parental opposition must be just and grave not only objectively, that is, considered in themselves, but also relatively to the marriage in question. The parents may have grave reasons for refusing their consent, for example, if the marriage would bring disgrace to the family; but, on the other hand, the minor may have even more serious reasons for contracting the marriage, for example, if the danger of incontinence needs to be counteracted. In this the opposition of the parents would be unreasonable.[27]

Objectively the parents would be justified in opposing the marriage if it would cause scandal or dissension within the family, if they would suffer disgrace or great material loss therefrom, or if the other party to the union is a drunkard, an atheist, or a member of a non-Catholic sect, or one who is indolent or in-

---

[24] Can. 1067.

[25] Payen, *De Matrimonio*, III, n. 524.

[26] Cf. can. 1087.

[27] Cletus F. O'Donnell, *The Marriage of Minors*, The Catholic University of America Canon Law Studies, n. 221 (Washington: The Catholic University of America Press, 1945), p. 155.

competent in the matter of supporting a wife and children.[28] On the other hand, objections based on reasons of avarice, ambition, social position, personal dislike and political differences are unreasonable and insufficient to justify opposition to the marriage.[29]

According to the Instruction *Sacrosanctum matrimonii*,[30] the pastor is to question minors as to whether they have obtained the consent of their parents to the marriage. If it is revealed that the parents have refused to give their consent, the pastor must investigate further to determine the cause of the refusal, and to decide whether or not the opposition is reasonable. Should the pastor find that the opposition is reasonable, he is bound to attempt to dissuade the young people from the marriage. If, however, they still insist on the marriage in spite of the pastor's efforts, he must refer the question to the ordinary, indicating the circumstances, the reasons of the parents for withholding their consent, and the reasons alleged by the minor for wishing to enter marriage.

When, on the other hand, after careful consideration of the reasons advanced by the unwilling parents, the pastor prudently judges that they are unreasonable in their dissent, he should urge the parents to give their permission for the marriage. If the parents remain adamant in their refusal despite the promptings of the pastor, the latter may assist at the marriage without consulting the ordinary.[31]

Alhough reference to the ordinary is not demanded by the Code in cases of unreasonable opposition on the part of the parents, there are times when prudence will prompt the pastor to do so. In certain localities the civil law requires parental consent for the marriage of a minor. Furthermore,

---

[28] Charles Augustine, *A Commentary on the New Code of Canon Law* (8 vols., Vol. V, 5 ed., 1935; Vol. VI, 3 ed., 1931; St. Louis: B. Herder Book Co., V, 80 (hereafter cited *Commentary)*.

[29] O'Donnell, The Marriage of Minors, 156.

[30] S. C. de Sacramentis, instr., 29 iun. 1941, Allegatum I, n. 1—*AAS*, XXXIII (1941), 311.

[31] Joseph Rossi, *De Matrimonii Celebratione iuxta Codicem Iuris Canonici* (Romae: F. Pustet, 1924), p. 54.

the parents may threaten civil suit if the pastor assists at a marriage to which they are opposed. In such instances it is manifest that the sensible course to be followed is that of consultation with the ordinary.[32] Cerato maintains that the pastor is obliged to do so in these circumstances.[33] Therefore, when parents unreasonably refuse to give their consent without which the civil authorities will not permit the marriage of a minor, then, because of the difficulties inherent in such cases and because of the adverse civil effects consequent thereto, the pastor should consult the ordinary as to the course to be taken.

When the parties assert that they have obtained parental consent to the marriage, the pastor should not accept the statement too readily, especially in the case of those who are not personally known to him. He should investigate this assertion to establish its veracity. In this regard the Sacred Congregation of the Sacraments has appended to the Instruction *Sacrosanctum matrimonii* a special questionnaire to be used by the pastor in making this inquiry.[34]

Accordingly, the parents appear before the pastor, who questions them under oath and writes down their responses. The parents are interrogated separately. Upon completion of the testimony, both the parents and the pastor affix their signatures to the separate documents. The pastor then adds the date and the place of the interrogation, together with the seal of the parish. If the parents are dead or if the minor is otherwise under the care of guardians, it is evident from the Instruction that the guardians must testify.

It seems, however, that it is unnecessary to obtain this prescribed documentary proof of the parental consent or refusal, if the parties to the marriage and the parents are well known to the pastor, since the Instruction demands it only in a case wherein the pastor has remained in doubt.

---

[32] O'Donnell, *The Marriage of Minors*, 158.

[33] *Matrimonium a Codice Iuris Canonici Integre Desumptum* (4 ed., Patavii: Typsis Seminarii Patavini, 1927), n. 25.

[34] 29 iun. 1941, Allegatum III—*AAS*, XXXIII (1941), 315

Article 5. Investigation Concerning the Reception of Baptism

Since the reception of the sacrament of baptism is the prime requisite in constituting a person as a subject capable of validly receiving any other sacrament,[35] the fact of its reception must be established with certainty prior to marriage. To this end the pastor is directed, unless baptism was conferred in his own parish, to demand testimony of the reception of baptism from both parties, or from the Catholic party only, when the marriage is to be contracted with a dispensation from the impediment of disparity of worship.[36] If a party was baptized in the parish of the pastor, the latter need only to consult his baptismal register to verify the baptism.[37]

The Instruction *Sacrosanctum matrimonii* attaches great importance to the procurement of a certificate of baptism, not only because it constitutes an authentic document attesting to the reception of the sacrament, but also because it should furnish proof of the freedom of the party from certain impediments. According to canon 470, § 2, there should be indicated in the parochial baptismal register the fact that the person baptized received confirmation, contracted marriage, was promoted to the subdiaconate or was solemnly professed and furthermore these annotations are to be appended to baptismal certificates whenever they are issued. In this same regard canon 1103, § 2, requires that the pastor, in accordance with canon 470, § 2, inscribe in the baptismal register that the parties contracted marriage on such a date. If one or both the parties were baptized elsewhere, the pastor of the place where the marriage was celebrated shall send notice of the marriage to the pastor of the place where the party or parties were baptized, either personally or through the Chancery Office.[38]

Similarly when a decree of nullity has been granted by an ecclesiastical tribunal, the ordinary of the place where the mar-

[35] Can. 737.

[36] Can. 1021, § 1; S. C. de Sacramentis, instr., 29 iun. 1941, n. 4 (c)—*AAS*, XXXIII (1941), 300.

[37] Gasparri, *Tractatus Canonicus de Matrimonio*, I, n. 144.

[38] S. C. de Sacramentis, instr., 29 iun. 1941, n. 11 (b)—*AAS*, XXXIII (1941), 305.

riage was celebrated is obliged to command the rector of the parish in which the celebration of the marriage has been entered in the parish register that he enter in this marriage register the record of the sentence of nullity and of any prohibitory clause which may perchance have been determined upon, as for example in the case of impotence, and further that he enter a similar record in the baptismal register, if either or both consorts had been baptized in his parish. If either or both parties were baptized elsewhere, the pastor thus informed by the ordinary is to apprise the pastors of the place or places of baptism of this information, which they in turn are obliged to record in their baptismal registers.[39]

With these various annotations the baptismal certificate becomes a valuable document, and hence the Sacred Congregation of the Sacraments is most solicitous that care be taken in the keeping of the baptismal register, and that all the information prescribed by law be recorded therein. Ordinaries are reminded to admonish pastors of their duty in this regard, and if necessary to punish the negligent in accord with the ruling that is stated in canon 2383.[40]

It is also important in this matter that the certificate be of recent issue, for then it proves to be a more reliable testimony of the free state of the party. The Instruction, therefore, rules that the certificate be issued no more than six months before the date of marriage.[41] In practice it is desirable that a certificate be requested and obtained precisely for the prenuptial investigation. In the request for the certificate it can then be indicated to the pastor of the place of baptism that any annotations inscribed in the register are to be appended.[42]

---

[39] S. C. de Sacramentis, instr., 15 aug. 1936, art. 225—*AAS*, XXVIII (1936), 357-358.

[40] S. C. de Sacramentis, instr., 29 iun. 1941, n. 11 (e)—*AAS*, XXXIII (1941), 306.

[41] *Ibid.*, n. 4 (c)—*AAS*, XXXIII (1941), 300.

[42] A De Smet, *De Sponsalibus et Matrimonio* (4 ed., Brugis: Car. Beyaert, 1927), n. 678; Eugene Sullivan, *Proof of the Reception of the Sacraments*, The Catholic University of America Canon Law Studies, n. 209 (Washington: The Catholic University of America Press, 1944), p. 82.

Besides attesting to the free status of the party concerned, the baptismal certificate directly bears witness to the all important fact that the party has received baptism. Since canon 1021, § 1, uses the phrase *"testimonium baptismi"* rather than *documentum*, there are certain authors who contend that a certificate of baptism is not necessarily required, and that any other means of proof will suffice.[43] The Instruction *Sacrosanctum matrimonii*, however, confirms the more common opinion, for it clearly indicates that a certificate of baptism is required.[44]

No other means of proof is acceptable if an authentic certificate can be procured.[45] At times, however, it may be very difficult or even impossible to secure this normally required documentary evidence. The records of the church where the baptism took place may have been kept inaccurately or may have been destroyed. Again, due to the fact that certain countries of Europe are ruled by factions hostile to the Church, requests for ecclesiastical documents go unanswered. In such instances, although no mention is made of them in the Instruction, other forms of proof must be utilized.

Proof of the reception of baptism can usually be had by means of oral testimony. The person whose baptism must be established as a fact may call upon his parents, godparents, relatives or anyone else who may have been present when he was baptized, as witnesses who will testify in favor of his reception of baptism. These witnesses, as long as they are trustworthy, can furnish sufficient evidence of the reception of the sacrament.[46] If a person was baptized in adult age, his testimony concerning his baptism, given under oath, will suffice to establish the fact.[47] It is the common opinion of canonists and moralists that the testimony of one reliable

---

[43] Donovan, *The Pastor's Obligation in the Prenuptial Investigation*, p. 149; S. Woywod, *A Practical Commentary on the Code of Canon Law* (7th printing, 2 vols., New York: Wagner, 1943), I, n. 993 (hereinafter cited as Woywod, *Practical Commentary*). .

[44] S. C. de Sacramentis, instr., 29 iun. 1941, n. 4 (c)—*AAS*, XXXIII (1941), 300

[45] Cappello, *De Matrimonio*, n. 148.

[46] Can. 779; Gasparri, *Tractatus Canonicus de Matrimonio*, I, n. 141.

[47] Can. 779.

witness will constitute sufficient proof of the reception of baptism,[48] because in this instance the rights of another are not jeopardized by the given testimony in the sense of canon 779.[49] The law does not require that those who testify to the baptism of another do so under oath; this is required only in the case in which one testifies concerning his own baptism.[50] The Instruction, however, requires that witnesses testify under oath, thus indicating that it is the mind of the Holy See that all important testimony be given in this manner.[51]

If the person is professedly a Catholic, yet can produce neither a certificate nor witnesses to establish the fact of baptism, the pastor must refer his doubtful case to the ordinary, indicating any presumptions in favor of the baptism, if there be such.[52] If the person can present a certificate of confirmation or of first Holy Communion, or if he was born of Catholic parents who were faithful to their religion and who brought their children up as Catholics, the presumption in favor of baptism seems strong enough to permit the celebration of the marriage.[53] The pastor, however, should await the decision of the ordinary as to the course to be followed.

The Instruction *Sacrosanctum matrimonii* warns the pastor not to accept too readily a denial of baptism by a party to a marriage, but rather to contact the pastor of the place of origin in order to ascertain if there be any record of the baptism of the person in question.[54] If he suspects that

---

[48] J. Chelodi, *Ius Matrimoniale iuxta Codicem Iuris Canonici* (3 ed., Tridenti: Libr. Edit. Tridentum, 1921), n. 21 (hereafter cited *Ius Matrimoniale*); Gasparri, *Tractatus Canonicus de Matrimonio*, I. n. 141; Cappello, *De Matrimonio*, n. 148; B. H. Merkelbach, *Summa Theologiae Moralis* (2. ed. 3 vols., Parisiis: Desclee, de Brouwer et Cie., 1936-1938), III, n. 837; Noldin-Schmitt, *Summa Theologiae Moralis*, III, n. 546.

[49] Sullivan, *Proof of the Reception of the Sacraments*, 86-88.

[50] Can. 779.

[51] S. C. de Sacramentis, instr., 29 iun. 1941, Allegatum II—*AAS*, XXXIII (1941), 313.

[52] Can. 1031, § 1, n. 1.

[53] Cappello, *De Matrimonio*, n. 148; Ayrinhac-Lydon, *Marriage Legislation*, n. 33.

[54] S. C. de Sacramentis, instr., 29 iun. 1941, n. 4 (c)—*AAS*, XXXIII (1941), 300.

despite the denial the person may have been baptized, in as much as he has a Catholic background or is known as a Catholic, the pastor should call upon the testimony of reliable witnesses to solve his doubt, and if the doubt remains insoluble, he must refer the case to the ordinary. If, on the other hand, the party is known to the pastor as a non-Catholic, and if the party asserts that he was never baptized, the pastor can proceed with the marriage after having obtained a dispensation from the impediment of disparity of worship.

If the non-Catholic claims to have been baptized, the pastor must attempt to establish the fact either by procuring a certificate thereof, or by obtaining he testimony of at least one reliable witness. Having established the fact of baptism, the question of the validity of the baptism demands the pastor's consideration. No general rule can be advanced as to the validity of baptisms conferred in any particular sect, since so many factors must be taken into account, viz., the ritual, the adherence to the ritual, the intention of the minister. To demand that the pastor investigate all these details in every case would be to place upon the pastor a task impossible to accomplish, and indeed an unwarranted burden, since the validity of the marriage can be safeguarded by the acquisition of a dispensation from mixed religion and from disparity of cult *ad cautelam.* In practice, therefore, unless the pastor be morally certain of the validity of the baptism of a non-Catholic, he should apply for the dispensation in this form.[55]

The certificates of baptism, or the written testimony of witnesses attesting to the baptism of a party, are to be preserved with the other documents pertaining to the prenuptial investigation.

Article 6. Investigation Concerning the Reception of Confirmation

According to canon 1021, § 2, Catholics who have not received the sacrament of confirmation are to do so before being

[55] Schenk, *Mixed Religion and Disparity of Cult*, nn. 203, 252; Donovan, *The Pastor's Obligation in the Prenuptial Investigation*, p. 236.

admitted to marriage, if this can be done without grave inconvenience. Herein there is placed upon the party a real obligation to receive this sacrament before marriage, yet one from which the party is excused for any just cause.[56] The fact that the bishop lives at some distance, in consequence of which expense and inconvenience are entailed for the person concerned, would be a sufficient reason to excuse from this obligation. Similarly the fact that the time in question is outside of the customary period at which the bishop is wont to administer the sacrament in a particular district would be a justifying cause.

The Instruction *Sacrosanctum matrimonii* requires that the pastor obtain from the parties certificates of confirmation if they assert that they have received this sacrament.[57] If a certificate of confirmation cannot be obtained or located, the reception of the sacrament may be evident from an annotation appended to the baptismal certificate,[58] or proof of it can be established through the testimony of at least one reliable witness, i.e., of the sponsor, of either of the parents, of anyone of the relatives, or of the party himself, if he received this sacrament in adult age.[59]

When it happens that a party to a marriage has not received confirmation, the pastor should ascertain whether the sacrament can be conveniently received before marriage, whether, for example, the bishop is to confer this sacrament in his own or in a neighbouring parish prior to the date of marriage.

---

[56] Cappello, De Matrimonio, n. 150.
[57] S. C. de Sacramentis, instr., 29 iun. 1941, n. 4 (c)—*AAS*, XXXIII (1941), 300.
[58] Canon 407, § 1, 2.
[59] Can. 800.

CHAPTER X

THE INVESTIGATION CONCERNING THE EXISTENCE OF IMPEDIMENTS

In this chapter it is the intention of the writer to consider individually the various impediments to marriage, recalling briefly the nature of each and indicating practical measures for the investigation of each. It is opportune, however, to preface this consideration with a few preliminary remarks on dispensations and on the causes required for their concession.

A dispensation is the relaxation of the law in a particular case, granted by the legislator, or by his successor or superior, or by one to whom the faculty of dispensing has been conceded.[1] For the concession of a dispensation from an ecclesiastical law there must be present a just and a reasonable cause, proportionate to the gravity of the law from which the dispensation is sought.[2]

If this cause is lacking, a dispensation granted by one inferior to the legislator is illicit and invalid, except in the case of matrimonial impediments of minor degree, in which no false statement or concealment of the truth will make the dispensation invalid, even if the one final or motive cause proposed be false.[3] The local ordinary, when empowered to grant certain matrimonial dispensations by means of his special faculties, requires such a cause not only for the lawful but also for the valid concession, with the exception of dispensations from the matrimonial impediments of minor degree as noted above.

It pertains to the one who grants the dispensation to judge the justness and reasonableness of the causes proposed for a dispensation, but since this superior is ordinarily not in personal contact with the petitioner, he must rely on the accuracy of the report of facts given to him by the pastor who actually

[1] Can. 80.

[2] Can. 84, § 1.

[3] Can. 1054. Cf. can. 1042, § 2, for a list of the matrimonial impediments of minor degree.

interviews the parties to the marriage. A most serious obligation, then, rests upon the pastor to investigate the presence and veracity of the reasons which are alleged in the petition for the dispensation, for at times the very validity of the marriage will depend upon the genuineness of these causes.

As a consequence, the pastor should be familiar with the various types of causes for dispensations. Causes may be *motivating* or *impulsive*. A *motivating* or *final* cause is one which, even when it exists alone, determines and moves the grantor to concede the dispensation; an *impulsive* cause is one which helps to move or dispose the grantor to do so. Oftentimes a single impulsive cause is insufficient to move the proper authority to grant the dispensation, whereas several such causes coexisting in a particular case may amount to final cause and bring about the concession of the dispensation.[4] Again causes which have been approved through the customary practice and habitual usage of the Roman Curia are known as *canonical* causes; all others are known as *non-canonical*. The exact force of these causes, that is, whether they are to be considered as final or impulsive, is determined by the practice of the Holy See.[5]

The Sacred Congregation for the Propagation of the Faith issued a list of the common canonical causes for matrimonial dispensation on May 9, 1877.[6] A further list was issued by the Apostolic Datary in the year 1901.[7] Of these various causes, the following are more commonly met with in practice: (1) the probable hope of the conversion of a non-Catholic party to the Catholic faith; (2) the danger of a civil marriage or of a marriage before a non-Catholic minister; (3) the convalidation of an invalid marriage; (4) the removal of grave scandal; (5) the serious danger of incestuous concubinage which can be removed only through the celebration of marriage; (6) excessive,

[4] Payen, *De Matrimonio*, I. n. 727; Augustine, Commentary, V. 125; William O'Mara, *Canonical Causes for Matrimonial Dispensations*, The Catholic University of America Canon Law Studies, n. 97 (Washington: The Catholic University of America, 1935), pp. 43, 44.

[5] Capello, *De Matrimonio*, n. 257.

[6] *Collectanea*, n. 1470.

[7] *Acta Sanctae Sedis*, (41 vols., Romae, 1865-1908), XXXIV (1901), 34, 35.

suspected and dangerous familiarity; (7) pregnancy and therefore the legitimation of the child; (8) the danger of apostasy if the dispensation is denied; (9) the cessation of notorious concubinage; and (10) the superadult age of a woman not a widow.

Although the commonly accepted canonical causes are more efficacious and should be expressed if they are present, the pastor should not refrain from mentioning in the petition other causes which may exist in a particular case. He should recall that the reasons set down for a dispensation should be proportionate to the gravity of the impediment from which the dispensation is sought.[8] Likewise, he will bear in mind that, since a dispensation is usually granted by means of a rescript, the condition "*si preces veritate nitantur*" is always understood, even if not actually expressed.[9]

The only exception to this regulation in matrimonial matters is that which, as is indicated in canon 1054, states that a dispensation granted from an impediment of minor degree is valid even if the single final cause mentioned is false. Consequently the pastor should take great care to mention in the petition for a dispensation only those causes which he has found through investigation to be actually present in the case at hand. The Instruction reminds the pastor that he must have certitude as to the existence of the causes alleged.[10] To attain this certitude the pastor may find it necessary to question witnesses, to consult documents,or to resort to circumstantial evidence.[11]

---

[8] Can. 84, § 1; S. C. de Sacramentis, instr., 29 iun. 1941, n. 5 (d)—*AAS*, XXXIII (1941), 302.

[9] Can. 40.

[10] S. C. de Sacramentis, instr., 29 iun. 1941, n. 5 (d)—*AAS*, XXXIII (1941), 301. It is proper to recall here the notion of moral certitude (which type of certitude is unquestionably required on the part of the pastor), as indicated by the present Holy Father, Pope Pius XII, in his Allocution to the Auditors of the Sacred Roman Rota on October 1, 1942. Therein he stated: "Moral certitude lies between the extremes of absolute certitude and quasicertitude. It is such that it excludes any well-founded or reasonable doubt, but not the possibility of the contrary . . . The Judge may be satisfied with the lowest degree of moral certitude, that which excludes all reasonable doubt concerning the truth provided that it is objective, and provided that the law or the unusual importance of the case do not require a higher degree." *AAS*, *XXXIV* (1942), 338; *The Jurist*, III (1943), 500-501.

[11] Donovan, *The Pastor's Obligation in the Prenuptial Investigation*, p. 144.

Article 1. The Impediment of a Simple Vow

A marriage is rendered unlawful for a person who is under the obligation of a simple vow of virginity, of perfect chastity, of not marrying, of receiving Sacred Orders, or of embracing the religious life. No simple vow, however, invalidates a marriage unless a special prescription of the Holy See has thus decreed.[12]

Although the number of persons who, outside of religious communities make such vows is small, the pastor should not neglect to question the party to marriage as to whether he has ever made such a promise to God. This is evident from the Instruction *Sacrosanctum matrimonii,* which directs pastors to inquire diligently as to whether the spouses are bound by any impediment, impedient or diriment, mentioning specifically the impediment of simple vow.[13]

In order to ascertain whether or not an impediment actually does exist when a party asserts that he has made such a vow, the pastor must keep in mind the precise notion of a vow, and more specifically the nature of the impedient vows mentioned in canon 1058. A vow is a deliberate and free promise made to God of some good that is possible and better than its opposite, and binding under the virtue of religion.[14] It is to be noted that the promise must be made to God, not to the Blessed Virgin or to the Saints, that the party intended morally to bind himself, not merely to make a resolution, that he was aware of what the promise entailed, that he consented to it only after deliberation, and that the party was completely free in making the promise.[15]

Concerning the impedient vows as mentioned in canon 1058, the pastor will recall that: (1) the vow of *virginity* is the vow to abstain from any act of complete sexual satisfaction, which in-

---

[12] Can. 1058.

[13] S. C. de Sacramentis, instr., 29 iun. 1941, Allegatum I, n. 9—*AAS,* XXXIII (1941), 311.

[14] Can. 1307.

[15] Coronata, *Institutiones Iuris Canonici,* II, n. 889; Augustine, *Commentary,* VI, 289, 290.

volves a physical carnal act;[16] (2) the vow of perfect chastity is the vow to refrain from all sexual pleasure, whether internal or external, whether lawful or unlawful;[17] (3) the vow of *not marrying* is, as it indicates, the vow of not entering the married state; (4) the vow of *receiving Sacred Orders* is the vow to receive the subdiaconate, the diaconate or the priesthood;[18] and (5) the vow of *embracing the religious life* is the vow to enter a religious institute, that is, a religious Order or congregation.[19]

If in accord with these notions the pastor determines that the party actually did make a vow which would impede marriage, he must then find out whether or not such a vow still binds. He will recall that a vow may cease to bind: (1) because of the lapse of the time for which a temporary vow was made; (2) because a condition upon which the vow was made is not fulfilled; (3) because of a cessation of the final cause for which the vow was made, for example, when one who made a vow of virginity has lost that virginity through a formally and materially completed act of sexual satisfaction; or (4) because the vow has been annulled, dispensed from or commuted to another good.[20]

If it is discovered through investigation that the vow still obliges the party, but that at the same time a sufficient cause is present to justify the marriage, the pastor should aid the party in applying for the necessary dispensation from the impediment. The nature of the vow will determine the authority who is empowered to grant the dispensation. If the vow is reserved, the Holy See alone can grant the dispensation.[21] Of the simple

[16] Gasparri, *Tractatus Canonicus de Matrimonio*, I, n. 427; Ayrinhac-Lydon, Marriage Legislation, n. 95.

[17] Gasparri, *op. cit.*, I, n. 428; Cappello, *De Matrimonio*, n. 300; Coronata, *De Matrimonio*, n. 249.

[18] Can. 949.

[19] Can. 487, 488; Cappello, *De Matrimonio*, n. 302.

[20] Can. 1311; Augustine, *Commentary*, VI, 297-299.

[21] Can. 1308, § 3. The faculties of Apostolic Delegates, however, include that of commuting or dispensing from all simple vows privately pronounced, even those reserved to the Holy See, provided that a just cause is present, and provided that there is no question of harm to a third party.—Chapter I, n. 15, Index of Faculties which . . . the Holy Father decreed to give . . . to Apostolic Delegates, all other faculties being abrogated.—T. Lincoln Bouscaren, *The Canon Law Digest* (2 vols., Milwaukee: Bruce, 1934, 1943), I, 178.

vows mentioned in canon 1058, only those of perfect and perpetual chastity, and of entering a religious community in which solemn vows are taken, are reserved. These vows, indeed, are reserved even if made privately, provided they be made absolutely by one who has completed his eighteenth year of age.[22] The local ordinary, however, by granting an indult of secularization, can directly dispense from the vow of perfect and perpetual chastity taken in an institute of diocesan approval.[23]

If the vows are non-reserved, then in accordance with canon 1313 they may be dispensed from for a just cause, provided the dispensation does not injure the acquired rights of others, (1) by the local ordinary, for his subjects and for non-subjects in his territory; (2) by the superior of an exempt clerical community, who may dispense not only the professed members and novices of his institute, but also such others who stay night and day at the religious house for the purpose of service or education, or because of sickness or even for the sake of hospitality;[24] and (3) by those who have been delegated by the Holy See to dispense.

Article 2. The Impediment of Legal Relationship

The impediment of legal relationship may be impedient, diriment, or non-existent, in so far as the nature of the canonical impediment depends on the prevailing civil law of the locality. Canon 1059 states: "In those regions in which relationship resulting from legal adoption is a prohibitive impediment by civil law, it is so also by canon law." Canon 1080 states: "Those whom the civil law considers as unable to intermarry in consequence of the legal relationship arising from adoption are by canon law incapable of contracting marriage validly"[25] In other words, the Church simply canonizes the civil law in this matter.[26]

---

[22] Can. 1309.

[23] Cf. can. 638, 640, § 1, n. 2; Schaefer, *Compendium de Religiosis ad Norman Codicis Iuris Canonici* (r. ed. Romae, 1947), n. 1540.

[24] Cf. can. 512. §1.

[25] Cf. Ayrinhac-Lydon, *Marriage Legislation*, pp. 97, 188.

[26] Payen, *De Matrimonio*, I, n. 844.

The first requisite on the part of the pastor for an effective investigation is a knowledge of the civil law on this point, in order that he may determine the existence and extent of the impediment, i.e., whether or not legal relationship arising from adoption exists as an impediment to marriage in his locality, and if so, whether it impedes or invalidates marriage.

If the parties are bound by a legal relationship which constitutes an impediment to marriage in his locality, the pastor may not proceed to witness their marriage until he has obtained the required dispensation. A dispensation obtained from the civil authorities alone is insufficient, for the binding force of the ecclesiastical impediment comes not from civil law but from Canon Law.[27]

Since legal relationship does not constitute an impediment to marriage in the United States or Canada,[28] pastors in these regions need not interrogate the parties concerning this matter. Woywod (1880-1941), however, advised caution in dealing with persons who have recently come from foreign countries in which the impediment of legal relationship exists, especially if their stay in this country is merely temporary.[29] Since they retain their former domicile, he states that they are still subject to the impediment, and this in conjunction with the fact that certain States demand that the requirements of the law of the party's domicile be observed will bring about the impediment of legal relationship. In such cases, should they confront the pastor, it is advisable that he consult a civil lawyer on the question.

Article 3. The Impediment of Nonage

According to canon 1067, a man may not enter a valid marriage before he has completed his sixteenth year of age, a woman before she has completed her fourteenth year. Furthermore, though a marriage entered into after these ages have been attained is valid, pastors shall take care to deter young people

---

27 Capello, *De Matrimonio*, n. 327; Payen, *De Matrimonio*, III, n. 844.

28 Ayrinhac-Lydon, *Marriage Legislation*, n. 96; Cappello, *De Matrimonio*, n. 324, ad IV.

29 *Practical Commentary*, I, n. 1037.

who have not reached the age at which, according to the custom of the country, marriage is usually contracted.

The pastor must recall, first of all, the canonical method of computing the age of the party for marriage, in order to ascertain by his investigation whether or not such a party is legally capable of contracting marriage. The years of age must be complete, as reckoned according to canon 34, § 3, n. 3, i.e., the day of birth is not counted, since the birth does not coincide with the beginning of the day, and the last day must be completed to the very last hour for validity.[30] Hence a boy born on January 5, 1932, is sixteen complete in the sense of the law only after midnight of his sixteenth birthday anniversary, that is, on January 6, 1948. If the marriage take place in the afternoon of the day on which he becomes sixteen years of age, it would be canonically null.

One of the first questions which the pastor is directed by the Instruction *Sacrosanctum matrimonii* to ask the party is that concerning his age.[31] Further evidence of age will be obtained from the baptismal certificate required by the same Instruction,[32] for although the law does not demand that the date of birth be recorded in the baptismal register, it is usually inscribed therein.[33] The baptismal certificate will not *prove* the date of birth, since that information is only accessorily contained in and not directly or primarily affirmed by the document.[34] Nevertheless, in conjunction with the sworn statement of the party, it affords the pastor sufficient certitude to allow the marriage to be contracted. If certitude cannot be attained, or if doubt or suspicion arises concerning the age of the party, the pastor should endeavor to ascertain the true age by securing an authentic birth certificate, by questioning parents or other reliable wit-

---

[30] Ayrinhac-Lydon, Marriage Legislation, n. 118; John C. O'Dea, *The Marriage Impediment of Nonage*, The Catholic University of America Canon Law Studies, n. 205 (Washington: The Catholic University of America Press, 1944), p. 52.

[31] S. C. de Sacramentis, instr., 29 iun. 1941, Allegatum I, n. 1—*AAS*, XXXIII (1941), 312.

[32] *Ibid.*, n. 4 (c)—*AAS*, XXXIII (1941), 300.

[33] Cf. can. 777, § 1.

[34] Can. 1816: Documenta publica fidem faciunt de iis quae directe et principaliter in eisdem affirmantur.

nesses or, as a last resort, through the suppletory oath of the party himself. If doubt should persist despite his efforts, the pastor must not assist at the marriage without consulting the ordinary.[35]

The pastor's obligation in relation to the impediment of nonage does not end with the assurance that the parties have attained the required minimum age for a valid marriage. According to canon 1067, § 2, he has the additional duty of dissuading the parties from marriage if they are below the customary age for marriage in the region. The age established as minimum for marriage by the civil law will usually serve as a norm in this regard.[36] Prudence suggests that such marriages be discouraged, since young persons below this age rarely have the maturity of judgment required for a happy and successful union.[37]

In certain cases grave reasons may exist in justification of the marriage, even though the parties have not reached the customary age for marriage in the region in which they live. The fact that parties are living in concubinage, or that there is grave danger of incontinence, or that they are habituated in the sin of fornication, or that there is need to legitimate their offspring, may furnish a reason which will excuse the pastor from deterring them from entering the union. In these cases and in others in which the parties refuse to heed the pastor's advice concerning the postponement of the marriage, the pastor should see to it that they obtain the permission required by the civil law for the marriage of those who are under the legally established age.[38] Furthermore, all that has been stated in the preceding chapter concerning the marriage of minors must be observed in these circumstances in the supposition that such parties are minors.[39]

The Church is wont to dispense from the impediment of nonage only under very limited conditions, for example, in

---

[35] Can. 1031, § 1, n. 3.

[36] Chelodi, *Ius Matrimoniale*, n. 68.

[37] Cappello, *De Matrimonio*. n. 335.

[38] Donovan, *The Pastor's Obligation in the Prenuptial Investigation*, 167.

[39] Can. 1034; cf. *supra*, pp.

missionary countries where marriage is contracted at a very early age.[40] The usual faculties granted to ordinaries by the Sacred Congregations do not include the faculty of dispensing from this impediment; rather, they specifically except it.[41] But the faculties given to Apostolic Nuncios and Apostolic Delegates include the faculty to dispense in a limited number of cases from all diriment impediments, except those which arise from affinity in the direct line when the marriage had been consummated, and from Sacred Orders and solemn religious profession. Hence the Apostolic Delegate can dispense from the impediment of nonage.[42]

Article 4. The Impediment of Impotence

Canon 1068 states that antecedent and perpetual impotence, whether on the part of the man or on the part of the woman, whether known or unknown to the other party, whether absolute or relative, invalidates marriage by the very law of nature. If the impediment is doubtful either by doubt of law or by doubt of fact, marriage is not to be prohibited. Finally, sterility neither invalidates nor prohibits marriage.

It is not the intention of the writer of this treatise to give an exhaustive explanation of the impediment of impotence. On this point one may gain all needed knowledge by consulting approved authors on the canonical legislation of marriage.[43] But a few fundamental notions will be stressed here for the sake of providing an aid to the pastor in recognizing the possible exis-

---

[40] Payen, *De Matrimonio*, I, n. 958.

[41] Formulae Facultatum quas S. C. de Prop. Fide Ordinariis in terris missionum procurat . . . n. 21—cf. Vermeersch-Creusen, *Epitome Iuris Canonici* (6. ed., 3 vols., Romae: Dessain, 1937-1946), I, n. 873 (hereafter cited *Epitome*). .

[42] Index of Faculties which, after the promulgation of the Code of Canon Law, the Holy Father decreed to give for the territories of their respective assignments, to the Apostolic Nuncios, internuncios and Delegates, all other faculties being abrogated, Chapter III, Faculties concerning Marriage, n. 30—Bouscaren, *The Canon Law Digest*, i, 181.

[43] Gasparri, *Tractatus Canonicus de Matrimonio*, I, pp. 299-338; Coronata, *De Matrimonio*, pp. 368-427; I. Rossi, *De Impedimento Impotentiae* (Romae: 1910); Vermeersch, *De Castitate et de Vitiis Contrariis* (Romae: Univ. Gregoriana, 1919), nn. 57-88.

tence of the impediment in the course of his investigations prior to marriage.

Two types of impotence are distinguished, the *impotentia coeundi* and the *impotentia generandi.* The *impotentia coeundi* is the inability of a man or a woman so to perform the conjugal act that by means of it a true male semen becomes deposited in the vagina of the woman in the natural way.[44] It is this type of impotence which renders marriage null.[45] The *impotentia generandi,* on the other hand, does not connote any such inability but simply precludes the possibility of the procreating of children. It is commonly known as *sterility,* which according to canon 1068, § 3, does not invalidate marriage.[46]

If impotence is to invalidate a marriage, it must exist prior to that marriage; it must be certain; it must be perpetual, i.e., it must be such that it is incurable through lawful means which at the same time do not involve a serious danger to life.[47] When these conditions are fulfilled, the canonical impediment of impotence exists, even though it be unknown to one or both parties, and irrespective of whether it be absolute or relative. It is absolute when it renders a person incapable of performing the conjugal act with any member of the other sex; it is relative when it renders him incapable in reference to a certain or even several members of the other sex.[48]

The investigation of the impediment of impotence presents a difficult task to the pastor. Donovan[49] aptly suggests that the investigation proves difficult "because society looks upon impotence as a serious human misfortune, due frequently to causes suggestive of sin, and as a result a nupturient may resent being interrogated on the subject, or if interrogated, may answer untruthfully; because there is so much ignorance concerning the fact that a diriment impediment exists, and because very fre-

---

[44] Payen, *De Matrimonio,* I, n. 981.

[45] Gasparri, *Tractatus Canonicus de Matrimonio,* I, n. 513.

[46] Gasparri, *op. cit.,* I, n. 522.

[47] Payen, *De Matrimonio,* I, nn. 992-997.

[48] V. Heylen, *Tractatus de Matrimonio* (9. ed., Mechliniae: Dessain, 1945), p. 529 (hereafter cited *De Matrimonio).*

[49] *The Pastor's Obligation in the Prenuptial Investigation,* p. 168.

quently a party cannot assert with certainty before marriage that he or she is not impotent."

Donovan, therefore, concludes that unless there is some positive indication or suspicion of its presence, the pastor may omit interrogating the nupturients concerning this impediment. The Instruction *Sacrosanctum matrimonii,* however, commands the pastor to inquire carefully as to whether the parties are bound by any impediment, particularly a diriment one.[50] In view of this insistence it seems necessary for the pastor to make some effort in all cases to assure himself of the absence of this impediment rather than entirely to omit reference to it. Thus in ordinary cases a single question such as, "Are you aware of any physical defect which would prevent the proper fulfillment of your marriage duties?", would suffice to elicit a statement of the parties' knowledge in this matter. At times prudence may suggest that the investigation take the form of instruction rather than interrogation.

In cases in which suspicion or serious doubt arises in the mind of the pastor concerning the possible existence of the impediment, a more detailed investigation will be necessary. The pastor, for example, would have grave reason to suspect the existence of impotence if the person had been party to a former marriage declared null on the grounds of impotence, or of a marriage dispensed from as *ratum et non-consummatum.* In such cases he would of necessity demand to see a copy of the declaration or of the dispensation,[51] because there is occasionally appended a *vetitum* or a prohibition which precludes one or the other of the parties from seeking to contract a future marriage on the ground of a definitely established status of impotence.[52] Due mention of such a *vetitum* should also appear on a baptismal certificate which has been copied from a properly annotated baptismal record.[53]

---

[50] S. C. de Sacramentis, instr., 29 iun. 1941, n. 5 (a)—*AAS*, XXXIII (1941), 301.

[51] S. C. de Sacramentis, instr., 29 iun. 1941, n. 4 (c)—*AAS*, XXXIII (1941), 300.

[52] Doheny, *Canonical Procedure*, II, 495.

[53] S. C. de Sacramentis, instr., 15 aug. 1936, art. 225—*AAS*, XXVIII (1936).

Similarly, if it is known or revealed that a man had an operation for sterilization, i.e., surgery of double vasectomy, although sterility itself does not denote impotence, grounds for suspicion would be present. In this and in other cases in which a party expresses doubt as to his physical aptitude for married life, the pastor should seek the aid of medical advice, directing the party to a reputable Catholic physician who, after examining the person, can provide for the pastor a written statement of his condition.[54] The pastor may find it advisable to refer the data obtained or any problems encountered to the ordinary or to the diocesan tribunal, since they are more expert in interpreting such matters.

If the investigation reveals that the person is incurably impotent, the pastor cannot allow the marriage to be contracted. Furthermore, there is no question of a possible dispensation, since the impediment derives from the natural law.[55] If, however, some doubt remains after all efforts to solve it have been fruitless, the marriage is not to be prohibited.[56]

Article 5. The Impediment of Previous Bond

Marriage is rendered invalid by the bond of a previous valid marriage even if only ratified, unless there has been applied the Privilege of the Faith. Although the previous marriage be invalid or dissolved for whatever reason, it is not lawful to contract another union before the nullity or the dissolution of the first has been legally and certainly established.[57]

If, therefore, it is ascertained that a party is bound by a previous and still-existing valid marriage bond, he is to be prevented from entering a new union under pain of nullity. The law of the Church thereby excludes the possibility of bigamous and polygamous unions, whether the plurality of marriage partners be simultaneous or successive, as in the case in which civil divorce has permitted a new civil contract.[58]

---

[54] Heylen, *De Matrimonio*, p. 530.
[55] Can. 1068, § 1.
[56] Can. 1068, § 3.
[57] Can. 1069.
[58] Gasparri, *Tractatus Canonicus de Matrimonio, I*, n. 552.

Canon 1069 states that an exception to this matrimonial law is had through the operation of the Privilege of the Faith. This privilege includes first of all the use of the Pauline Privilege, which under certain conditions permits a party to a marriage contracted in infidelity to enter a new marriage with a Catholic after he has been converted from infidelity.[59] Secondly, it embraces the dissolution in favor of the faith of the natural non-sacramental bond of marriage as effected through the ministerial power of the Roman Pontiff.[60] In cases in which the Pauline Privilege is applied, the first marriage is dissolved at the moment the second is contracted.[61]

The Instruction *Sacrosanctum matrimonii* urges pastors to be particularly watchful lest parties either in good faith or bad seek to enter upon new marriages while they are still held by the bond of a previous marriage.[62] This directive is especially apt in the present day when civil divorce with the legal right to remarry has become so prevalent in many countries, that at times even Catholics seek to disregard the sanctity of matrimony by entering new unions during the lifetime of their true partners. The possibility of contravening the law of the Church by deceitful means is enhanced by the apparent ease with which one can disguise his past history both from his future marriage partner and from the investigating priest. The need for diligent inquiry can hardly be over-emphasized, particularly if the parties are personally unknown to the pastor, if they have frequently changed their place of residence, or if they belong to other parishes.

The pastor, therefore, is to ask the party who appears before him for marriage whether he has previously entered marriage with another person according to the law of the Church, and, if so, how that marriage was dissolved. Moreover, since it is not beyond the sphere of practical possibility that a party, especially a non-Catholic, may assume that some sort of previous

---

[59] Can. 1120-1127.

[60] Cf. "Helena Case," Cappello, *De Matrimonio*, n. 791.

[61] Can. 1126.

[62] S. C. de Sacramentis, instr., 29 iun. 1941, n. 6—*AAS*, XXXIII (1941), 303.

union having the aspect of marriage was not a true marriage in the eyes of the Church, the pastor must attempt to uncover the existence of such unions by discreet questioning, avoiding mere general terminology. Particularly if one party is or has been a non-catholic, the pastor should inquire whether he has ever been partner to a union which was recognized as marriage by the civil law. When the party affirms the existence of such a union, the pastor should then determine its precise nature, and subsequently whether or not that party is now free to marry.[63]

For Catholics, the baptismal certificate to be procured according to Canon 1021, § 1, and the Instruction,[64] should serve to substantiate the statement of the party in this regard, if it contains the annotations required by law.[65] The fact that the certificate does not contain reference to a former marriage does not constitute full proof of freedom from the impediment of previous bond, since unfortunately some pastors are negligent in their duty of inscribing the record in their baptismal register or of forwarding such a record to the pastor of the place of baptism.[66]

In ordinary cases in which there is no doubt or suspicion in the mind of the pastor concerning the truth of the statements of the party, the absence of contrary annotations in the baptismal certificate seems to suffice. But when the party has frequently changed residence, the pastor should refer the matter to the ordinary, who in turn is to judge whether prudence demands that the banns be published, not only in the present parish of the party, but also in other parishes in which the party has lived for a period of six months or more, or whether other proofs or conjectures concerning his free status are to be gathered.[67] The ordinary may even demand that the banns be called in places in which the party has lived for less than six months

[63] S. C. de Sacramentis, instr., 29 iun. 1941, Allegatum I, n. 6—*AAS*, XXXIII (1941), 310.

[64] *Ibid.*, n. 4 (c)—*AAS*, XXXIII (1941), 303.

[65] Can. 470, 1103; S. C. de Sacramentis, instr., 29 iun. 1941, n. 11 (b) —*AAS*, XXXIII (1941), 305.

[66] S. C. de Sacramentis, instr., 4 iul. 1921—*AAS*, XIII (1921), 348.

[67] Can. 1023, § 2; S. C. de Sacramentis, instr., 29 iun. 1941, n. 6 (b)—*AAS*, XXXIII (1941), 303.

if some doubt has arisen regarding the party's freedom from the impediment.[68]

Furthermore, when doubt or suspicion is present, the Instruction directs the pastor to obtain the testimony of witnesses as a means of dispelling such doubt or suspicion.[69] These witnesses are to be questioned by the pastor according to the questionnaire given in Formula II of the Instruction.[70] Therein it is indicated that two witnesses known to the pastor must be secured for each party, although the same witnesses can serve for both parties provided that they testify separately for each spouse. Should the party be unable to produce witnesses personally known to the pastor, it then seems that witnesses whose reliability and truthfulness have been commended by their own pastor, or by some trustworthy person, can be admitted to testify. The pastor, having first reminded the witness of the sanctity of an oath and the severity of the punishment for perjury, will administer the oath and interrogate him according to the questions as indicated in the above-mentioned formula. He will consign the responses of the witness to writing, and both the witness and himself will sign the completed statement. Likewise the statement obtained from the parents of minors will contain reference to this impediment.[71]

As a last resort, when other means of proof are unobtainable or inconclusive, the suppletory oath of the party concerned may be accepted as indicative of freedom from the bond of previous marriage.[72] This sworn statement of the party is envisioned in canon 1031, § 1, n. 1, which directs the pastor to employ it only when other means of proof are lacking for the resolving of a doubtfully existing impediment. Formula IV of the Appendix of the Instruction, which is in reality the form to be used by the pastor in securing the suppletory oath, implies that this

---

[68] Can. 1023, § 3.

[69] S. C. de Sacramentis, instr., 29 iun. 1941, Allegatum I, n. 2—*AAS*, XXXIII (1941), 310.

[70] Allegatum II—*AAS*, XXXIII (1941), 313, 314.

[71] S. C. de Sacramentis, instr., 29 iun. 1941, n. 6 (b), Allegatum I, n. 2, Allegatum III—*AAS*, XXXIII (1941), 303, 310, 315.

[72] *Ibid.*, n. 6 (b), Allegatum I, n. 2, Allegatum IV—*AAS*, XXXIII (1941), 303, 310, 316; cf. also can. 1829-1831.

oath can be received only by the ordinary or his delegate, since it indicates that the document which contains the recorded oath must bear the signatures of the party and of the ordinary or his delegate. The text of the Instruction simply directs the pastor to obtain the oath only as a last resort; it makes no mention of his need of being delegated by the ordinary.[73] It seems to the writer that, since the law itself in canon 1031, § 1, n. 1, attributes to the pastor the right of accepting the suppletory oath of the party without a reference of the case to the ordinary, and since the Instruction does not directly demand such a previous reference, the pastor may resort thereto on his own initiative.

Before administering the oath, the pastor will admonish the party concerning the sanctity of the oath and concerning the severe penalties to be incurred by perjurers and by bigamists.[74] The oath when rendered and recorded is to be signed by the party and by the pastor. It may be noted that this recourse to the testimony of witnesses and to the suppletory oath is a vestige of the pre-code legislation of the decree *Cum alias,* which required the judicial examination of witnesses with a view to establishing proof of the free status of the parties prior to all marriages.[75]

When the party who is being questioned asserts that he had previously been married, but that the marriage has been declared null, or that a dispensation has been granted for entrance into a new union, documentary evidence to substantiate this statement must be produced. The pastor, therefore, must demand an authentic copy of the sentence of nullity given by an ecclesiastical tribunal, or of the dispensation granted by the Holy See in the case of a *ratum et non consummatum* marriage. Likewise he will obtain a copy of the official declaration of the ordinary that the party is entitled to use the Pauline Privilege.[76]

The baptismal certificate properly annotated should indicate that a sentence of nullity has been given, or that a

---

[73] *Ibid.*, n. 6 (b)—*AAS*, XXXIII (1941), 303.

[74] Can. 2323, 2356.

[75] S. C. S. Off., decr., *Cum alias*, 21 aug. 1670—*Fontes*, n. 742; cf. *supra*, Chap. V., p.

[76] S. C. de Sacramentis, instr., 29 iun. 1941, n. 4 (c) e—*AAS*, XXXIII (1941), 300, 301.

dispensation has been granted in the case of a *ratum et non consummatum* marriage, and should likewise reveal whatever prohibition or *vetitum* may have been appended to either the sentence or the dispensation.[77] The pastor must be particularly careful in seeing to it that any such prohibition contained in the sentence of dispensation is observed.

More commonly, however, the party will indicate that the marriage has been dissolved by the death of a former spouse. The pastor may not allow a new marriage to be contracted until he has moral certitude of the asserted death of the former partner.[78] There naturally arises the question as to when the pastor's decision will suffice for the legitimate establishment of the death of the first spouse, so that it will not be necessary for him to refer the matter to the ordinary.[79]

All authors agree that the pastor may proceed and need not consult the ordinary when he has personal knowledge of the death of the party, for example, when the person died in his parish, or when he assisted at the funeral, or if the record of death appears in his parish register, or if he has secured an authentic document certifying the death.[80] The majority of the authors likewise agree that in defect of personal knowledge or of an authentic documentation the question must be presented to the ordinary for settlement, so that it then lies beyond the province of the pastor to reach a decision.[81] Certain authors, however, permit the pastor to solve the case if he can obtain the testimony of two reliable eye-witnesses concerning the death.[82]

---

[77] S. C. de Sacramentis, instr., 29 iun. 1941, n. 11 (c)—*AAS*, XXXIII (1941), 305, 306; S. C. de Sacramentis, instr., 15 aug. 1936, art. 225—*AAS*, XXXIII (1936), 357; can. 1988.

[78] Doheny, *Canonical Procedure*, II, 592.

[79] Patrick W. Rice, *Proof of Death in Prenuptial Investigation*, p. 54.

[80] Gasparri, *Tractatus Canonicus de Matrimonio*, I, n. 723; Wernz-Vidal, *Ius Matrimoniale*, n. 371.

[81] Augustine, *Commentary*, V, 178; Chelodi, *Ius Matrimoniale*, n. 78.

[82] Payen, *De Matrimonio*, I, n. 1050; Vlaming, *Praelectiones Iuris Matrimonii ad norman Codicis Iuris Canonici* (3. ed., Bussum: Paul Brand, 1919-1921), I, n. 281; G. Vromant, *Ius Missionariorum*, Vol. V. *De Matrimonio* (Lovanii: Museum Lessianum, 1931), n. 44.

Cappello *(De Matrimonio*, n. 396) goes even so far as to permit the pastor to proceed *inconsulto Ordinario* when the death is certified by *one* eye-witness.

The writer of the present treatise is of the opinion that when the pastor can attain moral certitude of the death of a previous spouse at least through the testimony of two reliable eye-witnesses he may proceed to the marriage without consulting the ordinary. The law of the Code in canon 1031, § 1, n. 1, attributes to the pastor the right to accept the testimony of two reliable witnesses under oath in order to dispel doubt regarding a probably existing impediment, and in the present case, despite its extraordinary nature, there seems to be no reason for departing from this general rule.

If, however, he cannot secure moral certitude in this manner, he must then refer the case to the ordinary for a solution. The latter, according to the mind of the Holy See,[83] must then proceed in accordance with the ruling of the Pre-Code Instruction *Matrimonii vinculo* of the Sacred Congregation of the Holy Office when he seeks to establish the proof of death.[84] Following the norms indicated in this Instruction, the ordinary must in either an administrative or a judicial procedure gather the required proofs, and evaluate the evidence thereby obtained.[85]

A much more difficult problem confronts the pastor when the party asserts that the former consort has disappeared, so that no direct evidence of death is present. Because of the difficulties inherent in such cases, the pastor must refer the matter to the ordinary, who will institute an investigation according to the norms of the above-mentioned Instruction *Matrimonii vinculo*.[86] In referring these difficult problems to the ordinary, the pastor should include any information he may have gathered on the question, and stand in readiness to assist the ordinary in the consequent investigation. In any case, he may not proceed with the proposed marriage until he has received a favorable decision from the ordinary.

---

[83] S. C. de Sacramentis, instr., 18 nov. 1920—*AAS*, XIV (1922), 96; Bouscaren, *Canon Law Digest*, I, 508-511.

[84] 13 maii 1868—*Fontes*, n. 1002; cf. *supra*, Chap. VII, p.

[85] Doheny, *Canonical Procedure*, II, 596-608; Rice, *Proof of Death in Prenuptial Investigation*, pp. 43-51.

[86] Rice, *op. cit.*, pp. 80-105.

The Instruction *Sacrosanctum matrimonii* also requires the pastor to question the parties as to whether or not they have previously contracted a so-called civil marriage with each other or with a third person, and, if so, whether or not this marriage has been dissolved.[87] This question is directed at establishing not only the canonical freedom of the parties but also their freedom according to the civil law. Both in the case in which a party attempted a civil marriage with another person, and in the case in which an ecclesiastical decree of nullity has been given, the pastor should, in order to avoid conflict with the civil authorities and to safeguard the civil effects of the marriage, obtain from the party an authentic copy of the civil divorce decree. If no such civil dissolution has been obtained, he should consult the ordinary on the course to be followed.

Furthermore, this question will reveal whether a Catholic party has incurred an ecclesiastical penalty for attempting a marriage before a non-Catholic minister.[88]

Article 6. The Impediments of Mixed Religion and Disparity of Worship

The impediments of mixed religion and disparity of worship, undoubtedly the impediments most frequently encountered by pastors in conducting the prenuptial investigation, will be considered jointly in this single article because of the similarities existing between them. The canonical basis for the individual impediments will be considered separately, however, before there will be offered a discussion of the conditions required for a dispensation therefrom.

A. The Impediment of Mixed Religion

The Church most severely forbids everywhere marriages between two baptized persons, one of whom is a Catholic, and the other a member of a heretical or a schismatical sect. Further-

[87] S. C. de Sacramentis, instr., 29 iun. 1941, Allegatum I, n. 6—*AAS*, XXXIII (1941), 310.

[88] Can. 2319, § 1, n. 1; *Acta et Decreta Conc. Plen. Baltimorensis* III (1884) (Baltimorae: Typis Joannis Murphy Sociorum, 1886), decr. 127; *Acta et Decreta Conc. Plen. Quebecensis* I (1909) (Quebeci: Typis L'Action Sociale Limitee, 1912), decr. 533.

more, if there is danger of the preversion of the Catholic spouse and offspring, the marriage is forbidden also by the divine law.[89] Hence, an impediment which renders marriage unlawful exists between a baptized Catholic and a baptized member of a heretical or a schismatical sect.

Who are to be included in the term "Catholic"? According to Schenk,[90] the terms must be taken in the strict sense, and thus includes: (a) those who have been baptized in or converted to the Catholic Church and who at the time of the marriage are actually professed Catholics; (b) those Catholics who, although they have not joined a heretical or a schismatical sect, are occult heretics or are suspected of heresy; (c) those who have been excommunicated for moral delinquencies other than heresy or apostasy, and public sinners who refuse to be reconciled to the Church and (d) those Catholics who are members of condemned but not atheistic societies. In short, the term includes not only good and practising Catholics but also careless and fallen away Catholics, provided they have not joined another religious sect. Nevertheless, even though the impediment of mixed religion would not exist in the case in which a good Catholic wished to marry a person who belonged to any of the last three groups mentioned above, the prescripts of the law regarding the marriages of apostates, unworthy Catholics or public sinners must be observed.[91]

The terms "heretical or schismatical sect" should not be understood in the strict sense as derived from canon 1325, § 2, namely, as referring to purely Christian sects, but rather in a broader sense, which includes all organized religious groups which profess a false religion.[92] The stricter interpretation would be inconsonant with the purpose of the law, for the danger of perversion is equally present, if not more so, when the religious group is non-Christian. Moreover, according to a reply of the Pontifical Commission for the Authentic Interpretation of the

[89] Can. 1060.

[90] *Mixed Religion and Disparity of Cult*, pp. 83, 84.

[91] Can. 1065, 1066.

[92] Donovan, *The Pastor's Obligation in the Prenuptial Investigation*, 229.

Code as given on July 30, 1934, the impediment of mixed religion obtains between Catholics and those who are enrolled as members in an atheistic society,[93] just as much as it obtains between Catholics and those who belong or have belonged to a non-Catholic sect. Since Communism is undoubtedly an atheistic society, this impediment would forbid the marriage of a Catholic with a baptized person who is a full-fledged member of the Communist party.[94]

According to a reply of the Holy Office,[95] the following are to be considered as members of a heretical sect: (1) those who were baptized in the Catholic Church, but who from infancy have been brought up *in* heresy which they still profess;[96] (2) those who were baptized in the Catholic Church, but from infancy have been brought up by heretics, although with little or no heretical education and with infrequent attendance at worship, unless they formally sever relationship with the sect with which they have been identified; (3) those who were baptized in the Catholic Church, but who upon attaining the use of reason have fallen into the hands of heretics and have formally joined the sect; (3) those who were born of heretical parents and were baptized in a heretical sect, until they have formally separated from the sect by a positive act of the will, even though they did not actively profess that sect; and (5) those who in adult age apostatized from the Catholic faith and have formally joined a heretical sect.

Although the phrase "heretical sect" has been used throughout the preceding discussion, what has been said applies equally to a schismatical sect.

---

[93] *AAS*, XXVI (1934), 494.

[94] Bouscaren-Ellis, *Canon Law*, p. 459.

[95] Litt. (ad Ep. Harlemen.), 6 apr. 1859—*Fontes*, n. 950; Schenk, *Mixed Religion and Disparity of Cult*, pp. 88-91.

[96] Cf. can 1099, § 2. Children who, if born of non-Catholic parents, have indeed been baptized as Catholics, but have grown up from infancy in heresy or schism, in infidelity, or without any religion, are not bound by the Catholic form of marriage when they contract marriage with a non-Catholic, and it seems that they likewise are not bound by the impediment of mixed religion when they marry other baptized non-Catholics.

In conclusion, it is to be noted that baptized non-Catholics are presumed to be members of a sect until by a positive act of the will they have severed connections with it.[97]

B. The Impediment of Disparity of Worship

The marriage contracted by a non-baptized person with a person baptized in the Catholic Church or converted to it from heresy or schism is null.[98] The invalidating matrimonial impediment of disparity of worship presupposes that one party was never baptized and that the other was baptized in the Catholic Church or was converted to it after having been baptized in a heretical or a schismatical sect. Consequently a person baptized as a non-Catholic is no longer bound by the impediment of disparity of worship when marrying a non-baptized person, as he would have been prior to the Code.[99]

Furthermore, those who fall away from the Catholic faith after having been baptized in it, or after having been converted to it are still bound by this impediment. The same rule applies to those who were born of non-Catholic parents, then were baptized in the Catholic Church, but from infancy were reared in heresy or schism, in infidelity, or without any religion, even though they are exempted from the Catholic form of marriage when marrying non-Catholics.[100]

C. Determination of the Baptism or Non-baptism of the Non-Catholic

The determination of the reception or non-reception of baptism by the non-Catholic party to a mixed marriage is of paramount importance in establishing whether there is present the prohibiting impediment of mixed religion or the diriment impediment of disparity of worship.

---

[97] Ayrinhac-Lydon, *Marriage Legislation*, n. 97.

[98] Can. 1070, § 1.

[99] Bendictus XIV, ep. *Singulari*, 9 febr. 1749, § 1—*Fontes*, n. 394; Gasparri, *Tractatus Canonicus de Matrimonio*, I, n. 685.

[100] Can. 1099, § 2; Pont. Comm. Cod. Inter., 27 apr. 1940—*AAS*, XXXIII (1940), 212.

In the prenuptial investigation the pastor is to inquire of all parties who present themselves for marriage, the non-Catholics as well as Catholics, whether they have been baptized, and accordingly is to request a certificate of the reception of the sacrament whenever its reception is alleged.[101] The Instruction of 1941 warns the pastor not to accept too readily the statement of the party who asserts his non-baptism, unless this is already certain from some other source.[102] In this regard it is expedient to include among the questions which the pastor will ask the party in the prenuptial investigation a specific question regarding the religion of the parents both at the time of the investigation and at the time of the party's birth. The religious affiliation of the parents will serve to indicate the possibility that the person was or was not baptized, in so far as the parents belonged to a sect which believes and insists upon baptism, or to one which does not.

If the party asserts that he was not baptized, and it is ascertained that the parents either belonged to a sect which is not accustomed to confer baptism or did not profess any religious belief whatsoever, then the pastor would be justified in concluding that the party has never been baptized. If, on the other hand, the party indicates that he has not been baptized, but it is established that the parents were members of a sect which usually confers baptism, the pastor could reasonably doubt the party's statement of non-baptism, and should insist upon further evidence, such as reference to the records of the church with which the party's parents were affiliated. The pastor may at times suspect that the party may have been baptized as a Catholic. In such cases he is to inquire of the pastor of the place of birth whether there is any record of the baptism of the person in question.[103]

When a non-Catholic asserts that he has been baptized, the pastor is to ask for a certificate of the alleged baptism.[104] if no

---

[101] Can. 1021, § 1; S. C. de Sacramentis, instr., 29 iun. 1941, Allegatum I, n. 1—*AAS*, XXXIII (1941), 309.

[102] *Ibid.*, n. 4 (c)—*AAS*, XXXIII (1941), 300.

[103] S. C. de Sacramentis, instr., 29 iun. 1941, n. 4 (c)—*AAS*, XXXIII (1941), 300.

[104] *Loc. cit.;* Cappello, *De Matrimonio*, n. 149.

certificate is available, then the pastor is to establish the fact of baptism through the testimony of at least one reliable witness.[105]

The testimony of the parents or the godparents would be preferred in this matter, if such can be obtained.

After the pastor has established the fact of baptism in a non-Catholic sect, there still remains the question of the validity of the baptism. One can not set forth a general rule whereby the validity of non-Catholic baptisms can be readily established. As has been indicated in the preceding chapter,[106] various factors necessarily enter into the consideration of the validity of such a baptism, all of which would require appraisal for a complete and satisfactory solution of the problem, viz., the ritual ordinarily used by the sect in conferring baptism, the faithful observance of the ritual by the minister and the intention of the minister in performing the ceremony.

To place upon the pastor the obligation of investigating all these factors in every case in which a non-Catholic has asserted his reception of baptism appears an intolerable burden, and one which would be almost impossible of accomplishment. Marriages would be unduly delayed, and frequently even after the lengthy investigation, doubts would still persist. In short, the helpful results reasonably to be hoped for from this protracted examination do not warrant its institution. Wherefore, in practice, unless an investigation can easily be made, e.g., if the minister who is alleged to have baptized the party is personally known to the pastor and could easily be approached, it is not necessary for the pastor to conduct this lengthy inquisition. At the same time the pastor can safeguard the validity of the marriage by obtaining a dispensation from the impediment of mixed religion and also from the impediment of disparity of worship *ad cautelam*.[107]

Although the Holy See did not favor such petitions prior to the Code, they are now quite acceptable in view of the general

---

[105] Can. 779.

[106] cf. *supra*, Chap. IX, p.

[107] Schenk, *Mixed Religion and Disparity of Cult*, n. 203.

uncertainty of the validity of non-Catholic baptisms, and of the frequent impossibility of a suitable investigation.[108]

D. Investigation Concerning the Conditions Required for a Dispensation

The Church does not grant a dispensation from the impediment of mixed religion unless:

1. There be present just and grave causes;

2. The non-Catholic party has given guarantees which certify the obviation of the danger of perversion for the Catholic party, and both parties have promised and guaranteed that all the children will be baptized and brought up exclusively in the Catholic faith; and

3. There be moral certainty that the promises will be fulfilled.[109] These same conditions must be verified for a dispensation from the impediment of disparity of worship.[110]

1. Presence of a Just and Grave Cause

The question of the necessity of a just and grave cause has been considered at length above in the discussion of dispensations in general. Consideration has likewise been given to the duty of the pastor to ascertain with moral certitude the veracity of the alleged cause or causes.[111] The usual causes alleged for a dispensation from the impediments of mixed religion and disparity of worship are: (a) the serious promise of the non-Catholic party to embrace the Catholic faith; (b) the well-founded and probable hope of the conversion of the non-Catholic party; and (c) the danger of marriage before a civil magistrate or a non-Catholic minister, if the dispensation is denied.[112]

---

[108] Schenk, *op. cit.*, n. 252; cf. Quinquennial Faculties of Ordinaries . . . 1. Faculties from the Holy Office, n. 2—Bouscaren, *The Canon Law Digest*, II, 30.

[109] Can. 1061, § 1.

[110] Can. 1071.

[111] Cf. *supra*. Chap. X, p. 86

[112] Francis Ter Haar, *Mixed Marriages and Their Remedies* (New York: F. Pustet Co., 1933), pp. 66-68.

The last-mentioned is the cause most commonly found in petitions for dispensations from these impediments, but it is not on that score to be taken for granted as existing in all cases. The pastor must prudently determine its existence in each individual case, judging the relative determination of the parties to contract marriage even in spite of the refusal of a dispensation. A prudent judgment regarding the likelihood of an attempt at contracting marriage will suffice; the pastor need not have absolute certitude in this regard.[113] He must not provoke the parties to formal sin by asking them if they would marry before a minister or a civil official in the event that the dispensation would be denied.[114] The matter must be decided without recourse to direct questioning on the intentions of the parties in this regard, and the judgment based rather on the circumstances and the dispositions of the persons in question.

2. The Required Guarantees

The guarantees (*cautiones)*, as indicated in canon 1061, § 1, n. 1, are demanded in all cases with a view to offsetting the danger of perversion inherent in mixed marriages. Ordinarily these promises, as they are called, are to be put in writing and to be signed by both the Catholic and the non-Catholic party.[115] Diocesan statutes may require that the promises be signed in the presence of the priest or other witnesses.[116] In the absence of written law, the accepted diocesan practice must be taken as normative in this regard.

Written guarantees are required, because in written form they have probative value and can be produced as evidence should the validity of the promises be questioned subsequently.[117] Nevertheless in certain extraordinary cases, particularly in the

---

[113] S. C. de Prop. Fide, instr., 8 maii 1877—*Collectanea*, n. 1470.

[114] J. De Becker, *De Sponsalibus et Matrimonio Praelectiones Canonicae* (Lovanii: 1903), 330; Schenk, *Mixed Religion and Disparity of Cult*, n. 201.

[115] Can. 1061, § 2.

[116] Ter Haar *Mixed Marriages and Their Remedies*, p. 84.

[117] Cappello, *De Matrimonio*, n. 311; Gasparri, *Tractatus Canonicus de Matrimonio*, I, n. 452.

danger of death, oral guarantees or guarantees expressed by signs could be accepted.[118]

In no instance, however, may the exacting of the promises be omitted entirely, for they are absolutely necessary for the validity of the dispensation. Wherefore, if a dispensation were granted without the previous guarantees, the consequent marriage would be either unlawful or invalid according as the impediment actually existing at the time of the marriage was that of mixed religion or of disparity of worship.[119]

In the course of the instructions, which according to diocesan regulations usually precede a mixed marriage,[120] the pastor should explain clearly the nature and purpose of the guarantees to both the Catholic and the non-Catholic party. He should acquaint the non-Catholic party with the specific religious duties of the Catholic party which through his guarantees he is promising to respect. It should be impressed on both contracting parties that all the children are to be baptized and brought up as Catholics, since frequently there is made an agreement between the parties that the boys will be reared in the religion of the father, and the girls in the religion of the mother.[121]

The pastor should also explain that the obligation of providing for the Catholic upbringing of the children still remains in the event that the Catholic party should die. Finally, the Catholic party should be reminded of his obligation to do his

---

[118] Donovan, *The Pastor's Obligation in the Prenuptial Investigation*, p. 234.

[119] S. C. S. Off., 10 maii 1941—*AAS*, XXXIII (1941), 284; Chelodi, Ius Matrimoniale, n. 50; Ayrinhac-Lydon, *Marriage Legislation*, n. 104.

[120] Ter Haar, *Mixed Marriages and Their Remedies*, p. 106.

[121] Schenk, *Mixed Religion and Disparity of Cult*, n. 334. In this regard the response of the Holy Office on January 16, 1942, must be kept in mind. Therein it is stated that the promises are not required with reference to the children already born before the celebration of marriage, although the parties to the marriage are by all means to be warned of their grave obligation under the divine law to see to the Catholic education of also these children who have already been born. AAS, XXXIV (1942), 22; Bouscaren, *The Canon Law Digest*, II, 286.

The revised quinquennial faculties for ordinaries (Faculties from the Holy office, n. 2) state that the parties are to be warned of the grave obligation as deriving from the divine law, of providing for the Catholic education, and, if need be, for the conversion and baptism of the children born of an illicit union; in this regard an explicit promise is to be exacted of the Catholic party.—*The Jurist*, VI (1946), 536.

utmost to effect the conversion of the non-Catholic spouse to the true Church.[122]

3. Moral Certitude Concerning the Fulfillment of the Guarantees

Moral certitude in such that it excludes any wellfounded or reasonable doubt, but not the possibility of the contrary.[123] It is this type of certitude which the pastor must have concerning the fulfillment of the guarantees, according to canon 1061, § 1, n. 3. Absolute or perfect certitude, which excludes all doubt as to the truth of the fact, is not necessary; indeed it would be impossible to attain in every case.[124]

The disposition of the non-Catholic will indicate in some degree the hope of the fulfillment of the promises. The pastor will usually have a splendid opportunity to appraise the sincerity of the non-Catholic during the course of the accustomed instructions given prior to mixed marriages. If the party manifests genuine interest and co-operation together with his serious and considered expression of understanding and promise, the pastor will be justified in concluding that he will live up to his promises. An attitude of indifference, of apparent reluctance or even of open disapproval may indicate a routine and insincere signing of the guarantees. Each individual case must be judged on its own merits. The experience gained by a pastor in dealing with non-Catholics will usually equip him with sufficient judgment to discern sincerity or insincerity, and thus to reach a satisfactory verdict.

Likewise the character and the disposition of the Catholic party should be taken into consideration as indicative of the hope of the future Catholic education of children born of the marriage. If the Catholic is a strong character and regularly faithful to the practices of his religion, this hope will be great. If, on the other hand, the Catholic is careless about his religious

[122] Can. 1062.
[123] Allocutio Pii XII. 1 oct. 1942—*AAS*, XXXIV (1942), 338.
[124] Ter Haar, *Mixed Marriages and Their Remedies*, n. 82.

duties or poorly instructed, serious doubts may well rise in the pastor's mind.

If all the conditions required by the provisions of canon 1061 are present, the pastor will then forward the petition for the dispensation to the ordinary, who is empowered in his quinquennial faculties to concede it.[125] It is to be noted that these faculties do not permit the ordinary to grant the dispensation whenever the non-Catholic party is a Mohammedan. In such rare cases the petition must be forwarded to the Holy See, usually through the Chancery Office. Formerly the powers of the ordinary were restricted also in the case in which the non-Catholic party was a Jew, but the revised faculties which became effective on July 1, 1946, permit the ordinary to grant the dispensation from the impediment of disparity of worship in this case.[126]

Article 7. The Impediment of Sacred Orders

A marriage is invalid when attempted by clerics in sacred orders.[127] Sacred orders include the orders of subdiaconte, diaconate and priesthood.[128] Therefore the minor orders, through which a cleric becomes an acolyte, an exorcist, a lector or a porter, neither invalidate nor prohibit marriage, though a minor cleric who marries is automatically excluded from the clerical state.[129]

The diriment impediment of Sacred Orders arises from a valid ordination freely received by a cleric who was aware of the grave obligations attached thereto.[130] A cleric who has received Sacred Orders under compulsion of grave fear, and has not afterward, when the fear was removed, ratified the said ordination at least tacitly by exercising the Order with the intention

[125] Quinquennial Faculties of Ordinaries: Formula from the Holy Office, nn. 2, 3—Bouscaren, *The Canon Law Digest,* II, 30, 31.

[126] *The Jurist,* VI (1946), 535, 536.

[127] Can. 1072; cf. also can. 132, § 1.

[128] Can. 949.

[129] Can. 132, § 2.

[130] Cappello, *De Matrimonio,* n. 437; Ayrinhac-Lydon, *Marriage Legislation,* n. 140.

of thereby subjecting himself to the clerical obligations, may be reduced to the lay state, free from the obligations of celibacy and of the canonical hours, by the formal judgment of an ecclesiastical tribunal given upon legal proof of the compulsion and of the want of ratification. Such compulsion and want of ratification must be proved according to canons 1993-1998.[131] In order to obviate as far as possible later disputes concerning the possession of freedom in the reception of Orders, the Sacred Congregation of the Sacraments issued an important Instruction which directed that candidates for Orders must write personally to their ordinaries to ask for the reception of the Sacred Orders, and take an oath to the effect that they do so freely and that they understand the obligations attached to the Orders.[132]

The impediment ceases when a dispensation has been granted in the case of a validly received Order. As a general rule the concession of a dispensation from major Orders is reserved to the Holy Father. In the danger of death, according to canons 1043 and 1044, the power to dispense from the subdiaconate and the diaconate, but not from the priesthood, is granted by law to ordinaries, pastors, priests who assist at a marriage contracted under the circumstances contemplated in canon 1098, n. 2, and to confessors. But confessors can use their faculty solely in and for the internal sacramental forum. In the exceptional circumstances of canon 1045, the ordinary may grant similar dispensations, but pastors, priests who assist at a marriage as contemplated in canon 1098, n. 2, and confessors can do so only when the existence of the impediment is *de facto* occult.

Not infrequently does the Holy See dispense from the orders of subdiaconate and diaconate.[133] From the priesthood dispensations are rarely granted; in fact, the practice of the Holy See at the present time is to dispense only in accordance with the norms of canon 214, as considered above.[134] Under no

---

[131] Can. 214; S. C. de Sacramentis, instr., 9 iun. 1931—*AAS*, XXIII (1931), 457.

[132] 27 dec. 1930—*AAS*, XXIII (1931), 120.

[133] Gasparri, *Tractatus Canonicus de Matrimonio*, I, n. 619.

[134] Cappello, *De Matrimonio*, n. 442.

conditions is a dispensation ever granted to bishops.[135]

The pastor will rarely meet with the impediment of Sacred Orders in the prenuptial investigation. In the ordinary case he will satisfy the law of the Code and the directions of the Instruction *Sacrosanctum matrimonii,* which demand a diligent investigation concerning all impediments,[136] by asking the groom the question, "Are you bound by Sacred Orders?" The reception of the Orders of subdiaconate should be recorded in the baptismal register of the parish in which the candidate was baptized, and consequently should be annotated on the baptismal certificate which the pastor is to secure during the prenuptial investigation.[137] Wherefore, in the ordinary case in which there is no suspicion as to the existence of the impediment, the absence of such an annotation will serve as confirmatory evidence of the freedom of the groom from the impediment of Sacred Orders.

On rare occasions it is possible that some doubt may arise in the mind of the pastor regarding the presence of the impediment. It may have come to the pastor's attention, for example, that a man presenting himself for marriage had spent a long period of time in a seminary or religious institute, a period of sufficient duration to render the reception of major Orders a possibility. In such instances the pastor should investigate more extensively in order to attain moral certainty of the freedom of the groom from this impediment. Beyond the direct interrogation and the indirect evidence afforded through the baptismal certificate, he should inquire of the rector of the seminary, or of the superior of the religious community in which the man lived, regarding the possible conferral of Orders. The testimony of a reliable companion or classmate in the seminary can also prove satisfactory.[138] In accordance with the ruling of canon

---

[135] Gasparri, *loc. cit.;* hence the axiom of canonists regarding dispensations from Sacred Orders; *raro* (subdiaconate), *rarius* (diaconate), *rarissime* (priesthood), *nunquam* (episcopate)—Cappello, *loc. cit.;* Payen, *De Matrimonio,* I, n. 1242.

[136] Can. 1021, § 2; S. C. de Sacramentis, instr., 29 iun. 1941, n. 5—*AAS,* XXXIII (1941), 301, 311.

[137] Can. 470, § 2; 1011.

[138] Donovan, *The Pastor's Obligation in the Prenuptial Investigation,* p. 182.

1031, § 1, n. 3, when a prudent doubt remains despite his investigations, the pastor is not to assist at the marriage without consulting the ordinary.

If the groom asserts that he actually did receive major Orders, but that he was dispensed therefrom, or that the reception thereof has been declared invalid, the pastor must secure an authentic copy of the dispensation or of the decree of nullity, to be preserved together with the other pertinent documents of the marriage. Due to the extraordinary nature of such a case, it would be advisable for the pastor to present such documents to the ordinary for his "*nihil obstat.*"[139] Reference should be made to the ordinary in such cases in order that he may judge that no scandal or wonderment may be caused to the faithful through the marriage of one of whom it is known that he has received Sacred Orders.

Article 8. The Impediment of Solemn Vow.

Marriage is null when attempted by religious who have taken solemn vows, or even simple vows if these, through a special disposition of the Holy See, have been accorded the juridic force of invalidating a marriage.[140] Solemn vows are those which are taken by the members of religious orders, whether of men or of women.[141] Most of the women religious in the United States and Canada, however, take only simple vows.[142] By special privilege the simple profession of Jesuit scholastics, made upon completion of their two years' novitiate, invalidates

[139] The Sacred Congregation desires that the pastor apply for the "nihil obstat" prior to all marriages, and demands it whenever the pastors of the parties are of different dioceses.—Instr., 20 iun. 1941, n. 4 (a)—*AAS*, XXXIII (1941), 299.

[140] Can. 1073; cf. also can. 579.

[141] Can. 488, n. 2.

[142] J. Creusen-E. Garesche-A. Ellis state: "During the past century . . . the Holy See has allowed many nuns to take only simple vows, and has permitted the foundation of new monasteries on condition that the members take simple vows only. This is the condition of most nuns in Belgium, France and in the United States. In the United States there are only six monasteries of the Order of the Visitation and two of the Second Order of St. Dominic in which the nuns take solemn vows."—*Religious Men and Women in the Code*, 4. English ed. revised to conform to 5. French ed. (Milwaukee: Bruce, 1940), n. 223.

marriage.[143] Apart from this single exception, simple vows, whether taken in a religious Order or in a congregation, do not invalidate marriage, though they do render it unlawful.[144]

The impediment of solemn vow arises only from a valid profession made in accordance with the prescripts of the Code.[145] Furthermore, the vows must actually bind at the time of marriage in order to constitute an impediment. In this regard it is to be recalled that the vows may cease to bind in various ways.

(1) The indult of secularization, which is the permission to leave the religious institute permanently in order to return to secular life,[146] carries with it a dispensation from the vows taken in the institute.[147] If such an indult has been granted, the former solemnly professed religious is free to contract marriage, unless he were at the same time a cleric in major Orders, in which case he will still be bound by the diriment impediment of Sacred Orders.[148] In consequence of an indult of exclaustration, however, by which a religious is permitted to live temporarily outside of the houses of the institute, the religious is not dispensed from his vows.[149] Similarly an apostate religious, i.e., a professed religious with perpetual vows who unlawfully leaves the religious house with the intention of not returning,[150] and a fugitive religious, i.e., one who leaves the religious house without the permission of the superior, but with the intention of returning,[151] remains bound by their vows.[152]

(2) The solemnity of the vows ceases when a solemnly professed religious has with the permission of the Holy See completed his transfer to a religious congregation in which simple

---

[143] Gregorius XIII, const., *Ascendente Domino*, 25 maii 1584—*Fontes*, n. 153; Cappello, *De Matrimonio*, n. 447.

[144] Can. 1058, § 2, 579.

[145] Can. 572; 542; 555; Cappello, *De Matrimonio*, n. 448.

[146] Can. 638; Creusen-Garesche-Ellis, *Religious Men and Women in the Code*, n. 335.

[147] Can. 640, § 1, n. 2; Creusen-Garesche-Ellis, *op. cit.*, n. 336 (c); Cappello, *De Matrimonio*, n. 454.

[148] Can. 640, § 1, n. 2; 1072.

[149] Can. 638, 639; Creusen-Garesche-Ellis, *op. cit.*, n. 333.

[150] Can. 644, § 1.

[151] Can. 644, § 3.

[152] Can. 645, § 1.

vows are taken, unless other provision be made in the apostolic indult.[153]

(3) Scholastics of the Society of Jesus can be dispensed from their diriment simple vows by the Superior General of the Order. Likewise through a legitimate dismissal they are relieved of their vows, so that they may validly and lawfully contract marriage.[154]

(4) A decision in favor of the invalidity of the solemn profession may have been granted by the Holy See after the matter had been referred thither in accordance with canon 586, § 3.

(5) The Holy Father can grant a dispensation from the impediment of solemn vows, as the canonists say, *in sensu diviso,* but not *in sensu composito.*[155] A dispensation is granted *in sensu diviso* when the Holy Father dispenses a religious from his vows so that the recipient of the dispensation is no longer a religious, and thus can validly and lawfully contract marriage. It would be granted in *sensu composito* if the Holy Father were to permit the religious to validly and lawfully contract marriage while still remaining a professed religious of solemn vows. This the Roman Pontiff does not do, since the act would involve an inherent contradiction. Furthermore, the Holy Father usually grants such dispensations from solemn vows through the Sacred Congregation of Religious, which Congregation in practice no longer directly grants a dispensation for the contracting of marriage, but rather issues an indult of secularization.[156]

By virtue of the faculties in canons 1043 and 1044, ordinaries, pastors, priests who assist at marriage under the circumstances contemplated in canon 1098, n. 2, and confessors, but these in the internal sacramental forum only, may dispense from

---

[153] Can. 636.

[154] Gregorius XIII, const. *Ascendente Domino,* 25 maii 1584—*Fontes,* n. 153; Cappello, De Matrimonio, n. 454.

[155] Gasparri, *Tractatus Canonicus de Matrimonio,* I, n. 629; Cappello, *De Matrimonio,* n. 453; Wernz-Vidal, *Ius Matrimoniale,* n. 302.

[156] Gasparri, *op. cit.,* n. 631; Coronata, *De Matrimonio,* n. 370; Cappello *(op. cit.,* n. 453) seems to imply that the direct dispensation to enter marriage is granted by the Holy See, but Gasparri *(loc. cit.)* states that Cappello refers to the pre-Code practice.

the diriment impediment of solemn vows for a person who is in danger of death. In the extraordinary circumstances contemplated in canon 1045, a similar dispensation may be granted by ordinaries, and, if the existence of the impediment be *de facto* occult, by pastors, by priests in assistance at marriage as contemplated in canon 1098, n. 2, and by confessors. But the latter can do so only in the act of hearing confessions. It is postulated, of course, that the priests here mentioned have found it morally impossible to approach the ordinary for the dispensation.

In the ordinary cases which the pastor encounters in the prenuptial investigation, it will suffice if he inquires whether or not the party is bound by any solemn vows which he has taken in a religious institute. Although the pastor will rarely meet with this impediment, he should not on that account omit reference to it entirely, since the Instruction *Sacrosanctum matrimonii* in interpreting canon 1020, § 2, specifically mentioned the impediment of solemn vow.[157]

The baptismal certificate, if properly annotated, should contain a reference to solemn profession if such took place, since the record thereof is to be inscribed in the baptismal register of the parish in which the religious was baptized.[158] In cases in which there is no doubt or suspicion, the absence of an annotation to the effect that the party was solemnly professed will serve to substantiate the party's assertion of his freedom from the vow.

When a doubt does arise concerning the freedom of the party from this impediment, in consequence perhaps of the fact that he spent some time in a religious order, the pastor must investigate more extensively. If it is known in which religious house the party lived, the pastor should ascertain from the superior whether or not the party ever took solemn vows, and, if so, whether or not there was granted in his favor an indult by virtue of which he may lawfully and validly enter marriage. The testi-

[157] S. C. de Sacramentis, instr., 29 iun. 1941, Allegatum I n. 9—*AAS*, XXXIII (1941), 311.

[158] Can. 470, § 2; 576, § 2.

mony of two reliable witnesses given under oath could also afford the pastor sufficient grounds for moral certainty regarding the freedom of the party from this impediment.[159]

When the doubt remains unsolved despite the pastor's efforts to establish a sufficient certitude, he must not proceed with the marriage without consulting the ordinary.[160]

When the party upon being interrogated asserts that he had been solemnly professed, but that he has been released from his vows either through an indult of the Holy See, or in consequence of a declaration of the invalidity of the profession, an authentic document attesting thereto must be secured.

If it is discovered that the party is still bound by the impediment, and yet there is present a grave and urgent cause, whether public or private,[161] for the celebration of the marriage, a petition for a dispensation is to be sent through the ordinary to the Holy See. As has been discussed above, the Holy See in response to the petition will concede rather the indult of secularization than the dispensation for the contracting of marriage.

Article 9. The Impediment of Abduction

Between an abductor and the woman whom he has abducted with a view to marriage there can be no marriage as long as the abducted person is in the power of the abductor. If the abducted woman, however, is separated from the abductor and restored to a place of safety, then in the perfect freedom with which she can consent to have him for her husband, the impediment ceases. In regard to the nullity of marriage, equivalent to abduction is the violent detention of a woman, when, namely, a man violently detains her, with a view to marriage, in the place in which she resides or to which she has come of her own accord.[162]

It is evident that three elements combine to form this diriment impediment, viz., the abduction of a woman by a man, the

---

[159] Can. 1031, § 1, n. 1.
[160] Can. 1031, § 1, n. 3.
[161] Gasparri, *Tractatus Canonicus de Matrimonio*, I, n. 630.
[162] Can. 1074; Ayrinhac-Lydon, *Marriage Legislation*, pp. 158, 159.

factor of violence or force in connection with the abduction, and the intention of marrying on the part of the abductor.[163]

(1) The impediment of abduction is occasioned by the removal of the woman from a safe place to another in which she is in the power of the abductor, or by the detention of the woman in her place of residence or in a place to which she has come of her own free will.[164]

(2) The abduction or detention must be effected by force or violence on the part of the man against the will of the woman. The force may be not only physical but also moral, i.e., if the woman is influenced by threats of harm to herself or to the members of her family. When no violence is used, as for example when the woman is brought to the place by seduction, by flattery, by promises, by gifts and the like, the impediment does not arise.[165]

(3) The abduction must be effected with a view to marriage. If the woman is abducted for the purpose of turpitude or extortion, then the impediment does not arise.[166]

The impediment continues to exist as long as the woman remains in the abductor's power, even though she would at that time freely consent to marry him. It ceases only when she is separated from him and restored to a place of safety, where she is no longer under his influence.[167]

The pastor will seldom meet with this impediment in his prenuptial inquiries. Donovan suggests that the growing independence of women is not favorable to the abduction of women by men.[168] Since this impediment is related to the question of the

---

[163] Bartholomew F. Fair, *The Impediment of Abduction*, The Catholic University of America Canon Law Studies, n. 194 (Washington: The Catholic University of America Press, 1944), p. 31.

[164] Ayrinhac-Lydon, *Marriage Legislation*, n. 149.

[165] Fair, *The Impediment of Abduction*, p. 52. Fair discusses at some length (pp. 37-53) the question whether *dolus* gives rise to the impediment, and concludes with Kostler (*Das "Osterreichische Konkordats-Eherecht* [Wien: Springer, 1937], 61) that it does not suffice of itself to cause the impediment.

[166] Cappello, *De Matrimonio*, n. 468.

[167] Ayrinhac-Lydon, *Marriage Legislation*, n. 149.

[168] *The Pastor's Obligation in the Prenuptial Investigation.*, p. 187.

freedom of the woman's consent, ordinarily its possible presence may be revealed in the interrogation of the woman concerning her absolute freedom in entering marriage.

Occasionally, however, some doubt or suspicion may arise in the mind of the pastor with respect to the existence of the impediment. The attitude and dispositions of the parties may indicate its possible presence, i.e., the man may appear to be domineering and forceful, whereas the woman seems timid or manifests an aversion for her prospective husband, or appears to be dejected rather than cheerful at the prospect of marriage.[169] These factors, especially when considered in conjunction with the fact that the woman is living at some distance from her parental home, or has a limited number of friends, or is of minor age, will indicate to the pastor that a more extensive investigation should be made. He will endeavor to solve the doubt by first of all questioning the woman directly concerning the impediment. If necessary, he will also obtain the sworn testimony of reliable witnesses in this regard.[170] If a doubt persists despite his efforts to solve it, the pastor must refer the matter to the ordinary for his decision.[171]

When the investigation reveals that the impediment is actually present, the pastor may not permit the marriage until the woman is removed to a safe place from the place in which she has continued under the abductor's power. If after this removal she still wishes to marry the man, the marriage may be permitted. The Holy See rarely grants a dispensation from this impediment, because it is usually quite possible that the woman can be separated from the abductor and restored to safety. In the rare case in which this cannot be done, a dispensation is granted only for very serious reasons, and always with the proviso that the woman be absolutely free in her choice of marriage.[172]

---

[169] Donovan, *op. cit.*, p. 188.

[170] Can. 1031, § 1, n. 1.

[171] Can. 1031, § 1, n. 3.

[172] Payen, *De Matrimonio*, I, n. 1285; Gasparri, *Tractatus Canonicus de Matrimonio*, I, n. 662.

Article 10. The Impediment of Crime

There can be no valid marriage between: (1) those who within the continuance of one and the same lawful wedlock have committed adultery and also have promised to marry each other, or further have attempted a marriage, even by means of a merely civil act; (2) those who during the same lawful wedlock have committed adultery and one of them has in addition inflicted death upon the rightful spouse; and (3) those who by mutual co-operation, physical or moral, even apart from adultery, have caused the death of the rightful married partner.[173]

Accordingly four distinct species of the impediment of crime can occur:

1. Adultery along with the mutual promise of marriage.
2. Adultery along with an attempted marriage.
3. Adultery along with the killing of the spouse, the one or the accomplices causing the death.
4. The killing of the spouse even apart from adultery, both accomplices being instrumental in causing the death of the legitimate spouse.[174]

1. Adultery along with the Mutual Promise of Marriage

It is first of all noted that the adultery and the mutual promise of marriage must occur within the duration of one and the same lawful wedlock. The impediment would not arise if the adultery indeed took place during the marriage, but the mutual promise was exchanged only after its dissolution.[175] The adultery must be the normal act through which generation becomes possible;[176] materially it must be true adultery, i.e., at least one of the parties must be a validly married person; it must also be formal for both, i.e., the fact that the person with whom the sin is

---

[173] Can. 1075.

[174] John F. Donohue, *The Impediment of Crime*, The Catholic University of America Canon Law Studies, n. 69 (Washington: The Catholic University of America, 1931), p. 37.

[175] Ayrinhac-Lydon, *Marriage Legislation*, n. 152.

[176] Payen, *De Matrimonio*, I, n. 1330.

committed is married must be known to the other party.[177] The mutual promise must be a serious, free and reciprocally exchanged agreement, the fulfillment of which has for its object a true marriage, not free love or anything else.[178] If the promise was made conditionally, the impediment arises only when the condition is verified before the death of the lawful spouse.[179]

It is evident that there will be no necessity for the pastor to inquire into the possible existence of the impediment of crime except in cases in which at least one of the nupturients had for a time the status of a validly married person. This fact will be known to the pastor from his previous interrogation concerning the impediment of prior marriage bond. Since the impediment which arises from adultery together with the mutual promise of marriage is frequently occult, it poses difficulties to the investigating pastor. Nevertheless, when it is ascertained that the party was a previously validly married person, some effort should be made to establish freedom from this species of the impediment.[180] The question, "Did you during the lifetime of your wife/husband promise to marry your intended partner?", should be put to each party to the marriage in the separate interrogation. An affirmative reply will necessitate a further inquiry by the pastor for determining whether or not adultery was committed, and whether or not the adultery was such as to meet the various qualifications indicated in the preliminary discussion.

At times circumstances may lead the pastor to suspect the existence of the impediment, for example, if a man should shortly after the death of his wife marry a woman who has been living in the house with him in the capacity of a housekeeper or nurse during his wife's illness, and especially if there is no evident reason for an early re-marriage. Again, it may happen that in his neighborhood a man has the reputation of being unfaithful to his wife, or frequently was seen with other women at

---

177 Gasparri, *Tractatus Canonicus de Matrimonio*, I, n. 673; Augustine, *Commentary*, V. 196.

178 Augustine, *Commentary*, V, 197.

179 Cappello, *De Matrimonio*, n. 483, p. 460.

180 Can. 1021, § 2; S. C. de Sacramentis, instr., 29 iun. 1941, n. 5, Allegatum I, n. 9—*AAS*, XXXIII (1941), 301, 311.

places of amusement. In these and other similar instances in which there are indications of the possible presence of the impediment, the pastor should strive by prudent and careful questioning of the party himself, and of witnesses if necessary, to ascertain the true facts of the case, and the consequent freedom or lack of freedom of the parties to marry each other.[181]

The impediment will be multiplied if both adulterers are married and each one knows that there is a double marriage, since then there is a crime against two marriages.[182]

2. Adultery along with Attempted Marriage

This species of the impediment of crime arises when, during the same lawful wedlock, two parties commit adultery and attempt to intermarry.[183] The adultery must meet the qualifications that have been indicated in the preceding number. There must be a real attempt at marriage, i.e., it must be an intelligent act whereby two persons, aware of an existing marriage bond, truly and seriously and by means of words or signs give consent to a so-called marriage here and now.[184] It is not necessary that the marriage be attempted before a pastor and two witnesses, i.e., according to the canonical form; a marriage attempted before a non-Catholic minister or before a civil magistrate, or even an attempted common law marriage in which consent is exchanged privately, would suffice to establish the impediment.[185] Mere concubinage of itself would not give rise to the impediment unless the parties actually gave a verbal consent in that state, or unless it included a mutual promise of marriage.[186] The most frequent example of this species of the impediment of crime occurs when already validly married parties seek and obtain a civil divorce, enter a new civil marriage before a non-

[181] Can. 1031, § 1, n. 1; Donovan, *The Pastor's Obligation in the Prenuptial Investigation*, p. 190.

[182] Ayrinhac-Lydon, *Marriage Legislation*, n. 155.

[183] Can. 1075, § 1.

[184] Cappello, *De Matrimonio*, n. 486; Donohue, *The Impediment of Crime*, p. 53.

[185] Gasparri, *Tractatus Canonicus de Matrimonio*, I, n. 675.

[186] Cappello, *De Matrimonio*, n. 486, 2b; Donohue, *The Impediment of Crime*, p. 54.

Catholic minister or civil official, and consummate this latter attempted marriage.[187]

Here again, as in the preceding species of the impediment, it will not be necessary for the pastor, with reference to the possible presence of the impediment, to inquire of all who present themselves for marriage. Since the fact of a previous valid marriage constitutes a basic element for the possible emergence of the impediment, there is no need for the interrogation when no such marriage has existed. When it has been discovered that at least one of the nupturients had been a partner to a valid marriage, then in the separate interrogation of each of the parties the question, "Did you during the lifetime of the legitimate spouse attempt marriage with your intended partner?", should be asked. An affirmative reply will direct the pastor to determine whether or not adultery preceded the attempted marriage, or whether the attempted marriage has been consummated.

When parties present themselves to the pastor in order to have a previous civil marriage convalidated, he must be vigilant to discern the possible presence of this impediment, seeking to find out whether or not either of the parties had been validly married prior to the civil marriage. If such was the case, he must establish whether or not the present civil marriage took place during the valid marriage, and whether or not there had been previous adultery, or whether the attempted marriage had been consummated prior to the death of the lawful spouse. Once marriage has been attempted and cohabitation has followed, the presumption is that the marriage has been consummated.[188] The pastor should be vigilant particularly in instances in which the Pauline Privilege is being used, since the conditions for this species of the impediment may be verified in such cases.

If both adulterers had been validly married, and each one knew of the double marriage, there would exist a double impediment, since then there would have been perpetrated a sin against two marriages.[189]

---

[187] Donohue, *op. cit.*, p. 54.

[188] Can. 1015, § 2.

[189] Ayrinhac-Lydon, *Marriage Legislation*, n. 155.

3. Adultery along with the Killing of the Spouse

As in the two previous species of the impediment of crime, the adultery must be true and formal. Moreover, it is evident that the adultery must have been committed before the murderous attack was effected. Hence the impediment would not arise if the carnal act took place after the murder of the lawful spouse, for the legitimate marriage would then have been already dissolved. It is postulated that the killing of the spouse was perpetrated by one of the accomplices in the adultery, whether the act of killing was executed personally or through the agency of another.[190] It is likewise postulated that the murder was intentional, and that it was effected with the purpose of gaining freedom for marrying the accomplice.[191]

Because of the seriously criminal nature of this species of the impediment, the pastor must be extremely prudent and cautious in his investigation. In ordinary cases, when it has been revealed that at least one of the parties was previously validly married, it will suffice in the separate interrogation of the prospective spouse to ask, "Did you in any way cause the death of the former partner in marriage?" The answer to this question will indicate to the pastor whether or not further investigation will be necessary.

As Donovan wisely suggests,[192] the pastor should use the occasion to instruct the parties on the impediment and its basis, thereby leaving it to the conscience of parties, who may be loath to reveal the impediment to the pastor, to mention it in the sacrament of penance prior to marriage.

If each of the two guilty parties is married, and each one has killed his or her lawful spouse, then there is a double impediment of crime.[193]

4. The Killing of the Spouse through Concerted Effort

In this species of the impediment of crime, unlike the preceding three, the law abstracts entirely from the element of

---

[190] Heylen, *De Matrimonio*, p. 576.
[191] Cappello, *De Matrimonio*, n. 489.
[192] *The Pastor's Obligation in the Prenuptial Investigation*, p. 194.
[193] Ayrinhac-Lydon, *Marriage Legislation*, n. 155.

adultery. Here the impediment arises between two parties who have co-operated, either physically or morally, in killing the lawful spouse of one of them, in order that they may be free to marry each other.[194] The murderous attack must be real, intentional and effective.[195] There must be a real co-operation in the committing of the murder, i.e., the aid of the accomplice must contribute, not only facilitatingly, but also effectively, to the commission of the crime.[196] In other words, there must be a mutual co-operation by which the two accomplices actually, efficaciously, and with mutual intent and counsel concur in inflicting death on the lawful spouse. If one accomplice merely approves or ratifies the murder after it has been committed, the impediment is lacking.[197] Furthermore the perpetrated murder must be planned with the mutual intention of becoming free to marry the accomplice. Wherefore, if the murder was committed through anger, revenge or for any other motive, the impediment does not arise.[198] This is also true if the murder was committed in order that the murderer could wed a person other than the accomplice.

In ordinary cases in which one of the nupturients was previously validly married, the pastor should ask each spouse in the separate interrogation , "Did you and she/he co-operate in any way to cause the death of the lawful marriage partner?" When confronted with the rare case of the murder of the rightful spouse, the pastor must determine through prudent and cautious questioning whether or not all the elements required for the contracting of the impediment are present.

When both conspirators are married and both legitimate spouses are killed in consequence of the mutual cooperation of the conspirators, there is a twofold impediment of crime.[199]

---

194 Can. 1075, § 3.

195 Cappello, *De Matrimonio*, n. 494.

196 Ayrinhac-Lydon, *Marriage Legislation*, n. 154.

197 Gasparri, *Tractatus Canonicus de Matrimonio*, I, n. 679.

198 Wernz-Vidal, *Ius Matrimoniale*, n. 332.

199 Ayrinhac-Lydon, *Marriage Legislation*, n. 155.

5. Dispensation from the Impediment of Crime

If the pastor ascertains from his investigation that the impediment of crime actually exists, and there are sufficiently grave reasons for the celebration of the marriage, a dispensation must be obtained before he may proceed with it. In formulating petitions for such dispensations, he must take care to express the precise species of the impediment from which the dispensation is sought, and whether or not it is single or multiple.

If the impediment has arisen either from the fact of adultery accompanied with the murder of the spouse by one of the guilty parties, or from the concerted act of the murder of the spouse by the two accomplices, the Holy See will not grant a dispensation if the crime is public; if it is occult, a dispensation will be granted only for very serious reasons.[200] The impediment arising from adultery along with the mutual promise of marriage, or from adultery along with an attempted marriage, is an impediment of minor degree from which a dispensation is more easily granted.[201] The faculties given to ordinaries by the Sacred Congregation of the Sacraments permit them to dispense from the minor impediments of crime.[202] Petitions for dispensations from the more serious species of the impediment must be forwarded to the Holy See through the local ordinary.

Article 11. The Impediment of Consanguinity

In the direct line, consanguinity invalidates marriage between all ascendants and descendants, whether legitimate or only natural. In the collateral line marriage is invalid to the third degree inclusively, but the impediment becomes multiple only with the multiplication of the common ancestry. Marriage is never permitted when doubt exists whether the parties are related in some degree of the direct line, or in the first degree of the collateral line.[203]

---

[200] Cappello, *De Matrimonio*, n. 504.
[201] Can. 1042, § 1, n. 5; Cappello, *loc. cit.*
[202] Bouscaren, *The Canon Law Digest*, II, 33.
[203] Can. 1076.

Consanguinity, then, constitutes a diriment impediment to marriage between all persons related by blood in the direct line, and between persons related to the third degree inclusively of the collateral line, i.e., between brother and sister, between first cousins, between second cousins, between aunt and nephew, between uncle and niece, between great-aunt and grand nephew, and between great-uncle and grand-niece. According to the present law as contained in canon 1076, § 3, the impediment is multiplied only when the common ancestry from which the persons descend is multiple.

The investigating pastor should inquire of all nupturients whether or not they are related by ties of blood. The Instruction *Sacrosanctum matrimonii* considers at some length this particular obstacle to a valid marriage,[204] stating that the principal marriage cases referred to the Sacred Congregation of the Sacraments for simple convalidation or for a *sanatio in radice* regard marriages celebrated with an impediment in the second degree of consanguinity, or more frequently still of consanguinity in the third degree simply or in the third degree touching the second of the collateral line, and without a canonical dispensation. It therefore urges pastors to be diligent in their inquiry, by considering carefully the surnames of the parties and of their parents for an indication of blood-relationship. Special consideration should be given to the baptismal certificates as indicative of such a relationship.

If the pastor detects a certain reticence in the parties' attitude and suspects concealment of blood-relationship, then with a view to a more accurate investigation the Instruction directs him to employ credible and reputable witnesses who shall testify under oath.[205] In this matter the testimony of parents, grandparents or other close relatives would naturally be preferred.

For the sake of clarity it is advisable for the pastor to draw up a chart of the genealogical trees of the parties whenever consanguinity is detected or is suspected. In fact, the Instruction

---

[204] S. C. de Sacramentis, instr., 29 iun. 1941, n. 5—*AAS*, XXXIII (1941), 301.

[205] S. C. de Sacramentis, instr., 29 iun. 1941, n. 5, Allegatum II—*AAS*, XXXIII (1941), 301, 313; can. 1031, § 1, n. 1.

requires that such a diagram accompany all petitions for dispensations from this impediment in order to obviate errors in computing the degrees of relationship.[206]

Since the impediment includes natural or illegitimate as well as legitimate children, care must be taken when such a person presents himself for marriage.[207] The pastor should endeavor diligently to discover who the parents of the illegitimate party are. If the mother is living and can be approached, she will be able to indicate whether relationship exists between the two nupturients. Usually the baptismal certificate will be of little help, since the father's name is ordinarily not indicated.[208] In practice it is safe for the pastor to proceed with the marriage even though the father's name be unknown, unless there remain a prudent doubt as to the presence of the impediment.

Similarly, extreme care must be taken when it is known that the groom had illicit relations with the mother of the prospective bride, especially if the ages of the parties indicate that she may actually be the offspring of the illicit relations, and consequently related to the groom in the first degree of the direct line. In this case the pastor must ascertain the girl's paternity, or at least establish with moral certainty that the groom was not her father. If prudent doubt should persist, then according to a reply of the Code Commission the marriage is not to be permitted.[209]

If the investigation reveals that the impediment of consanguinity bars the parties from a valid marriage, the pastor will not proceed until a dispensation has been obtained. The Instruction reminds pastors of the necessity of care in petitioning for dispensations.[210] As has been mentioned, it states that a diagram of the genealogical trees of the parties must accompany the petitions forwarded to the Holy See, in order to obviate errors that sometimes creep into the computation of consan-

[206] *Loc. cit.* .

[207] Can. 1076, § 1.

[208] Can. 777, § 2.

[209] Pont. Comm. Interp. Cod., 3 iun. 1918—*AAS*, X (1918), 346.

[210] S. C. de Sacramentis, instr., 29 iun. 1941, n. 5—*AAS*, XXXIII (1941), 302.

guinity. Further, it discourages ambiguous descriptions of impediments when spouses are bound by double impediments.

Moreover, the Instruction recalls that for a valid dispensation from an impediment of major degree there is required a canonical reason, proportionate to the gravity of the impediment and actually existing in the case.[211] Particular reference is made to the Instruction of the Sacred Congregation of the Sacraments of August 1, 1931, an Instruction which dealt specifically with dispensations from the impediment of consanguinity in the first degree of the collateral line mixed with the second, and considered the legitimate causes approved by the long-continued practice of the Holy See as sufficient for the dispensation. Regarded as sufficient in these cases were the prevention of notable scandal, the settlement of important questions concerning the succession of property, and the relief of distressing family conditions. Finally, such petitions were to be accompanied with a letter of recommendation written by the ordinary in his own hand.[212]

Apart from these exceptional cases, the Instruction *Sacrosanctum matrimonii* points to the earlier Instruction of the Sacred Congregation for the Propagation of the Faith of May 9, 1877,[213] and to approved authors for a list of the commonly accepted causes for dispensations.[214] It is noted that, when the reason "*aetas superadulta mulieris, non vidua*" is advanced, there is required the completion of the twenty-fourth year of age.[215]

No dispensation will be granted from an impediment that derives from the natural law, i.e., consanguinity in the direct line.[216] If the impediment derives from the ecclesiastical law, the Holy See will grant a dispensation, but the closer the relationship, the more difficult it is to obtain the dispensation, and the more serious is the reason required. Consanguinity in the

[211] *Loc. Cit.*
[212] *AAS*, XXIII (1931), 413.
[213] *Collectanea*, n. 1470.
[214] S. C. de Sacramentis, instr., 29 iun. 1941, n. 5 d—*AAS*, XXXIII (1941), 302.
[215] *Ibid.*, n. 5, e—*AAS*, XXXIII (1941), 302.
[216] Capello, *De Matrimonio*, n. 525.

third degree of the collateral line is an impediment of minor degree.[217]

The quinquennial faculties granted by the Sacred Congregation of the Sacraments to ordinaries of the United States include those of dispensing from consanguinity in the second and third degree touching the first, provided that there be no wonderment therefrom, and from consanguinity in the second degree of the collateral line.[218] Further, by virtue of the same faculties, ordinaries can dispense from the minor impediment of consanguinity, i.e., the impediment which arises from the third degree of relationship in the collateral line.[219] Wherefore, petitions for dispensations from these impediments may be sent to the ordinary; for dispensations from the closer degrees of relationship, the petition is to be sent to the Holy See through the ordinary.

Article 12. The Impediment of Affinity

Affinity in the direct line annuls marriage in any degree; in the collateral line it annuls marriage to the second degree inclusively. The impediment is multiplied whenever the impediment of consanguinity from which it proceeds is multiplied, and also by successive marriages with blood-relatives of the deceased spouse up to and inclusive of the second degree in the collateral line.[220]

Unlike the pre-Code law, affinity now arises only from a valid marriage, whether ratified simply or ratified and consummated.[221] It exists between the man and the blood relations of the woman, and vice versa. Affinity is so reckoned that the blood-relations of the woman are related to her husband by affinity in the same line and degree in which they are related to the woman by consanguinity, and vice versa.[222] Wherefore, a man is forbidden under pain of invalidity to marry the mother, daughter, grandmother or granddaughter of his wife; and a

[217] Can. 1042, § 2, n. 1; Cappello, *loc. cit.*
[218] Bouscaren, *The Canon Law Digest,* II, 34.
[219] Bouscaren, *op. cit.*, II, 33.
[220] Can. 1077.
[221] Can. 97, § 1; Ayrinhac-Lydon, *Marriage Legislation,* n. 165.
[222] Can. 97, § 2, 3.

woman is forbidden to marry the father, son, grandfather or grandson of her husband. In the collateral line a man may not marry his wife's sister, aunt, niece or first cousin, and a woman may not marry her husband's brother, uncle, nephew or first cousin.

The pastor will not always find it necessary to question the nupturients concerning this impediment in the prenuptial investigation. If it is definitely known that neither party has ever been previously married, or if the previous marriage has been invalid on any score, it is evident that the impediment of affinity is non-existent. In this latter regard, however, interrogation on the impediment of public decency will be in order.[223]

In cases in which a party has been previously validly married, the pastor should question both parties separately whether they are related by that previous marriage, and, if so, precisely to what extent of that relationship. When doubt arises, he should question credible witnesses under oath, preferably the parents or other close relatives of the parties, in order to attain more accurate information.[224] In such cases of doubt the pastor may obtain a partial proof by comparing the baptismal certificates of the former spouse and of the present intended partner, especially from a perusal of the names of the parents.

The observations of the Instruction concerning the impediment of consanguinity are directed also to the impediment of affinity, and the precautions it indicates concerning petitions for dispensations are to be adhered to as well. The diagram of the genealogical trees of the parties is to be appended to such petitions, in order that the precise relationship may be clearly indicated.[225]

Since affinity is an impediment of ecclesiastical origin, the Holy See can dispense from it in all its degrees, but in practice it does not grant dispensations from affinity in the direct line when the marriage has been consummated.[226] The extensive

---

[223] Can. 1078.

[224] Can. 1031, § 1, n. 1; S. C. de Sacramentis, instr., 29 iun. 1941, n. 5 (a)—*AAS*, XXXIII (1941), 302.

[225] *Loc. cit.*

[226] Cappello, *De Matrimonio*, n. 539.

faculties implied in canons 1043-1045 exclude the right to dispense from the impediment when these circumstances are verified. In the collateral line, dispensations are granted without difficulty for reasonable causes, whether public or private.[227] Affinity in the second degree of the collateral line is an impediment of minor degree.[228]

By virtue of the quinquennial faculties granted to ordinaries of the United States by the Sacred Congregation of the Sacraments, these ordinaries may dispense, not only from the impediment of affinity of minor degree, but also from affinity in the first degree of the collateral line, either simple or mixed with the second degree[229] under the conditions noted therein.

Article 13. The Impediment of Public Decency

The impediment of public decency arises from an invalid marriage, whether or not it has been consummated, and from a public or notorious concubinage; it invalidates marriage in the first and second degrees of the direct line between the man and the blood-relatives of the woman, and vice versa.[230]

A man, therefore is by way of a diriment impediment prohibited from marrying the mother, grandmother, daughter or granddaughter of the woman with whom he contracted an invalid marriage, or with whom he lived in public or notorious concubinage. Similarly a woman may not marry the father, son, grandfather or grandson of the man. The impediment does not exist in the collateral line.[231]

It matters not on what score the marriage was invalid, whether it was from lack of form, from defect of consent, or from the existence of a diriment impediment, provided that the union had the appearance and semblance of a marriage.[232] According to a reply of the Pontifical Commission of Interpretation, as given

227 Cappello, *loc. cit.*
228 Can. 1042, § 2, n. 2.
229 Bouscaren, *The Canon Law Digest*, II, 33, 34.
230 Can. 1078.
231 Ayrinhac-Lyon, *Marriage Legislation*, n. 175.
232 Cappello, *De Matrimonio*, n. 543.

on March 12, 1929, a mere civil marriage does not give rise to the impediment independently of cohabitation.[233] From this cohabitation the impediment would follow by reason of the concubinage described in canon 1078, and not by reason of the invalid status of the marriage, since a civil marriage does not present the appearance of a marriage when it has been contracted by a Catholic.[234]

Before concubinage can give rise to the impediment, it must be a true concubinage, i.e., a union that implies an agreement between the man and the woman to maintain marital relations in a permanent manner despite the accompanying lack of all external appearance of marriage.[235] It would exist, for example, if a man kept a mistress even though she did not live in the same house with him. The relationship, however, must be a habitual one. Mere isolated acts of fornication do not connote the existence of a concubinary union.

Moreover, the concubinage must be public or notorious. It would be public if knowledge of it has already been published, or if the circumstances are such that it can and must be prudently judged that it will easily be divulged.[236] It would be notorious by notoriety of law after a sentence of a competent judge which has become irrevocable, or after the judicial confession of one of the parties in court.[237] It would be notorious by notoriety of fact if it is publicly known and the circumstances are such that it cannot be concealed by means of any subterfuge.[238]

In the course of the prenuptial investigation, the interrogation concerning the impediment of previous marriage bond should reveal the presence of a prior invalid marriage, and to this information the pastor can add a question regarding the relationship, if such should exist, of the intended spouse to the previous married partner, thus obtaining a response indicating whether or

---

[233] *AAS*, XXI (1929), 170.

[234] Payen, *De Matrimonio*, I, n. 1538.

[235] Payen, *op. cit.*, I, n. 1540; Ayrinhac-Lydon, *Marriage Legislation*, n. 174.

[236] Can. 2197, n. 1.

[237] Can. 2197, n. 2.

[238] Can. 2197, n. 3.

not the impediment of public decency arising from an invalid marriage exists.

If the parties are well known to the pastor, for example, if one or both are faithful members of his parish concerning whom he would be likely to know of any scandalous conduct, the pastor need not question them unless some doubt or suspicion warrants it. If the parties are not personally known to the pastor, a general question concerning the impediment will suffice to reveal its possible existence.

When there is cause for prudent doubt in the mind of the pastor, a more extensive investigation will be required. If the reputation of the party is such that the pastor may well suspect the possibility of public or notorious concubinage, or if there are rumors to that effect in the locality, the pastor should not hesitate to investigate, both by interrogating the party himself, and by prudently questioning reliable witnesses under oath.[239]

If it is ascertained that the impediment actually does exist, the pastor may not permit the marriage until a dispensation has been granted. A dispensation can be obtained from the impediment in both forbidden degrees, since it is an impediment which exists solely in consequence of the ecclesiastical law.[240] In the second degree, public decency is an impediment of minor degree.[241]

By virtue of the quinquennial faculties granted to ordinaries by the Sacred Congregation of the Sacraments, these ordinaries may dispense from both degrees of the impediment, provided that there is no possibility that the one party be the offspring of the other.[242]

Article 14. The Impediment of Spiritual Relationship

Only that spiritual relationship which arises from baptism and exists between the person baptized and the person baptizing, and between the person baptized and the sponsor, invalidates marriage.[243] Therefore, though a spiritual relationship arises

[239] Can. 1031, § 1, n. 1.
[240] Cappello, *De Matrimonio*, n. 554.
[241] Can. 1042, § 2, n. 3.
[242] Bouscaren, *The Canon Law Digest*, II, 33, 34.
[243] Can. 1079, 768.

also from the sacrament of confirmation,[244] it does not constitute an impediment to marriage, for the Code nowhere lists this relationship as a matrimonial impediment.

Ordinarily very little difficulty will be encountered by the pastor in his investigation concerning this impediment, for it is not of frequent occurrence, and usually its presence or absence can be established by means of the baptismal certificate, which should contain the names of the minister, and of the sponsors, if the party was baptized a Catholic.[245] If the baptismal certificates reveal that both parties were validly baptized in infancy, and if their ages are approximately the same, it will not be necessary to question them concerning the impediment.

If the baptismal certificate cannot be obtained, though it is known that the parties were baptized, then the pastor should ask the parties who the minister and the sponsors were. In a case of doubt he must resort to the testimony of reliable witnesses given under oath to obtain this information.[246] Parents, members of the family of the party, close friends of the family or the priest who administered the sacrament, are preferred as witnesses.

If the party asserts that he was baptized privately in a case of necessity, the pastor must carefully ascertain who conferred the baptism and who the sponsors were. Similarly, he must take care to determine the sponsor when the party was baptized in adult age, for the intended partner, as a close friend of the party, could readily have acted as sponsor at the baptism.

If the pastor through his investigation determines that the impediment exists, he will not proceed to the marriage until he has obtained a dispensation therefrom. Since the impediment of spiritual relationship is one of minor degree,[247] the ordinary may dispense from it in virtue of his quinquennial faculties, granted to him by the Sacred Congregation of the Sacraments.[248]

---

[244] Can. 797.
[245] Can. 777, § 1.
[246] Can. 1031, § 1, n. 1.
[247] Can. 1042, § 2, n. 4.
[248] Bouscaren, *The Canon Law Digest*, II, 33.

Article 15. Investigation in Marriages of Unworthy Catholics

Not infrequently the pastor will be confronted with prospective marriages in which one or both of the contracting parties are notoriously or publicly unworthy Catholics. Now, if both parties have been baptized in the Catholic Church, and neither has joined a schismatical or a heretical sect, obviously they are not prevented by the impediment of mixed religion or of disparity of worship from entering marriage.[249] Such marriages, however, are regulated by the special prescripts of canons 1065 and 1066.

The unworthiness mentioned in these canons does not constitute an impediment to marriage,[250] but it does establish a certain legal inequality between such unworthy Catholics and a faithful Catholic, who is presumably in the state of grace.[251]

A. Unworthy Catholics of Canon 1065

According to canon 1065, the faithful are to be deterred from contracting marriage with those who have notoriously rejected the Catholic faith, although they have not joined a non-Catholic sect, and with those who belong to societies condemned by the Church.[252]

The first group included in this canon comprises those who through apostasy, heresy, or schism have seceded from communion with the Church though they have not joined a non-Catholic sect.[253] It does not refer to mere careless Catholics.[254] A delict is implied, i.e., an external and a morally imputable violation of the law,[255] and a notorious one, i.e., one which is already widely known or almost certainly bound to become known

---

[249] Can. 1060-1064; 1070-1071.

[250] Chelodi, *Ius Matrimoniale*, n. 65; Wernz-Vidal, *Ius Matrimoniale*, n. 173; Gasparri, *Tractatus Canonicus de Matrimonio*, I, n. 474.

[251] John Heneghan, "The Marriage of Unworthy Catholics: Canons 1065 and 1066"—*The Jurist*, V (1945), 389.

[252] Heneghan, *The Marriages of Unworthy Catholics*, The Catholic University of America Canon Law Studies, n. 188 (Washington: The Catholic University of America Press, 1944), p. 83.

[253] Cf. Can. 1325, § 2.

[254] Ayrinhac-Lydon, *Marriage Legislation* n. 115.

[255] Can. 2195, § 1.

because of the circumstances.[256] Belonging to this group of unworthy Catholics are those who have become materialists, rationalists, indifferentists or free thinkers.[257]

The second group comprises those who have notoriously joined societies condemned by the Catholic Church. Condemned societies are those which the Church declares to be unlawful, and in which, under penalty of censure or of grave sin without censure, it forbids its subjects to take membership.[258] Among the societies condemned under censure are included those of the Freemasons, Anarchists, Extreme Socialists, Orders of Knights Templar, Masonic Cremation Societies and their female affiliates, e.g., The Order of the Eastern Star.[259] Societies condemned under penalty of grave sin include the Oddfellows, Knights of Pythias, Sons of Temperance, non-Catholic Bible Societies, and theosophical societies.[260] The prescripts of canon 1065 apply to both types of condemned societies.

The Instruction *Sacrosanctum matrimonii* recalls these prescripts of the law and directs the pastor to inquire prudently regarding the existence of these dangers.[261]

If the party is well known to the pastor, for example, if he is a member of his parish, the pastor should have little difficulty in recognizing or establishing the party's worthiness for marriage. If the party is a stranger to the pastor, a more diligent inquiry will be necessary. The Instruction directs the pastor to inquire of the other party to the marriage whether or not the intended partner has rejected the Catholic faith or has joined a condemned society. Frequently the attitude of the party during the interview with the pastor will serve to indicate whether he is a faithful Catholic, or perhaps cause the pastor to suspect

[256] Can. 2197, n. 3; Heneghan, *op. cit.*, p. 58.

[257] Heylen, *De Matrimonio*, p. 187.

[258] Can. 2335, 684; Joseph Quigley, *Condemned Societies*, The Catholic University of America Canon Law Studies, n. 82 (Washington: The Catholic University of America Press, 1932), p. 7.

[259] Heneghan, *The Marriages of Unworthy Catholics*, p. 100.

[260] Heneghan, *loc. cit.*
XXXIII (1941), 311.

[261] S. C. de Sacramentis, instr., 29 iun. 1941, Allegatum I, n. 8—*AAS*,

that he has abandoned the faith. In a case of doubt the pastor should not hesitate to call upon the testimony of reliable witnesses to determine the presence or absence of the conditions enumerated in canon 1065.

When it is established that the party is unworthy according to canon 1065, § 1, the pastor's first duty is to endeavor to dissuade the faithful Catholic from such a marriage. Ordinarily, however, such dissuasion is of little avail when the parties have already determined to marry and appear before the priest to arrange for the celebration of their marriage. Young people should be warned through sermons and instructions of the dangers inherent in such unions, and consequently be put on their guard against associations which might lead to this type of marriage. If dissuasion is of no avail and it is evident to the pastor that the parties are determined to marry, he must immediately refer the case to the ordinary, explaining its particular facts.[262]

The ordinary in turn will not grant the required permission to proceed with the marriage until, having considered the facts of the case, he prudently judges that the Catholic education of the children will be provided for and that the danger of perversion to the Catholic party is removed, and moreover that a grave cause is present for the celebration of the marriage. The pastor, therefore, should previously investigate concerning these requirements in order that he may present a completed account of the case to the ordinary.

Causes which are considered as sufficient for the concession of a dispensation from the impediments of mixed religion and disparity of worship are likewise of sufficient gravity to warrant the cessation of the prohibition of this canon.[263] In some dioceses formal written promises, similar to those required for mixed marriages, are demanded, and, if so, the pastor must comply with these regulations.[264]

---

[262] Can. 1065, § 2.

[263] Heneghan, *The Marriages of Unworthy Catholics*, p. 158.

[264] Heneghan, *op. cit.*, p. 168.

B. Unworthy Catholics of Canon 1066

According to canon 1065, branded as unworthy Catholics are also those who are public sinners or who are notoriously bound by a censure. A public sinner is one who is guilty of grave sin, and whose sinful condition is known to the community, or according to solid and prudent judgment will inevitably be known to the community from the circumstances which accompany the sin.[265] Cappello mentions as an example of a public sinner a Catholic who seriously neglects his religious duties and whose negligence is publicly known, such as one who habitually fails to fulfill the annual Easter precept. Notoriously censured Catholics are those upon whom the penalty of an excommunication or of a personal interdict rests in such a manner that their condition cannot be concealed.[266]

It is the duty of the investigating pastor to determine whether or not a prospective spouse belongs to this class of unworthy Catholics. The pastor may know from personal knowledge that a person comes within the scope of canon 1066. Frequently, however, he knows very little about the person before him. The Instruction directs the pastor to endeavor to learn these things from the bridegroom concerning the bride, and vice versa, and in general from persons other than the party himself.[267]

Here again the attitude of the party during the interrogation may serve to indicate to the pastor whether the party is a faithful, practising Catholic, or whether further investigation should be made. If necessary, he will call upon reliable witnesses who will be able to inform him whether the party is actually a public sinner or notoriously bound by a censure, or whether he is free from serious sin and penal censure in the eyes of the community.

If the pastor ascertains that the party actually comes within the prohibition of canon 1066 as a public sinner or as

[265] Cf. can. 2197, n. 1.
[266] Cf. can. 2197, nn. 2, 3; Payen, *De Matrimonio*, I, n. 922.
[267] S. C. de Sacramentis, instr., 29 iun. 1941, Allegatum I, n. 8—*AAS*, XXXIII (1941), 311.

a notoriously censured person, he should attempt to persuade the person to reconcile himself with the Church. Should the party refuse to go to confession or to have the censure removed, the pastor may not assist at the marriage unless a grave cause is present, concerning which he has, if possible, consulted the ordinary.[268]

---

[268] Cf. Cappello, *De Matrimonio*, n. 332.

CHAPTER XI

INVESTIGATION CONCERNING THE PARTIES' MATRIMONIAL CONSENT AND KNOWLEDGE OF CHRISTIAN DOCTRINE

Part I. Matrimonial Consent

The second general reason for investigation, as ordered by canon 1020, § 2, concerns the freedom of the parties in consenting to the marriage. Although the canon mentions only the freedom of consent, it is evident that the pastor would be remiss in his duty if he were to omit reference to the other qualities of matrimonial consent as determined in Title VII, Chapter V, of the Third Book of the Code.[1] In the following articles a brief consideration will be given to these various qualities, through the appraisal of which by means of his investigation the pastor may hope to determine whether or not an integral consent for the marriage is present.

Article 1. Freedom of Consent

According to canon 1087, § 1, marriage is invalid if a person has contracted it through force or grave fear that unjustly has been brought to bear on him by an external agent, with the result that the person has elected to enter marriage with the intent of freeing himself from this force or fear.

The qualities of force and fear which invalidate marriage must be clearly understood by the pastor, for it remains for him to recognize their existence in a particular case. From the canon just quoted, it is evident that the fear must be grave, i.e., real and serious, not imaginary or slight. This grave fear may be absolute, i.e., of such a nature that it would move any normal resolute person to do something

[1] S. C. de Sacramentis, instr., 29 iun. 1941, n. 9—*AAS*, XXXIII (1941), 304.

he does not wish to do; or it may be relative, i.e., of such a nature that it depends on the characters of the persons involved, and on the relationship existing between them, with reference to the nature of the evil that is threatened.[2] Secondly, the force and fear must be unjustly inflicted. It may be unjust either because the offender has no right in justice to inflict it, or because, though he have a right to do so, he inflicts it in an unjust manner.[3] Thirdly, it is postulated that the force and fear be inflicted by an external agent, i.e., the fear must arise from the action of a person other than the one suffering the fear; it must not arise merely from the workings of one's mind, or as the result of some act of nature.[4] Finally, if they are to invalidate the marriage, the force and fear must be the motive cause of the person's entry into marriage.[5]

Despite the greater freedom and independence of young people these days, cases of alleged force and fear are not infrequent; the validity of many marriages is still impugned on this basis. A study of such cases reveals the variety of motives which prompt others to force young people into marriage. When a man is the victim of force, it is usually because illicit relations have taken place, and either the girl or her family, or possibly also the guardian of the law will coerce the man into marriage. When the girl is the victim of force, the situation is usually brought on by domineering parents, who for one reason or another insist on their own selfish choice rather than allow the girl to follow the dictates of her heart. The parents may be moved by good and honest motives; they may think that they know better what is for her good. Or they may so act because of selfish or un-

---

[2] James P. Kelly, 11 Force and Fear Affecting Matrimonial Consent"—*The Jurist*, V. (945), 515.

[3] S. R. R., *Nullitatis Matrimonii*, 23 febr., 1927, coram R. P. D. Ubaldo Mannucci, Dec. VIII—*S. Romanae Rotae Decisiones seu Sententiae* Quae Prodierunt 1909-1939 (31 vols., Romae Civitate Vaticana: Typis Polyglottis Vaticanis, 1912-1948), XIX (1927), 57-58 (hereafter cited *Decisiones).*

[4] S. R. R., *Nullitatis Matrimonii*, 21 iulii 1910, coram R. P. D. Gulielmo Sebastian elli, Dec. XXVIII, n. 2—*Decisiones*, II (1910), 289.

[5] S. R. R., *Nullitatis matrimonii*, 10 nov. 1927, coram Iulio Grazioli, Dec. L, n. 2—*Decisiones*, XIX (1927), 445-446.

worthy motives, such as the seeking of wealth or social status. Occasionally the prospective husband forces the girl into marriage with his threats of the infliction of physical or moral harm, e.g., with his threat to reveal illicit intimacies in which the girl had a part.[6]

In accordance with canon 1020, § 2, the Instruction *Sacrosanctum matrimonii* directs the pastor to establish the freedom of the consent of the parties to the marriage.[7] Particular reference is made to the freedom of the woman, since it is more likely that she can easily be subjected to the influences of force and fear. Nevertheless the freedom of the man is likewise to be established.

The pastor must first of all question the parties themselves regarding the matter of their freedom in entering the marriage. He will ask them whether they are being compelled either directly or indirectly by the threats, the pleadings or the persuasions of some other person, or whether they are completely free in their choice of marriage. The wisdom of the separate interrogation of the nupturients can readily be seen in this matter, for in this private interview with the pastor a party is more apt to reveal undue influence than in the presence of another. The pastor should elicit the confidence of the party being questioned by impressing upon him the fact that any information given to him on this point will be guarded with the utmost discretion and circumspection, so that the party will have nothing to fear as a consequence. He should also assure the party that perhaps some other way out of the difficulty will be found.[8]

The circumstances of the marriage and the dispositions of the parties are important factors to be kept in mind as indicative of the freedom of the parties or of the compulsion exercised on them. The fact that one or the other of the parties is entering marriage to obviate some difficulty or to forestall some penalty

---

[6] Kelly, "Force and Fear Affecting Matrimonial Consent"—*The Jurist*, V (1945), 319-320.

[7] S. C. de Sacramentis, instr., 29 iun. 1941, n. 7, Allegatum I, n. 10—*AAS*, XXXIII (1941), 304, 311.

[8] S. C. de Sacramentis, instr., 29 iun. 1941, Allegatum I, n. 10—*AAS*, XXXIII (1941), 311.

of the law should certainly move the pastor to a more than ordinarily cautious investigation. If the ordinary signs of affection are lacking, or if the party seems despondent over the forthcoming marriage, the pastor should be on his guard for evidence of force and fear. In such dubious cases, he should certainly call upon the sworn testimony of witnesses, especially of the parents, of members of the party's family, or of close friends, in order to attain assurance of the liberty of both parties.[9]

The Instruction adds to further precaution by insisting that the pastor interrogate the groom concerning the freedom of the bride, and vice versa. The party thus interrogated is to be asked from what source compulsion comes, whenever it is alleged.[10]

If his investigations reveal that there are indications of force and fear, the pastor should determine whether or not it is of such a nature that it would invalidate the marriage. If the force and fear fulfills the conditions mentioned earlier in this article as sufficient to invalidate the union, the pastor must absolutely refuse to assist at the marriage. If the force and fear is not sufficient to nullify the marriage, he should nevertheless endeavor to dissuade the parties from the marriage, for it is the mind of the Church that a person be perfectly free in entering this state.[11]

If doubt remains in the pastor's mind in respect of the freedom of consent or with regard to the sufficiency of the force or fear to invalidate the marriage, prudence dictates that he consult the ordinary concerning his difficulties. Although the Code, in canon 1031, § 1, n. 3. demands reference to the ordinary only in cases in which doubt remains regarding the presence of an impediment, nevertheless, since force and fear constitute an impediment in the broad sense,[12] and place the validity of the marriage in jeopardy, a parallel reason is present for the necessity of such consultation.

---

[9] S. C. de Sacramentis, instr., 29 iun. 1941, n. 7—*AAS*, XXXIII (1941), 304; can. 1031, § 1, n. 1.

[10] *Ibid.*, Allegatum I, n. 11—*AAS*, XXXIII (1941) 311.

[11] Donovan, *The Pastor's Obligation in the Prenuptial Investigation*, p. 209.

[12] Cappello, *De Matrimonio*, n. 195.

Article 2. Invalidating Intentions and Conditional Consent

The Instruction *Sacrosanctum matrimonii* refers to other phases of matrimonial consent which demand the careful consideration of the investigating pastor, namely, those of conditional and substantially defective consent.[13] It states that "there are some, especially in large cities, who in defiance of canon law dare to contract marriage with a condition or intention which either suspends or invalidates it, and thus supply themselves with a subterfuge for later shaking off the yoke and remarrying".[14]

Marriage consent, then, may be vitiated either because of a condition attached thereto, or because of a contrary intention.

A condition is a circumstance attached to a contract, upon which the value of the contract depends.[15] The condition may render the contract void or it may suspend the value of the contract pending the condition's fulfillment. With regard to conditions attached to matrimonial consent, canon 1092 states:

"When a condition has been placed and not withdrawn,

1. If it concerns the future and is necessary, impossible or immoral, but not contrary to the substance of marriage, let it be regarded as non-existing;

2. If it concerns the future and is contrary to the substance of marriage, it invalidates the marriage;

3. If it concerns the future and is permissible, it suspends the validity of the marriage;

4. If it concerns the past or present, the marriage is either valid or invalid according as that which underlies the condition does or does not exist.[16]

Thus some conditions certainly invalidate marriage, that is, such conditions as concern the future and at the same time are contrary to the substance of marriage, e.g., when marriage is

---

[13] S. C. de Sacramentis, instr., 29 iun, 1941, n. 9—*AAS*, XXXIII (1941), 304.

[14] Bouscaren, *The Canon Law Digest*, II, 261.

[15] Cappello, *De Matrimonio*, n. 625.

[16] Ayrinhac-Lydon, *Marriage Legislation*, p. 223.

contracted with the stipulation that divorce may be obtained when it is desired, and also such conditions as concern the past or the present if they are unfulfilled, e.g., when marriage is contracted on the condition that the woman is a virgin, and this condition is without basis in fact. Other conditions suspend the validity of the marriage pending the verification of the condition, such as permissible conditions which concern the future. Conditions regarding the future which are necessary, impossible or immoral are presumed not to exist, but if in fact they were seriously placed, they suspend the validity pending the fulfillment of both the necessary and immoral conditions as set, but nullify the marriage outright in that the achievement of impossible conditions can never be realized.[17]

Secondly, marriage consent may be vitiated by contrary intentions, or, in other words, because of essential defects in the consent, i.e., defects which are the result of a person's positively excluding from his consent some essential part of marriage. In this regard canon 1086, 2, states: "If either or both of the parties with a positive act of the will should exclude the marriage itself, or all right to the conjugal act, or some property that is essential to the marriage, the contract is made invalidly." Thus defects in the matrimonial consent are fourfold: (1) The intention not to enter a true marriage; (2) the positive exclusion of the obligation of indissolubility; (3) the positive exclusion of the obligation of fidelity; (4) the positive exclusion of the right to proper conjugal relations.[18]

The Instruction directs the pastor to remind the prospective spouses that those who enter marriage with conditions or intentions in any way opposed to its validity commit a sacrilege, enmesh themselves in an almost endless series of sins, and moreover, cannot attack the marriage to obtain a declaration of nullity.[19] He is to warn them that concealment

---

[17] Cappello, *De Matrimonio*, n. 629.

[18] Andrew F. Quinn, "Defects in Marriage Consent"—*The Jurist*, V (1945), 543.

[19] Can. 1086. § 2; 1092, n. 2; 1971, § 1, n. 1; S. C. de Sacramentis, instr., 29 iun. 1941, Allegatum I, n. 16—*AAS*, XXXIII (1941), 312; S. C. de Sacramentis, instr., 15 aug. 1936, artt. 35-37—*AAS*, XXVIII (1936), 321-322.

or deceit in this matter will in no way change the situation or help them.

The pastor, then, should question the parties directly concerning this phase of their consent with a view to establishing the absence of invalidating conditions and intentions. If the party declares that he has placed or intends to place a condition or intention which the pastor recognizes as invalidating, the pastor must make every effort to induce the party to retract it; if the party declines to do so, the pastor must refuse to assist at the marriage. If, on the other hand, the party changes his mind, the pastor is to indicate in the written deposition a declaration of this change of intention. He should likewise ask the party whether he knows of any such condition or intention having been made by the other party to the marriage, and if so of what nature this condition or intention is. If the response is in the affirmative, the procedure indicated above must be followed with the second party regarding the retraction of the condition or intention. In the event of the party's refusal to evince a change of mind, the pastor is not to assist at the marriage.[20]

Furthermore, if either or both the parties, upon being interrogated concerning this matter, declare that they have attached or intend to attach to their consent some permissible condition concerning the past, present or future, which in effect could suspend the validity of the marriage, the pastor should prudently inquire as to how they propose to satisfy themselves of the verification of the condition. If the parties admit that they intend to do so by means that are forbidden, the pastor should strive to deter them from placing the condition, or to persuade them to revoke it if already placed; otherwise he may not assist at the marriage. It seems that if the pastor were to allow the parties to enter marriage with such a condition which they proposed to verify through sinful means, he would directly permit the commission of the sin upon which the ascertainment of the validity or invalidity of the marriage depends. If, on the other hand, the parties

[20] S. C. de Sacramentis, instr., 29 iun. 1941, Allegatum I, n. 16—*AAS*, XXXIII (1941), 312; Bouscaren, *The Canon Law Digest*, II, 269.

declare that they intend to verify the condition through means that are morally lawful, and if the pastor finds the condition a reasonable one, he is to consult the ordinary and abide by his decision.[21]

Article 3. Other Qualities of Consent

True consent cannot be given to a marriage unless a person has a sufficient use of reason.[22] The pastor, therefore, must determine through his investigation whether a party has the proper mental capacity to consent to the marriage. Since mental disorders of one kind or another are not uncommon, it is not unlikely that the pastor may occasionally be confronted with those whose attitude or behavior cause him to doubt their mental fitness. Naturally, direct questioning of the party concerning this matter would be imprudent and probably offensive. Moreover, the pastor can usually solve his doubts by weighing the responses of the party to the other questions of the examination, particularly those which deal with the nature of marriage and its consequent duties. In cases of prudent doubt it would be expedient for the pastor to resort to the testimony of witnesses, especially the parents, the members of the family, or the friends of the party, to ascertain whether the party has ever suffered from any serious mental disorder, and whether, for example, he has ever been confined to an institution on that account. If the case warrants it, the pastor should refer the person to a reliable expert on mental disorders, who can report on whether the party has a sufficient discretion for the giving of a proper matrimonial consent.[23]

Again, a person may indeed have a sufficient use of reason, but may be ignorant of the nature and the obligations of the sacrament of matrimony. In order to give a true matrimonial consent, a party must at least know that marriage is a permanent society of a man and a woman for the procreation and

[21] S. C. de Sacramentis, instr., 29 iun. 1941, Allegatum I, n. 17—*AAS*, XXXIII (1941), 312, 313; Bouscaren, *The Canon Law Digest*, II, 269.

[22] Cappello, *De Matrimonio*, n. 579.

[23] Donovan, *The Pastor's Obligation in the Prenuptial Investigation*, p. 210.

education of children.[24] The absence of this minimum knowledge is not presumed after the party has reached the age of puberty.[25] The interrogation of the parties concerning their knowledge of Christian doctrine and of the rights and duties of married life, which is to be considered in the next article of this chapter, may well be employed for the sake of discovering whether they have or have not a knowledge that suffices for the giving of a true consent for marriage.

Part II. Knowledge of Christian Doctrine

According to canon 1020, § 2, the final phase on which the pastor is to interrogate the contracting parties concerns their knowledge of Christian doctrine. The Instruction *Sacrosanctum matrimonii* recalls this legislation, and directs pastors to ascertain whether the parties are sufficiently instructed in Christian doctrine, and especially in the chief purposes, the rights and the obligations of marriage.[26]

Article 4. Knowledge of the Rudiments of the Faith

Parties entering marriage must be sufficiently instructed in the essential elements of the Catholic faith, especially concerning the truths necessary for salvation whether essentially as a means or preceptively as a command.[27] This obligation arises not only from the ecclesiastical law but also from the divine law, which imposes upon parents the duty of instructing their children in the truths necessary for salvation.[28]

To be considered as *sufficiently instructed*, parties should be acquainted with the principal truths of the Catholic religion as contained in the Apostles' Creed; they should be familiar with the Ten Commandments and the six principal precepts of the Church, and the seven Sacraments: they should know

---

[24] Can. 1082, § 1.

[25] Can. 1082, § 2.

[26] S. C. de Sacramentis, instr., 29 iun. 1941, n. 8; Allegatum I, n. 13—*AAS*, XXXIII (1941), 304, 311.

[27] Payen, *De Matrimonio*, I, n. 412.

[28] Heylen, *De Matrimonio*, p. 76.

the Our Father, the Hail Mary and the Acts of Faith, Hope, Charity and Contrition.[29]

In order to verify this sufficiency of religious instruction, the pastor must interrogate the parties concerning their knowledge of the aforemenioned essentials, unless the qualitative character of the parties makes this inquiry unnecessary.[30] Naturally, with certain classes of nupturients the pastor will already be assured of their sufficient religious instruction. It would be unnecessary to question those who in his knowledge have been faithful members of his parish, who have attended parish schools, who have regularly been present at Mass, and thus have heard the doctrines of the Church explained in the customary sermons. Likewise he may usually presume that those who have been active in Christian Doctrine discussion groups, or who are graduates of Catholic colleges, are well instructed in their faith.

Accordingly, in approaching this phase of the interrogation, rather than ask direct questions concerning the parties' knowledge of the rudiments of the faith, the pastor will, as a thing more feasible, seek to determine the Catholic background and upbringing of the persons in question. The evidence thus produced will indicate to the pastor whether or not the more detailed inquiry concerning the parties' knowledge of the principal tenets of the Catholic religion is necessary. The pastor, then, should ask the parties to indicate the schools which they attended and the religious instruction which they received. If doubt arises regarding their possession of the requisite religious knowledge, he should not hesitate to question them directly regarding Christian doctrine.

If the pastor finds through his inquiry that the parties are ignorant of Christian doctrine, it is his duty to instruct them in the essential elements thereof prior to the marriage. Should they refuse to submit to such instruction, he may not repel them from marriage, but should admit them in accordance with the rulings

---

[29] Augustine, *Commentary*, V. 54; Cappello, *De Matrimonio*, n. 152, ad 3; Heylen, *loc. cit.*

[30] Can. 1020, § 2; S. C. de Sacramentis, instr., 29 iun. 1941, n. 8—*AAS*, XXXIII (1941), 304.

of canon 1066.[31] In such instances of refusal, the pastor should warn the parties of their grave obligations by which they are bound to acquire a sufficient knowledge, in order that they may properly instruct their offspring, and he should attempt to defer the marriage until such time as he has succeeded in imparting this knowledge. But if they absolutely refuse to postpone the marriage, the pastor may assist thereat if there be present a grave cause concerning which, if possible, he has consulted the ordinary.[32]

Article 5. Knowledge of the Nature of Marriage and Its Obligations

The Instruction *Sacrosanctum matrimonii* reminds the pastor of the further duty of inquiring whether the parties are aware of the sanctity and indissolubility of the contract of marriage, and of the duties of the married state.[33] In conjunction with this the prescripts of canon 1033 must be kept in mind. Therein is placed upon the pastor the obligation of instructing the prospective parties of a marriage concerning the sanctity of the marriage contract, and regarding the mutual obligations of the married couple towards each other and towards their children.

Needless to say, it is of the utmost importance for those who seek to enter the married life to have the proper concept of Christian marriage and its obligations, especially in these days when so many pagan and materialistic notions are commonly accepted to the detriment of the institute of marriage and of the welfare of family life. The pastor, therefore, should question the parties directly concerning their knowledge of the essential qualities of marriage. He should ask them whether they understand that the marital union is permanent and exclusive and that it can be ended only through the death of one of the parties, in order that he may thus eliminate from their minds all possible

---

[31] Pont. Comm. Cod. Inter., 3 iun. 1918, IV, 3—*AAS*, X (1918), 345; S. C. de Sacramentis, instr., 29 iun. 1941, n. 8—*AAS*, XXXIII (1941), 304.

[32] Can. 1066; Cappello, *De Matrimonio*, n. 155.

[33] S. C. de Sacramentis, instr., 29 iun. 1941, n. 8—*AAS*, XXXIII (1941), 304.

thought of divorce. Further, he should ask them whether they understand that the prime purpose of marriage is the procreation and education of children, and whether they are aware of their mutual rights and obligations as man and wife. In the separate interrogation, then, the pastor is to question each party regarding his own personal understanding of these essentials.

If the pastor discovers from their attitude and responses that the parties are ignorant or vague in their knowledge of these points, he must proceed to inform them of their rights and obligations as man and wife and as parents towards their children,[34] emphasizing the lawfulness of the conjugal act and the duty of acceding to the reasonable request of the partner in this regard.[35] For such who are poorly informed, it is helpful for the pastor to give them some suitable book or pamphlet on marriage, written in accordance with Catholic principles of morality, whereby the necessary information may be obtained.

Although some prenuptial investigation questionnaires demand that the pastor elicit from the contracting parties a promise that they will lead a married life in conformity with the teachings of the Catholic Church regarding birth control, such a promise or proviso is not required by the Instruction *Sacrosanctum matrimonii*. In view of the prevalence of the practice of birth prevention, however, the pastor should not omit reference to it; he should refute it as seriously immoral, and so therefore contravening the law of God; he should stress the Catholic principles as reflecting an imperative harmony with the natural law.[36]

Parties may reveal that they intend to postpone the having of children for the first few years after marriage, or that they intend definitely to limit the size of their family, even at the cost of abusing the marital right. The pastor is not infrequently faced with this vexing problem. In attempting to solve it, the

[34] Can. 1033.

[35] Donovan, *The Pastor's Obligation in the Prenuptial Investigation*, p. 218.

[36] S. C. de Sacramentis, instr., 29 iun. 1941, Allegatum I, n. 13—*AAS*, XXXIII (1941), 311.

pastor must first of all recall that there is an essential distinction between the strict right to the marital act and the exercise of that right; an agreement or an intention to abuse the marital right, although seriously sinful, does not invalidate the marriage as long as the right itself to the proper conjugal acts is mutually exchanged in the matrimonial contract.[37]

The pastor must judiciously question the parties with reference to their precise intention or agreement in this matter. If the interrogation reveals that there is a definite exclusion of the marital right itself, he may not permit the marriage until the intention or agreement is revoked, since it stands contrary to the very substance of marriage.[38] If the pastor learns that the intention or the agreement is one of abusing the marital rights, and thus connotes the presence of a grave sin, he must warn the parties that to marry with this intention would be to involve themselves in an endless series of sins, to render themselves unfit for the reception of the sacraments, and thus to deprive themselves of the graces so sorely needed in the married state.

Moreover, he must earnestly endeavor to dissuade them from their sinful intentions. But if they should refuse to follow his suggestions, it does not seem that he can refuse to permit the marriage, for if public sinners are not to be impeded from marriage when a grave cause is present,[39] neither should they whose sinful condition is not generally known.[40] Wherefore, if there be present for the celebration of the marriage a grave cause about which he has, if possible, consulted the ordinary, the pastor may permit the marriage. Furthermore, it seems expedient in such cases, inasmuch as they are analogous to the cases in which the parties withdrew an invalidating condition or intention, for the pastor to place an annotation in the acts of the prenuptial investigation to the effect that the parties indeed intend to convey to each other the mutual

---

[37] Heneghan, *The Marriages of Unworthy Catholics*, p. 127.

[38] Can. 1081, § 2; 1086, § 2; 1092, n. 2.

[39] Can. 1066.

[40] Cappello, *De Matrimonio*, n. 332, ad 1; Heneghan, *The Marriages of Unworthy Catholics*, p. 129.

rights and obligations, even though they reflect a desire to abuse the same.[41]

Article 6. The Conclusion of the Interrogation

When the pastor has completed the interrogation of the party, he is to read the written replies which have been given to his questions, as is customary upon the completion of similar depositions given judicially.[42] The pastor should then ask the party if he has anything else to declare about his intended marriage,[43] and thus there will be afforded to the latter an opportunity to reveal any pertinent information of which perchance no note was made, or to discuss any problem or difficulty regarding which a more definite solution is sought.

If the party declares that he has nothing to add to his statements, the pastor upon reminding him that the answers have been given under the oath of telling the truth, shall ask the person if he is willing to sign the sworn statement.[44] The party is then to affix his signature to the document, and the pastor upon inscribing the name of the place in which the interrogation was conducted, and listing the day, the month and the year, shall also add his own signature beneath that of the party. If the party does not know how or is unable to write, he is to trace the mark of a cross on the document, and the pastor is to make a note of this fact in the document.

Finally, the seal of the parish is to be affixed to or impressed on the completed questionnaire.[45]

---

[41] S. C. de Sacramentis, instr., 29 iun. 1941, Allegatum I, n. 16—*AAS*, XXXIII (1941), 312.

[42] Can. 1780, § 1.

[43] S. C. de Sacramentis, instr., 29 iun. 1941, Allegatum I, n. 18—*AAS*, XXXIII (1941), 313.

[44] *Ibid.*, n. 19—*AAS*, XXXIII (1941), 313.

[45] *Loc. cit.*

CHAPTER XII

THE REQUIRED DOCUMENTS, THEIR TRANSMISSION AND PRESERVATION

In conjunction with the information obtained through the oral testimony of the parties and witnesses examined by the pastor, the prenuptial investigation embraces also certain documentary evidence. As has been discussed in a previous chapter,[1] the Code and the Instruction *Sacrosanctum matrimonii* demand that the pastor obtain the baptismal and confirmation certificates of the parties during the investigation.[2] Similarly the pastor must have on hand documents which prove the death of a former spouse,[3] which contain the declaration of the nullity of a former marriage,[4] or the concession of a dispensation, should the prospective marriage warrant the obtaining of one or other of these documents.

Furthermore the Instruction requires that the responses of the parties and of witnesses to the inquiries of the pastor be committed to writing and be attested to by the signatures of the pastor and of said persons, and moreover that the resulting documents be preserved for future reference.[5]

In addition to the aforementioned documents, two others are necesary in special instances, viz., testimonial letters and the *nihil obstat.*

Article 1. Testimonial Letters and the *Nihil obstat.*

It is necessary briefly to recall here precisely who are the "*nupturientium parochi*", for upon this notion depends a correct understanding of the legal instruments of testimonial let-

---

[1] Cf. *Supra*, Chapter IX, p. 81

[2] Can. 1021, 1; S. C. de Sacramentis, instr., 29 iun. 1941, n. 4—*AAS*, XXXIII (1941), 300.

[3] Cf. *supra*, Chapter X, pp. 81, 85; S. C. de Sacramentis, instr., 29 iun. 1941, n. 4 (c)—*AAS*, XXXIII (1941), 300.

[4] Instr. cit., loc. cit.

[5] S. C. de Sacramentis, instr., 29 iun. 1941, Allegatum I, n. 19—*AAS*, XXXIII (1941) 313.

ters and the *nihil obstat*. Briefly, then, the pastors of the parties are those who have a right to assist at their marriage in accordance with canon 1097, 1. Therefore the pastor of the groom is the pastor of the parish in which the groom has a domicile, a quasi-domicile, residence of a month's duration prior to the marriage, or in the case of a *vagus,* the parish in which he actually resides at the time of marriage; likewise the pastor of the bride is the pastor of that parish in which the bride has a domicile, a quasi-domicile, a month's residence prior to marriage, or if she be a *vaga,* of the parish in which she actually resides at the time of the marriage. Anyone of these various pastors has a right to assist at the marriage; naturally only one will be chosen to do so, and this will usually be the pastor of the bride in accordance with the preference attributed to him in canon 1097, 2. Both this pastor of the bride whom she chooses to assist at her marriage and the pastor of the groom have the right and obligation to conduct the prenuptial investigation.

At times it happens that the pastor of the groom and the pastor of the bride belong to different dioceses. In these cases, the Instruction demands that testimonial letters be issued by the chancery office of the diocese of the groom's pastor, whenever the marriage is to take place before the pastor of the bride, and vice versa, when the marriage is to take place before the pastor of the groom.[6]

Testimonial letters, as the name indicates, are to bear witness to the freedom of the party in question to enter marriage, and are granted by the chancery office on the strength of the investigation regarding this freedom as conducted by the pastor of the party.

Conversely, the pastor who is to assist at the marriage, usually the pastor of the bride, but at times the pastor of the groom, is to obtain from the chancery of his diocese a *nihil obstat,* as it is called, that is, the written permission of the episcopal curia for the celebration of the marriage. The Sacred Congregation of the Sacraments greatly desires that this permission be obtained

---

[6] S. C. de Sacramentis, instr., 29 iun. 1941, n. 4 (a)—*AAS*, XXXIII (1941) 299.

for all marriages, but orders that this be done when the pastors of the parties are of different dioceses.[7]

The *nihil obstat,* since it implies that the chancery finds no obstacle to the marriage, presupposes a knowledge and consideration of the status of the nupturients on the part of the chancery. To this end the Instruction directs pastors who have conducted the prenuptial investigation to forward all the documents which they have thereby secured, together with a summary account of the status of the parties as exemplified in Formula V of the Appendix of the Instruction.[8]

Thus the pastor who has the right and who intends to assist at the marriage is to send in good time to the chancery office whatever documents he has received concerning the marriage, such as, the baptismal and confirmation certificates, the copies of the declaration of nullity of a former marriage, the documents proving the death of a former spouse, and any other written acts pertinent to the case. The summary transcript is to denote the status of the parties as ascertained through the interrogation, to contain an inventory of the documents which prove the freedom of the parties and to indicate the fact that the banns were or were not published, in the first instance stating the dates of the proclamations.[9]

This transcript is used by the chancery in the concession of its permission for the celebration of the marriage. The customary diocesan forms prepared according to Formula V of the Instruction provide a space on the reverse side of the transcript for the *nihil obstat* of the curia, which when completed bears the signatures of the ordinary and of the chancellor, as well as the episcopal seal.

The transcript is likewise to be used by the pastor, namely the one who has a right to assist at the marriage, when he gives to a priest who has all the requisite faculties for valid assistance[10] the permission to assist at the marriage, if it is to be

[7] *Loc. cit.*

[8] S. C. de Sacramentis, instr,. 29 iun. 1941, n. 4 (a)—*AAS*, XXXIII (1941), 299.

[9] *Ibid.*, Allegatum V—*AAS*, XXXIII (1941), 317.

[10] Can. 1095.

celebrated outside of the parish of the pastor who has the right to assist thereat.[11]

Therefore, the *nihil obstat* must be obtained from the curia of the diocese of the pastor who has the right and who intends to assist at the marriage, whenever the pastor of the bride and the pastor of the groom pertain to different dioceses. In all other marriages, that is, in marriages in which the pastors of the parties belong to the same diocese, the Sacred Congregation desires that the *nihil obstat* be secured, but does not command that this be done.

Article 2. Transmission of the Documents

In cases in which the pastors of the parties to a prospective marriage pertain to different dioceses, the transmission of pertinent documents from one pastor to another must be made not directly, but through the chancery office of the diocese of the forwarding pastor.[12] The pastor of the groom who is to be married in another diocese is to send to his chancery the pertinent documents indicating the freedom of the groom to marry, e.g., the certificates of baptism and confirmation, the proof of the death of a former spouse, the declaration of the nullity of a previous marriage, and the completed deposition of the groom, if he has interrogated the party.

On the strength of these documents, the ordinary through his episcopal curia grants the required testimonial letter of the freedom of the groom to marry, and forwards the dossier to the pastor of the bride who is to assist at the marriage. This latter pastor, when he has completed the interrogation of the bride and has gathered the documents relative to her freedom to marry, is to fill out the summary transcript and forward all to his own chancery, which in turn will issue the *nihil obstat*.[13] If the pastor of the groom is to assist at the marriage, the situation is re-

[11] Can. 1097, 1, n. 3; S. C. de Sacramentis, instr., 29 iun. 1941, Allegatum V—*AAS*, XXXIII (1941), 318. As is evident, this permission as granted by the pastor who has the right to assist at the marriage is required not for the sake of validity, but for the sake of lawfulness in the celebration of the marriage.

[12] S. C. de Sacramentis, instr., 29 iun. 1941, n. 4 (a)—*AAS*, XXXIII (1941), 299.

[13] Heylen, *De Matrimonio*, p. 121.

versed, i.e., the pastor of the bride transmits the documents pertinent to the freedom of the bride to the chancery of his diocese for the testimonial letters, and the pastor of the groom upon receiving these letters and odcuments then applies to his own chancery for the *nihil obstat*.

The question now arises: What is to be done in a particular case if it is impossible to obtain the testimonial letters or the *nihil obstat?* Occasionally, because of the distance and the irregular postal service between the pastor and his own chancery, or between the pastor and the chancery of another diocese, it is impossible to obtain these required documents in time for the marriage. Vlaming (1935),[14] when he treated of similar testimonial letters attesting to the completion of the publication of the banns, stated that the pastor should use every means at his disposal to obtain the same. If, however, no satisfaction can thus be obtained, the pastor who is to assist at the marriage should consult the ordinary and follow his advice. Finally, if even this latter course is impossible, the pastor, provided he is morally certain of the freedom of the parties as a result of his investigations, may proceed to the marriage. As an extraordinary means pastors frequently resort to the telegram service for confirmation of the free status of the prospective spouse or for permission to proceed in such cases.

De Smet (1868-1927)[15] suggested that the ordinary or the pastor on his own authority could demand a suppletory oath from the party in question. The Instruction directs the pastor to obtain such an oath from a party who cannot show testimonial letters of the ecclesiastical curiae of the different dioceses in which he has lived.[16]

If it is impossible to forward the required documents to the chancery, and to receive the *nihil obstat* in time for the marriage, the pastor should contact the ordinary if time permits. If even this course cannot be followed, the pastor may proceed with the

---

[14] *Praelectiones Iuris Matrimonii*, I, n. 177.

[15] *De Sponsalibus et Matrimonio* (4. ed., Brugis, 1927), n. 686.

[16] S. C. de Sacramentis, instr. 29 iun. 1941, Allegatum IV—*AAS*, XXXIII (1941), 316.

marriage, provided that as a result of his investigations he is morally certain of the freedom of the parties to intermarry.

Article 3. Preservation of the Documents

The Instruction *Sacrosanctum matrimonii*[17] repeats the insistent demands of the Code that the proper registration of marriages be made both in the marriage register of the parish in which the marriage took place[18] as well as in the baptismal registers of the parishes in which each party was baptized.[19] Ordinaries, either personally or through suitable ecclesiastical persons, are to look into this matter diligently to see that the prescripts of the law are being observed. To this end they are to make frequent visitations—every six months, if possible or at least within intervals of not longer than a year—during which they are to inspect every registration of marriages and baptisms, placing thereon a special sign to indicate this examination.[20]

In addition to the registration of the marriage in the proper parochial books, it is essential that the sworn depositions of the parties resulting from the pastor's interrogations, as also the documents pertinent to the marriage, be preserved for future reference. A note appended to Formula I of the Instruction indicates the primary reason for the retention of these documents, namely, that in the event of a subsequent impugning of the validity of the marriage, they can be forwarded to the competent tribunal as evidence.[21]

[17] *Ibid.*, n. 11—*AAS*, XXXIII (1941), 305.

[18] Can. 1103, 1.

[19] Can. 1103, 2; Can. 470, 2. The Instruction (n. 11, (b) and (d)—*AAS*, XXXIII 1941, 306) directs the pastor who assisted at the marriage to notify the pastor of the parish in which the party was baptized, in order that the latter may inscribe a notification thereof in the baptismal register, and furthermore warns the former not to rest content until he has received notice of the transcription in the baptismal register. The same Instruction in n. 11 (d) advises ordinaries that, when the baptism was conferred outside the parish of origin, they be watchful that in addition to the recording of the baptism in the baptismal register of the parish of baptism a transcript of the baptism be entered also in the register of the parish of origin.

The Instruction of the Sacred Congregation of the Sacraments of the year 1921 concerning the marriages of emigrants from Europe (*AAS*. XIII, 348) also reminds pastors of the duty of sending a notice of marriage to the parish of baptism.

[20] S. C. de Sacramentis, instr., 29 iun. 1941, n. 11 (f)—*AAS*, XXXIII (1941), 306.

The Instruction, however, does not indicate directly in which parish these prenuptial documents are to be preserved. There is nevertheless evidence to substantiate the view that it is the mind of the Sacred Congregation of the Sacraments that they be kept in the parish in which the marriage was celebrated. In speaking of the duty of the pastor who assisted at the marriage, namely his duty of notifying the pastor of the place of baptism of each party concerning its celebration in order that a record to that effect be placed in the baptismal register, the Instruction states that the pastor of assistance is not to rest content until he receives a written notice which attests the fact that this transcription has been made. When he has received this notice, he is to attach it to the bundle of papers relating to the marriage.[22]

The Instruction, therefore, supposes that the pastor who assisted at the marriage has all the pertinent documents. Since nothing further is stated regarding any later disposition of the documents, it can be legitimately concluded that he is to retain them. Furthermore, the preservation of the papers at the church where the marriage was actually contracted seems more consonant with the main purpose which is to be served, for, if the marriage should be called into question at a later date, it would be of greater convenience to have the pertinent documents at the church where the marriage was celebrated than to have them at the parishes in which the investigation was conducted. The regulations of many dioceses, enacted in conformity with the directions of the Instruction, require that the papers which were gathered in the course of the prenuptial investigation be preserved at the church wherein the marriage was contracted.

In the event that the marriage takes place in a non-parochial church, it is preferable that the papers be presented in the parochial church of the parish in which the marriage was celebrated. A note to this effect should be appended to the registration of the marriage in the register of the church of celebration.

---

[21] *Ibid.*, Allegatum 1—*AAS*, XXXIII (1941) 313.

[22] S. C. de Sacramentis, instr., 29 iun. 1941, n. 11 (b)—*AAS*, XXXIII (1941) 305.

CONCLUSIONS

1. The prescripts of the Instruction *Sacrosanctum matrimonii* of the Sacred Congregation of the Sacraments is to be observed in all dioceses as the official explanation of the application of the legislation of the Code concerning the prenuptial investigation.[1]

2. The pastors who have a right to assist at the marriage and to conduct the prenuptial investigation are the pastors of the parishes in which the bride and groom have a domicile, a quasi-domicile, a month's residence prior to marriage, or, in the case of *vagi,* actual residence at the time of marriage. Although the pastor of the bride has a preferred right to assistance at the marriage, it is the mind of the Holy See that the pastor of the groom should investigate the free state of the groom.[2]

3. A certificate attesting to the reception of confirmation should be secured from each party. If this cannot be conveniently done, a baptismal certificate bearing an annotation concerning the reception of confirmation is acceptable as sufficient proof thereof.[3]

4. In cases concerning the alleged baptism of a non-Catholic party to a marriage, the helpful result reasonably to be hoped for does not warrant the extensive investigation which is required for establishing with moral certainty the validity of the baptism. Therefore, for a reasonable cause, the pastor is absolved from the detailed investigation, but he must take care to safeguard the validity of the marriage by seeking a dispensation from the impediment of mixed religion and from the impediment of disparity of worship *ad cautelam.*[4]

---

[1]Cf. *supra,* Chap. IX, p. 52
[2]Cf. *supra,* Chap. IX, p. 57
[3]Cf. *supra,* Chap. X, p. 85
[4]Cf. *supra,* Chap. XI, p. 110

5. The pastor may accept as sufficient proof of the death of a former spouse the sworn testimony of at least two eye-witnesses of the death. With the possession of such proof he no longer needs to refer the case to the Ordinary.[5]

6. When it is impossible to obtain the *nihil obstat* of the Chancery concerning a marriage, the pastor is, whenever that is possible, to contact the ordinary; if this cannot be done, he may proceed with the marriage, provided that he is morally certain of the freedom of the parties to intermarry.[6]

7. All documents gathered in the course of the prenuptial investigation are to be preserved at the parish church in which the marriage was celebrated.[7]

---

[5]Cf. *supra*. Chap. XI, p. 104

[6]Cf. *supra*, Chap. XII, p. 164

[7]Cf. *supra*, Chap. XII, p. 166

BIBLIOGRAPHY

SOURCES

Acta Apostolicae Sedis, Commentarium Officiale, Romae, 1909-1929; Civitate Vaticana, 1929-.

Acta et Decreta Concilii Plenarii Baltimorensis III (1884), Baltimorae: Typis Joannis Murphy Sociorum, 1886.

Acta et Decreta Concilii Plenarii Quebecensis I (1909), Quebeci: Typis "L'Action Sociale Limitee", 1912.

Acta et Decreta Sacrorum Counciliorum Recentiorum, Collectio Lacensis, 7 vols., Friburgi Brisgoviae, 1870-1890.

Acta Sanctae Sedis, 41 vols., Romae, 1865- 1908.

Bouscaren, T. Lincoln, *The Canon Law Digest*, 2 vols., Milwaukee: Bruce Publishing Co., 1934, 1943.

Bruns, Hermann Theodor, *Canones Apostolorum et Conciliorum Saeculorum IV-VII*, 2 vols., Berolini, 1839.

Bullarium Clementis XI, Romae: Typographia Rev. Camerae Apostolicae, 1723.

Bullarum Diplomatum et Privilegiorum Sanctorum Romanorum Pontificum Tauriensis Editio, 25 vols., Augustae Taurinorum, 1857-1872.

Codex Iuris Canonici Pii X Pontificis Maximi iussu digestus, Benedicti Papae XV auctoritate promulgatus, Romae: Typis Polyglottis Vaticanis, 1917.

Codicis Iuris Canonici Fontes, cura Emi Petri Card. Gasparri editi, 9 vols., Romae (postea Civitate Vaticana): Typis Polyglottis Vaticanis, 1923-1939 (Vols. VII-IX ed. cura et studio Emi Iustiniani Card. Seredi.

Collectanea S. Congregationis de Propaganda Fide, 2 vols., Romae: Typographia Polyglotta S. C. de Propaganda Fide, 1907.

Concilii Plenarii Baltimorensis II Acta et Decreta, ed. altera, Baltimorae: John Murphy, 1894.

Corpus Iuris Canonici, ed. Lipsiensis 2. post Aemilii Ludovici Richteri curas . . . instruxit Aemilius Friedberg, 2 vols., Lipsiae: Tauchnitz, 1879-1881; ed. anastatice repetita, 1928.

Corpus Iuris Civilis, 3 vols., Vol. I, Institutiones, recognovit Paulus *Krueger*, 15. ed., *Digesta*, recognovit Theodorus Mommsen, retractavit Paulus Krueger, 15. ed.; Vol. II, *Codex Iustinianus*, recognovit et retractavit Paulus Krueger, 10. ed.; Vol. III, *Novellae*, recognovit Rudolphus Schoell, absolvit Gulielmus Kroll, 5. ed., Berolini: Apud Weidmannos, 1928-1929.

Corpus Scriptorum Ecclesiasticorum Latinorum, 68 vols., Pragae, Vindobonae, Liusiae, 1866-.

Decretales D. Gregorii Papae IX suae integritati una cum glossis restitutae, Romae, 1582.

Decretum Gratiani emendatum et observationibus illustratum una cum glossis, 2 vols., Romae, 1582.

Funk, F. X., *Patres Apostolici*, 2. ed,, 2 vols., Tubingae, 1901.

Hardouin, Jean, *Acta Conciliorum et Epistolae Decretales ac Constitutiones Summorum Pontificum*, 12 vols., Parisiis, 1714-1715.

Jaffe, Philippus, *Regesta Pontificum Romanorum ab Condita Ecclesia ad annum post Christum natum MCXCVIII*, 2. ed., correctam et auctam auspiciis Gulielmi Wattenbach curaverunt F. Kaltenbrunner, P. Ewald, S. Lowenfeld, 2 tomes in 1 vol., Lipsiae, 1885-1888.

Mandement collectif au sujet des investigations prenuptialies, Quebec: Librairie de l'Action Catholique, 1943.

Mansi, Ioannes, *Sacrorum Conciliorum Nova et Amplissima Collectio*, 53 vols., in 60, Parisiis-Arnhem-Lipsiae, 1901-1927.

Monumenta Germaniae Historica, Epistolarum Tom. VI, *Epistolae Karolini Aevi*, Tom. IV, edidit Ernestus Perels, Berolini, apud Weidmannos, 1925.

Monumenta Germaniae Historica, Legum Section II, *Capitularia Regum Francorum*, Tom. I, edd. Alfredus Boretius et Victor Krause, Hannoverae, 1883.

Monumenta Germaniae Historica, Legum Sectio III, *Concilia Aevi Merowingici*, Tom. I, ed. Albertus Werminghoff, Hannoverae, 1893.

Pallottini, S., *Collectio omnium conclusionum et resolutionum quae in causis propositis apud Sacram Congregationem Cardinalium S. Concilii Tridentini interpretum prodierunt ab eius institutione anno MDLXIV ad annum MDCCCLX, distinctis titulis alphabetico ordine per materias digesta*, 18 vols., Romae, 1868-1895.

Potthast, A., Regesta Pontificum Romanorum inde ab an no post Christum MCXCVIII ad annum MCCCIV, 2 vols., Berolini, 1874-1875.

S. Romanae Rotae Decisiones seu Sententiae Quae Prodierunt 1909-1939, 31 vols., Romae (Civitate Vaticana): Typis Polyglottis Vaticanis, 1912-1948.

Schroeder, H. J., *Canons and Decrees of the Council of Trent*, St. Louis: B. Herder, 1941.

Thesaurus Resolutionum Sacrae Congregationis Concilii, 167 vols., Romae, 1718-1908.

Thiel, A., *Epistolae Romanorum Pontificum Genuinae a S. Hilario usque ad Pelagium II*, vol. I, Brunsbergae, 1868.

Author

Augustine, Charles, *A Commentary on the New Code of Canon Law*, 8 vols., Vol V, 5. ed., 1935; Vol. VI, 3. ed., 1931, St. Louis: B. Herder Book Co.

Ayrinhac, H. A., *Marriage Legislation in the New Code of Canon Law*, revised and enlarged by P. J. Lydon, New York: Benziger, 1943.

Benedictus XIV (Prosper Lambertini), *De Synodo Dioecesana*, 2 vols., Romae, 1805.

Boich, Henricus, *Commentaria In Quinque Decretalium Libros*, Venetiis, 1576.

Bouix, D., *Tractatus de Judiciis Ecclesiasticis*, 2. ed., 2 vols., Parisiis, 1855.

Bouscaren, T. Lincoln, and Ellis, Adam C., *Canon Law. A Text and Commentary*, Milwaukee: The Bruce Publishing Co., 1946.

Cappello, Felix M., *Tractatus Canonico-Moralis de Sacramentis*, Vol. V, *De Matrimonio*, 5. ed., Romae: Marietti, 1947.

Carberry, John J., *The Juridical Form of Marriage*, The Catholic University of America Canon Law Studies, n. 84, Washington: The Catholic University of America, 1934.

Cerato, P., *Matrimonium a Codice Iuris Canonici Integre Desumptum*, 4, ed., Patavii: Typis Seminarii Patavini, 1927.

Chelodi, Ioannes, *Ius Matrimoniale iuxta Codicem Iuris Canonici*, 3 ed., Tridenti: Libr. Edit. Tridentum, 1921.

Coburn, Vincent P., *Marriages of Conscience*, The Catholic University of America Canon Law Studies, n. 191, Washington: The Catholic University of America Press, 1944.

Corbett, Percy Ellwood, *The Roman Law of Marriage*, Oxford: Clarendon Press, 1930.

Coronata, Matthaeus Conte a, *Institutiones Iuris Canonici*, ed. altera, 5 vols., Taurini-Romae: Marietti, 1939-1947.

———*Tractatus Canonicus de Sacramentis*, 3 vols., Taurini-Romae: Marietti, 1943-1946.

Creusen, J., *Religious Men and Women in the Code*, trans. by E. Garesche 4. English ed. revised and edited by A. Ellis to conform with 5 French ed., Milwaukee: Bruce, 1940.

De Becker, Julius, *De Sponsalibus et Matrimonio*, Brugis, 1909; 4. ed., Brugis: Car. Beyaert, 1927.

Dodwell, Edward J., *The Time and Place for the Celebration of Marriage*, The Catholic University of America Canon Law Studies, n. 154, Washington: The Catholic University of America Press, 1942.

Doheny, William J., *Canonical Procedure in Matrimonial Cases*, Vol. II, *Informal Procedure*, Milwaukee: Bruce, 1944.

Donohue, John F., *The Impediment of Crime*, The Catholic University of America Canon Law Studies, n. 69, Washington: The Catholic University of America, 1931.

Kleist, J., *The Epistles of St. Clement of Rome and St. Ignatius of Antioch*, *Ancient Christian Writers*, n. 1, ed., J. Quasten and J. C. Plumpe, Washington: Newman Bookshop, 1946.

Kostler, Rudolf, *Das osterreichische Konkordats-Eherecht*, Wein: Springer, 1937.

Leage, R., *Roman Private Law*, 2. ed., edited by C. H. Ziegler, London: Macmillan, 1932.

McSorley, Joseph, *Outline History of the Church by Centuries*, St. Louis: B. Herder Book Co., 1945.

Marbach, Joseph F., *Marriage Legislation for the Catholics of the Oriental Rites in the United States and Canada*, The Catholic University of America Canon Law Studies, n. 243, Washington: The Catholic University of America Press, 1946.

Merkelbach, B. H., *Summa Theologiae Moralis*, 2. ed., 3 vols., Parisiis: Desclee, de Brouwer et Cie, 1936-1938.

Migne, P. J., *Patrologiae Cursus Completus*, Series Latina, 221 vols., Parisiis, 1844-1864.

Monacelli, Fr., *Formularium Legale Practicum Fori Ecclesiastici*, 4 vols., in 3, Romae, 1844.

Muratori, Ludovicus, *Liturgia Romana Vetus*, 2 vols., Venetiis, 1748.

Noldin, H.-Schmitt, A., *Summa Theologiae Moralis*, 26. ed., 3 vols., Ratisbonae: Pustet, 1940.

Feije, Henricus J., *De Impedimentis et Dispensationibus Matrimonialibus*, 3. ed., 2 vols., Lovanii, 1885.

Ferraris, Lucius, *Prompta Bibliotheca, Canonica, Iuridica, Moralis. Theologica necnon Acsetica, Polemica, Rublicistica, Historica*. 9 vols., ed., novissima, Romae, 1885-1899.

Gasparri, Petrus, *Tractatus Canonicus de Matrimonio*, 3. ed., 2 vols., Parisiis, 1904.

———*Tractatus Canonicus de Matrimonio*, ed. nova ad mentem Codicis Iuris Canonici, 2 vols., Romae: Typis Polyglottis Vaticanis, 1932.

Gonzalez-Tellez, E., *Commentaria Perpetua in Singulos Textus Quinque Librorum Decretalium Gregorii IX*, 5 vols. in 4, Lugduni, 1715.

Heylen, V., *Tractatus de Matrimonio*, 9 ed., Mechliniae: Dessain, 1945.

Hinschius, Paulus, *Decretales Pseudo-Isidorianae et Capitula Angilramni*, Lipsiae, 1863.

Hostiensis, Cardinalis (Henricus de Segusio), *Commentaria in Quinque* Decretalium Libros, 5 vols. in 3, Venetiis, 1581.

Henegan, John, J., *The Marriages of Unworthy Catholics*, The Catholic University of America Canon Law Studies, n. 188, Washington: The Catholic University of America Press, 1944.

Donovan, James, J., *The Pastor's Obligation in the Prenuptial Investigation*, The Catholic University of America Canon Law Studies, n. 115, Washington: The Catholic University of America, 1938.

Esmein, A.-Genestal, R.-Dauvillier, J., *Le Mariage en Droit Canonique*, 2. ed., 2 vols., Paris: Recueil Sirey, 1929-1935.

Fair, Bartholomew, F., *The Impediment of Abduction*, The Catholic University of America Canon Law Studies, n. 194, Washington: The Catholic University of America Press, 1944.

Fanfani, L., *De Iure Parochorum ad normam Codicis Iuris Canonici*, Taurini-Romae, Marietti, 1924.

Rossi, Joseph, *De Impedimento Impotentiae*, Romae, 1910.

———*De Matrimonii Celebratione iuxta Codicem Iuris Canonici*, Romae: F. Pustet, 1924.

Sanchez, Thomas, *De Sancto Matrimonii Sacramento Disputationum Libri* Tres, 3 tomes, Venetiis, 1607.

Santi, Franciscus, *Praelectiones Iuris Canonici iuxta Ordinem Decretalium Gregorii IX*, 4. ed., 5 vols., a M. Leitner recognita Ratisbonae: Pustet, 1903-1905.

Schenck, Francis J., *The Matrimonial Impediments of Mixed Religion and Disparity of Cult*, The Catholic University of America Canon Law Studies, n. 51, Washington: The Catholic University of America, 1929.

O'Dea, John C., *The Matrimonial Impediment of Nonage*, The Catholic University of America Canon Law Studies, n. 205, Washington: The Catholic University of America Press, 1944.

O'Donnell, Cletus Francis, *The Marriages of Minors*, The Catholic University of America Canon Law Studies, n. 221, Washington: The Catholic University of America Press, 1946.

O'Mara, William A., *Canonicial Causes for Matrimonial Dispensations*. The Catholic University of America Canon Law Studies, n. 96, Washington: The Catholic University of America, 1935.

Panormitanus, Abbas (Nicolaus de Tudeschis), *Commentaria in Quinque Decretalium Lobros*, 5 vols., in 7, Venetiis, 1588.

Payen, G., *De Matrimonio in Missionibus ac Potissimum in Sinis Tractatus Practicus et Casus*, 2. ed., 3 vols., Z.-ka-wei: In Typographia T'ou-se-we, 1935-1936.

Quigley, Joseph, A., *Condemned Societies*, The Catholic University of America Canon Law Studies, n. 46, Washington: The Catholic University of America, 1927.

Rice, Patrick W., *Proof of Death in the Prenuptial Investigation*, The Catholic University of America Canon Law Studies, n. 123, Washington: The Catholic University of America Press, 1940.

Roberts, James B., *The Banns of Marriage*, The Catholic University of America Canon Law Studies, n. 64, Washington: The Catholic University of America, 1931.

Schroeder, H. J., *Disciplinary Decrees of the General Councils*, Text, Translation and Commentary, London-St. Louis: Herder, 1937.

Sullivan, Eugene Henry, *Proof of the Reception of the Sacraments*, The Catholic University of America Canon Law Studies, n. 209, Washington: The Catholic University of America Press, 1944.

Ter Haar, Francis, *Mixed Marriages and Their Remedies*, New York: F. Pustet Co., 1933.

Van Hove, A., *Commentarium Lovaniense in Codicem Iuris Canonici*, Vol. I, Tom. I, *Prolegomena*, 2. ed., Mechliniae-Romae: Dessain, 1945.

Vermeersch, A., *De Castitate et de Vitiis Contrariis*, Romae: Univ. Gregoriana, 1919.

Vermeersch, A.-Creusen, J., *Epitome Iuris Canonici*, 6. ed., 3 vols., Mechliniae-Romae, Dessain, 1937-1946.

Vlaming, Th. M., *Praelectiones Iuris Matrimonii ad Norman Codicis Iuris Canonici*, 3. ed., Bussum: Paul Brand, 1919-1921.

Vromant, G., *Ius Missionariorum*, Vol. V., *De Matrimonio*, Lovanii: Museum Lessianum, 1931.

Wahl, Francis X., *The Matrimonial Impediments of Consanguinity and Affinity*, The Catholic University of America Canon Law Studies, n. 90, Washington: The Catholic University of America, 1934,

Watkins, Oscar D., *Holy Matrimony*, New York, 1895.

Wernz, Franciscus X., *Ius Decretalium*, 6 vols., Romae, 1898-1905; Vol. IV, *Ius Matrimoniale*, 1904.

Wernz, F. X.-Vidal, P., *Ius Canonicum*. 7 vols., in 8, Romae: Apud Aedes Universititatis Gregorianae, 1928-1946; Vol. V, *Ius Matrimoniale*, 3. ed., a P. Aguirre recognita, 1946.

Woywod, S., *A Practical Commentary on the Code of Canon Law*, 7th printing, ed. by Callistus Smith, 2 vols, New York: Wagner, 1943.

Articles

Aguirre, Ph., "Brevis explanatio Instructionis"—*Periodica*, XXX (1941), 370-385.

Bastnagel, C., "Parish Assistants and the Prenuptial Investigation"—*The Jurist*, VII (1947), 171-174.

Donnelly, Francis B., "Fraud and Estoppel of Canon 1971, 1, n. I"—*The Jurist*, VI (1946), 378-400.

Gulovich, Stephen C., "Matrimonial Laws of the Catholic Eastern Churches"—*The Jurist*, IV (1944), 200-245.

Heneghan, John, "The Marriages of Unworthy Catholics: Canons 1065-1066"—*The Jurist*, V (1945), 389-437.

Kelly, James P., "Force and Fear Affecting Matrimonial Consent"—*The Jurist*, V. (1945), 514-532.

Quinn, Andrew F., "Defects in Marriage Consent"—*The Jurist*, V. (1945), 532-551.

Periodicals

American Ecclesiastical Review, The, Vols. I-XXXII, Philadelphia, 1895-1905; *The Ecclesiastical Review*, Vols. XXXIII-CIX, Philadelphia, 1905-1943; *The American Ecclesiastical Review*, Vol. CX, Washington, 1944-.

Jurist, The, Washington, 1941-.

Jus Pontificium, Romae, 1921-1940.

Periodica de Re Canonica, Morali, Liturgica, Brugis, 1927-.

Abbreviations

AAS—*Acta Apostolicae Sedis.*

C—*Codex Iustinianus.*

Coll. Lac.—*Collectio Lacensis.*

D—*Digesta Iustinianum.*

Fontes—*Codicis Iuris Canonici Fontes* cura . . . Gasparri editi.

JE—Jaffe, *Regesta Pontificum Romanorum* . . . section ed. by Ewald.

JK—Jaffe, op. cit., section ed. by Kaltenbrunner.

JL—Jaffe, *op. cit.*, section ed. by Loewenfeld.

Mansi—*Sacrorum Conciliorum Nova et Amplissima Collectio.*

MGH—*Monumenta Germaniae Historica.*

MPL—Migne, *Patrologia Latina.*

Pont. Comm. Cod. Inter.—Pontificia Commissio ad Codicis Canones Interpretandas.

S. C. C.—Sacra Congregatio Concilii.

S. C. de Sacramentis—Sacra Congregatio de Disciplina Sacramentorum.

S. C. S. Off.—Sacra Congregatio Sancti Officii.

BIOGRAPHICAL NOTE

Thomas B. Fulton was born on January 13, 1918, in St. Catharines, Ontario, Canada. He completed his elementary education at St. Nicholas' Separate School in that city. He received his secondary education at St. Catharines Collegiate Institute and Vocational School, from which institution he graduated in June, 1935. In September of the same year he entered St. Augustine's Seminary, Toronto, where he pursued his philosophical and theological studies. On June 7, 1941, he was ordained to the priesthood in St. Michael's Cathedral, Toronto. For the next four years he was assistant priest in the parishes of St. Paul the Apostle and St. Vincent de Paul, in Toronto. In September, 1945, he was enrolled in the School of Canon Law of the Catholic University of America in Washington, D.C., where he received the degree of the Baccalaureate in Canon Law in June, 1946, and the degree of the Licentiate in Canon Law in June, 1947.

INDEX

CANON LAW STUDIES*

1. Frebiks, Rev. Celestine A., C.PP.S., J.C.D., Religious Congregations in Their External Relations, 121 pp., 1916.
2. Galliher, Rev. Daniel M., O.P., J.C.D., Canonical Elections, 117 pp., 1917.
3. Borkowski, Rev. Aurelius L., O.F.M., J.C.D., De Confraternitatibus Ecclesiasticis, 136 pp., 1918.
4. Castillo, Rev. Cayo, J.C.D., Disertacion Historico-Canonica sobre la Potestad del Cabildo en Sede Vacante o Impedida del Vicario Capitular, 99 pp., 1919 (1918).
5. Kubelbeck, Rev. William J., S.T.B., J.C.D., The Sacred Penitentiaria and Its Relation to Faculties of Ordinaries and Priests, 129 pp., 1918.
6. Petrovits, Rev. Joseph J. C., S.T.D., J.C.D., The New Church Law on Matrimony, X-461 pp., 1919.
7. Hickey, Rev. John J., S.T.B., J.C.D., Irregularities and Simple Impediments in the New Code of Canon Law, 100 pp., 1920.
8. Klekotka, Rev. Peter J., S.T.B., J.C.D., Diocesan Consultors, 179 pp., 1920.
9. Wanenmacher, Rev. Francis, J.C.D., The Evidence in Ecclesiastical Procedure Affecting the Marriage Bond, 1920 (Printed 1935).
10. Golden, Rev. Henry Francis, J.C.D., Parochial Benefices in the New Code, IV-119 pp., 1921 (Printed 1925).
11. Koudelka, Rev. Charles J., J.C.D., Pastors, Their Rights and Duties According to the New Code of Canon Law, 211 pp., 1921.
12. Melo, Rev. Antonius, O.F.M., J.C.D., De Exemptione Regularium, X-188 pp., 1921.
13. Schaaf, Rev. Valentine Theodore, O.F.M., S.T.B., J.C.D., The Cloister, X-180 pp., 1921.
14. Burke, Rev. Thomas Joseph, S.T.D., J.C.D., Competence in Ecclesiastical Tribunals, IV-117 pp., 1922.
15. Leech, Rev. George Leo, J.C.D., A Comparative Study of the Constitution "Apostolicae Sedis" and the "Codex Juris Canonici," 179 pp., 1922.
16. Motry, Rev. Hubert Louis, S.T.D., J.C.D., Diocesan Faculties According to the Code of Canon Law, II-167 pp., 1922.
17. Murphy, Rev. George Lawrence, J.C.D., Delinquencies and Penalties in the Administration and the Reception of the Sacraments, IV-121 pp., 1923.
18. O'Reilly, Rev. John Anthony, S.T.B., J.C.D., Ecclesiastical Sepulture in the New Code of Canon Law, 11-129 pp., 1923.

*Below n. 100 only the following numbers are sitll avalable: Nn. 3, 4, 9, 25, 34, 57 and 75. Beginning with n. 100 only the following are unavailable: Nn. 100-111 inclusive, and n. 113.

19. MICHALICKA, REV. WENCESLAS CYRIL, O.S.B., J.C.D., Judicial Procedure in Dismissal of Clerical Exempt Religious, 107 pp., 1923.
20. DARGIN, REV. EDWARD VINCENT, S.T.B., J.C.D., Reserved Cases According to the Code of Canon Law, IV-103 pp., 1924.
21. GODFREY, REV. JOHN A., S.T.B., J.C.D., The Right of Patronage According to the Code of Canon Law, 153 pp., 1924.
22. HAGEDORN, REV. FRANCIS EDWARD, J.C.D., General Legislation on Indulgences, II-154 pp., 1924.
23. KING, REV. JAMES IGNATIUS, J.C.D., The Administration of the Sacraments to Dying Non-Catholics, V-141 pp., 1924.
24. WINSLOW, REV. FRANCIS JOSEPH, O.F.M., J.C.D., Vicars and Prefects Apostolic, IV-149 pp., 1924.
25. CORREA, REV. JOSE SERVELION, S.T.L., J.C.D., La Potestad Legislativa de la Iglesia Catolica, IV-127 pp., 1925.
26. DUGAN, REV. HENRY FRANCIS, A.M., J.C.D., The Judiciary Department of the Diocesan Curia, 87 pp., 1925.
27. KELLER, REV. CHARLES FREDERICK, S.T.B., J.C.D., Mass Stipends, 167 pp., 1925.
28. PASCHANG, REV. JOHN LINUS, J.C.D., The Sacramentals According to the Code of Canon Law, 129 pp., 1925.
29. PIONTEK, REV. CYRILLUS, O.F.M., S.T.B., J.C.D., De Indulto Exclaustrationis necnon Saecularizationis, XIII-289 pp., 1925.
30. KEARNEY, REV. RICHARD JOSEPH, S.T.B., J.C.D., Sponsors at Baptism According to the Code of Canon Law, IV-127 pp., 1925.
31. BARTLETT, REV. CHESTER JOSEPH, A.M., LL.B., J.C.D., The Tenure of Parochial Property in the United States of America, V-108 pp., 1926.
32. KILKER, REV. ADRIAN JEROME, J.C.D., Extreme Unction, V-425 pp., 1926.
33. McCORMICK, REV. ROBERT EMMETT, J.C.D., Confessors of Religious, VIII-266 pp., 1926.
34. MILLER, REV. NEWTON THOMAS, J.C.D., Founded Masses According to the Code of Canon Law, VII-93 pp., 1926.
35. ROELKER, REV. EDWARD G., S.T.D., J.C.D., Principles of Privilege According to the Code of Canon Law, XI-166 pp., 1926.
36. BAKALARCZYK, REV. RICHARDUS, M.I.C., J.U.D., De Novitiatu, VIII-208 pp., 1927.
37. PIZZUTI, REV. LAWRENCE, O.F.M., J.U.L., De Parochis Religiosis, 1927. (Not Printed.)
38. BLILEY, REV. NICHOLAS MARTIN, O.S.B., J.C.D., Altars According to the Code of Canon Law, XIX-132 pp., 1927.
39. BROWN, MR. BRENDAN FRANCIS, A.B., LL.M., J.U.D., The Canonical Juristic Personality with Special Reference to its Status in the United States of America, V-212 pp., 1927.
40. CAVANAUGH, REV. WILLIAM THOMAS, C.P., J.U.D., The Reservation of the Blessed Sacrament, VIII-101 pp., 1927.
41. DOHENY, REV. WILLIAM J., C.S.C., A.B., J.U.D., Church Property: Modes of Acquisition, X-118 pp., 1927.
42. FELDHAUS, REV. ALOYSIUS H., C.PP.S., J.C.D., Oratories, IX-141 pp., 1927.

43. Kelly, Rev. James Patrick, A.B., J.C.D., The Jurisdiction of the Simple Confessor, X-208 pp., 1927.
44. Neuberger, Rev. Nicholas J., J.C.D., Canon 6 or the Relation of the Codex Juris Canonici to the Preceding Legislation, V-95 pp., 1927.
45. O'Keefe, Rev. Gerald Michael, J.C.D., Matrimonial Dispensations, Powers of Bishops, Priests, and Confessors, VIII-232 pp., 1927.
46. Quigley, Rev. Joseph A. M., A.B., J.C.D., Condemned Societies, 139 pp., 1927.
47. Zaplotnik, Rev. Johannes Leo, J.C.D., De Vicariis Foraneis, X-142 pp., 1927.
48. Duskie, Rev. John Aloysius, A.B., J.C.D., The Canonical Status of the Orientals in the United States, VIII-196 pp., 1928.
49. Hyland, Rev. Francis Edward, J.C.D., Excommunication, Its Nature, Historical Development and Effects, VIII-181 pp., 1928.
50. Reinmann, Rev. Gerald Joseph, O.M.C., J.C.D., The Third Order Secular of Saint Francis, 201 pp., 1928.
51. Schenk, Rev. Francis J., J.C.D., The Matrimonial Impediments of Mixed Religion and Disparity of Cult, XVI-318 pp., 1929.
52. Coady, Rev. John Joseph, S.T.D., J.U.D., A.M., The Appointment of Pastors, VIII-150 pp., 1929.
53. Kay, Rev. Thomas Henry, J.C.D., Competence in Matrimonial Procedure, VIII-164 pp., 1929.
54. Turner, Rev. Sidney Joseph, C.P., J.U.D., The Vow of Poverty XLIX-217 pp., 1929.
55. Kearney, Rev. Raymond A., A.B., S.T.D., J.C.D., The Principles of Delegation, VII-149 pp., 1929.
56. Conran, Rev. Edward James, A.B., J.C.D., The Interdict, V-163 pp., 1930.
57. O'Neill, Rev. William H., J.C.D., Papal Rescripts of Favor, VII-218 pp., 1930.
58. Bastnagel, Rev. Clement Vincent, J.U.D., The Appointment of Parochial Adjutants and Assistants, XV-257 pp., 1930.
59. Ferry, Rev. William A., A.B., J.C.D., Stole Fees, V-136 pp., 1930.
60. Costello, Rev. John Michael, A.B., J.C.D., Domicile and Quasi-Domicile,VII-201 pp., 1930.
61. Kremer, Rev. Michael Nicholas, A.B., S.T.B., J.C.D., Church Support in the United States, VI-136 pp., 1930.
62. Angulo, Rev. Luis, C.M., J.C.D., Legislation de la Iglesia sobre la intencion en la application de la Santa Misa, VII-104 pp., 1931.
63. Frey, Rev. Wolfgang Norbert, O.S.B., A.B., J.C.D., The Act of Religious Profession, VIII-174 pp., 1931.
64. Roberts, Rev. James Brendan, A.B., J.C.D., The Banns of Marriage, XIV-104 pp., 1931.
65. Ryder, Rev. Raymond Aloysius, A.B., J.C.D., Simony, IX-151 pp., 1931.
66. Campagna, Rev. Angelo, Ph.D., J.U.D., Il Vicario Generale del Vescovo, VII-205 pp., 1931.

67 Cox, Rev. Joseph Godfrey, A.B., J.C.D., The Administration of Seminaries, VI-124 pp., 1931.

68. Gregory, Rev. Donald J., J.U.D., The Pauline Privilege, XV-165 pp., 1931.

69. Donohue, Rev. John F., J.C.D., The Impediment of Crime, VII-110 pp., 1931.

70. Dooley, Rev. Eugene A., O.M.I., J.C.D., Church Law on Sacred Relics, IX-143 pp., 1931.

71. Orth, Rev. Clement Raymond, O.M.C., J.C.D., The Approbation of Religious Institutes, 171 pp., 1931.

72. Pernicone, Rev. Joseph M., A.B., J.C.D., The Ecclesiastical Prohibition of Books, XII-267 pp., 1932.

73. Clinton, Rev. Connell, A.B., J.C.D., The Paschal Precept, IX-108 pp., 1932.

74. Donnelly, Rev. Francis B., A.M., S.T.L., J.C.D., The Diocesan Synod, VIII-125 pp., 1932.

75. Torrente, Rev. Camilo, C.M.F., J.C.D., Las Procesiones Sagradas, V-145 pp., 1932.

76. Murphy, Rev. Edwin J., C.PP.S., J.C.D., Suspension Ex Informata Conscientia, XI-122 pp., 1932.

77. MacKenzie, Rev. Eric F., A.M., S.T.L., J.C.D., The Delict of Heresy in its Commission, Penalization, Absolution, VII-124 pp., 1932.

78. Lyons, Rev. Avitus E., S.T.B., J.C.D., The Collegiate Tribunal of First Instance, XI-147 pp., 1932.

79. Connolly, Rev. Thomas A., J.C.D., Appeals, XI-195 pp., 1932.

80. Sangmeister, Rev. Joseph V., A.B., J.C.D., Force and Fear as Precluding Matrimonial Consent, V-211 pp., 1932.

81. Jaeger, Rev. Leo A., A.B., J.C.D., The Administration of Vacant and Quasi-Vacant Episcopal Sees in the United States, IX-229 pp., 1932.

82. Rimlinger, Rev. Herbert T. J.C.D., Error Invalidating Matrimonial Consent, VII-79 pp., 1932.

83. Barrett, Rev. John D. M., S.S., J.C.D., A Comparative Study of the Third Plenary Council of Baltimore and the Code, IX-221 pp., 1932.

84. Carberry, Rev. John J., Ph.D., S.T.D., J.C.D., The Juridical Form of Marriage, X-177 pp., 1934.

85. Dolan, Rev. John L., A.B., J.C.D., The Defensor Vinculi, XII-157 pp., 1934.

86. Hannan, Rev. Jerome D., A.M., S.T.D., LL.B., J.C.D., The Canon Law of Wills, IX-517 pp., 1934.

87. Lemieux, Rev. Delise A., A.M., J.C.D., The Sentence in Ecclesiastical Procedure, IX-131 pp., 1934.

88. O'Rourke, Rev. James J., A.B., J.C.D., Parish Registers, VII-109 pp., 1934.

89. Timlin, Rev. Bartholomew, O.F.M., A.M., J.C.D., Conditional Matrimonial Consent, X-381 pp., 1934.

90. Wahl, Rev. Francis X., A.B., J.C.D., The Matrimonial Impediments of Consanguinity and Affinity, VI-125 pp., 1934.

91. White, Rev. Robert J., A.B., LL.B., S.T.B., J.C.D., Canonical Ante-Nuptial Promises and the Civil Law, VI-152 pp., 1934.
92. Herrera, Rev. Antonio Parra, O.C.D., J.C.D., Legislacion Eclesiastica sobra el Ayuno y la Abstinencia, XI-191 pp., 1935.
93. Kennedy, Rev. Edwin J., J.C.D., The Special Matrimonial Process in Cases of Evident Nullity, X-165 pp., 1935.
94. Manning, Rev. John J., A.B., J.C.D., Presumption of Law in Matrimonial Procedure, XI-111 pp., 1935.
95. Moeder, Rev. John M., J.C.D., The Proper Bishop for Ordination and Dimissorial Letters, VII-135 pp., 1935.
96. O'Mara, Rev. William A., A.B., J.C.D., Canonical Causes for Matrimonial Dispensations, IX-155 pp., 1935.
97. Reilly, Rev. Peter, J.C.D., Residence of Pastors, IX-81 pp., 1935.
98. Smith, Rev. Mariner T., O.P., S.T.Lr., J.C.D., The Penal Law for Religious, VII-169 pp., 1935.
99. Whalen, Rev. Donald W., A.M., J.C.D., The Value of Testimonial Evidence in Matrimonial Procedure, XIII-297 pp., 1935.
100. Cleary, Rev. Joseph F., J.C.D., Canonical Limitations on the Alienation of Church Property, VIII-141 pp., 1936.
101. Glynn, Rev. John C., J.C.D., The Promoter of Justice, XX-337 pp., 1936.
102. Brennan, Rev. James H., S.S., M.A., S.T.B., J.C.D., The Simple Convalidation of Marriage, VI-135 pp., 1937.
103. Bunini, Rev. Joseph Bernard, J.C.D., The Clerical Obligations of Canons 139 and 142, X-121 pp., 1937.
104. Connor, Rev. Maurice, A.B., J.C.D,. The Administrative Removal of Pastors, VIII-159 pp., 1937.
105. Guilfoyle, Rev. Merlin Joseph, J.C.D., Custom, XI-144 pp., 1937.
106. Hughes, Rev. James Austin, A.B., A.M., J.C.D.,. Witnesses in Criminal Trials of Clerics, IX-140 pp., 1937.
107. Jansen, Rev. Raymond J., A.B., S.T.L., J.C.D., Canonical Provisions for Catechetical Instruction, VII-153 pp., 1937.
108. Kealy, Rev. John James, A.B., J.C.D., The Introductory Libellus in Church Court Procedure, XI-121 pp., 1937.
109. McManus, Rev. James Edward, C.SS.R., J.C.D., The Administration of Temporal Goods in Religious Institutes, XVI-196 pp., 1937.
110. Moriarty, Rev. Eugene James, J.C.D., Oaths in Ecclesiastical Courts, X-115 pp., 1937.
111. Rainer, Rev. Eligius George, C.SS.R., J.C.D., Suspension of Clerics, XVII-249 pp., 1937.
112. Reilly, Rev. Thomas F., C.SS.R., J.C.D., Visitation of Religious, VI-195 pp., 1938.
113. Moriarity, Rev. Francis E., C.SS.R., J.C.D., The Extraordinary Absolution from Censures, XV-334 pp., 1938.
114. Connolly, Rev. Nicholas P., J.C.D., The Canonical Erection of Parishes, X-132 pp., 1938.
115. Donovan, Rev. James Joseph, J.C.D., The Pastor's Obligation in Prenuptial Investigation, XII-322 pp., 1938.

116. HARRIGAN, REV. ROBERT J., M.A., S.T.B., J.C.D., The Radical Sanation of Invalid Marriages, XII-236 pp., 1939.

117. BOFFA, REV. CONRAD HUMBERT, J.C.D., Canonical Provisions for Catholic Schools, VII-211 pp., 1939.

118. PARSONS, REV. ANSCAR JOHN, O.M.Cap., J.C.D., Canonical Elections,XII-236 pp., 1939.

119. REILLY, REV. EDWARD MICHAEL, A.B., J.C.D., The General Norms of Dispensation, XII-156 pp., 1939.

120. RYAN, REV. GERALD ALOYSIUS, A.B., J.C.D., Principles of Episcopal Jurisdiction, XII-172 pp., 1939.

121. BURTON, REV. FRANCIS JAMES, C.S.C., A.B., J.C.D. A Commentary on Canon 1125, X-222 pp., 1940.

122. MIASKIEWICZ, REV. FRANCIS SIGISMUND, J.C.D., Supplied Jurisdiction According to Canon 209, XII-340 pp., 1940.

123. RICE, REV. PATRICK WILLIAM, A.B., J.C.D., Proof of Death in Prenuptial Investigation, VIII-156 pp., 1940.

124. ANGLIN, REV. THOMAS FRANCIS, M.S., J.C.D., The Eucharistic Fast, VIII-183 pp., 1941.

125. COLEMAN, REV. JOHN JEROME, J.C.D., The Minister of Confirmation, VI-153 pp., 1941.

126. DOWNS, REV. JOSEPH EMMANUEL, A.B., J.C.D., The Concept of Clerical Immunity, XI-163 pp., 1941.

127. ESSWEIN, REV. ANTHONY ALBERT, J.C.D., Extrajudicial Penal Powers of Ecclesiastical Superiors, X-144 pp., 1941.

128. FARRELL, REV. BENJAMIN FRANCIS, M.A., S.T.L., J.C.D., The Rights and Duties of the Local Ordinary Regarding Congregations of Women Religious of Pontifical Approval, V-195 pp., 1941.

129. FEENEY, REV. THOMAS JOHN, A.B., S.T.L., J.C.D., Restitutio in Integrum, VI-169 pp., 1941.

130. FINDLAY, REV. STEPHEN WILLIAM, O.S.B., A.B., J.C.D., Canonical Norms Governing the Deposition and Degradation of Clerics, XVII-279 pp., 1941.

131. GOODWINE, REV. JOHN, A.B., S.T.L., J.C.D., The Right of the Church to Acquire Property, VIII-119 pp., 1941.

132. HESTON, REV. EDWARD LOUIS, C.S.C., PH.D., S.T.D., J.C.D., The Alienation of Church Property in the United States, XII-222 pp., 1941.

133. HOGAN, REV. JAMES JOHN, A.B., S.T.L., J.C.D., Judicial Advocates and Procurators, XIII-200 pp., 1941.

134. KEALY, REV. THOMAS M., A.B., LITT.D., J.C.D., Dowry of Women Religious, IX-152 pp., 1941.

135. KEENE, REV. MICHAEL JAMES, O.S.B., J.C.D., Religious Ordinaries and Canon 198, V-164 pp., 1942.

136. KERIN, REV. CHARLES A., S.S., M.A., S.T.B., J.C.D., The Privation of Christian Burial, XVI-279 pp., 1941.

137. LOUIS, REV. WILLIAM FRANCIS, M.A., J.C.D., Diocesan Archives, X-101 pp., 1941.

138. MCDEVITT, REV. GILBERT JOSEPH, A.B., J.C.D., Legitimacy and Legitimation, X-247 pp., 1941.

139. McDonough, Rev. Thomas Joseph, A.B., J.C.D., Apostolic Administrators, X-217 pp., 1941.

140. Meier, Rev. Carl Anthony, A.B., J.C.D., Penal Administration Procedure Against Negligent Pastors, XI-240 pp., 1941.

141. Schmidt, Rev. John Rogg, A.B., J.C.D., The Principles of Authentic Interpretation in Canon 17 of the Code of Canon Law, XII-331 pp., 1941.

142. Slafkosky, Rev. Andrew Leonard, A.B., J.C.D., The Canonical Episcopal Visitation of the Diocese, X-197 pp., 1941.

143. Swoboda, Rev. Innocent Robert, O.F.M., J.C.D., Ignorance in Relation to the Imputability of Delicts, IX-271 pp., 1941.

144. Dube, Rev. Arthur Joseph, A.B., J.C.D., The General Principles for the Reckoning of Time in Canon Law, VIII-299 pp., 1941.

145. McBride, Rev. James T., A.B., J.C.D., Incardination and Excardination of Seculars, XX-585 pp., 1941.

146. Krol, Rev. John T., J.C.D., The Defendant in Ecclesiastical Trials, XII-207 pp., 1942.

147. Comyns, Rev. Joseph J., C.SS.R., A.B., J.C.D., Papal and Episcopal Administration of Church Property, XIV-155 pp., 1942.

148. Barry, Rev. Garrett Francis, O.M.I., J.C.D., Violation of the Cloister, XII-260 pp., 1942.

149. Bolduc, Rev. Gatien, C.S.V., A.B., S.T.L., J.C.D., Les Etudes dans les Religions Cléricales, VIII-155 pp., 1942.

150. Boyle, Rev. David John, M.A., J.C.D., The Juridic Effects of Moral Certitude on Pre-Nuptial Guarantees, XII-188 pp., 1942.

151. Canavan, Rev. Walter Joseph, M.A., Litt.D., J.C.D., The Profession of Faith, XII-143 pp., 1942.

152. Desrochers, Rev. Bruno, A.B., Ph.L., S.T.B., J.C.D., Le Premier Concile Plénier de Québec et le Code de Droit Canonique, XIV-186 pp., 1942.

153. Dillon, Rev. Robert Edward, A.B., J.C.D., Common Law Marriage, X-148 pp., 1942.

154. Dodwell, Rev. Edward John, Ph.D., S.T.B., J.C.D., The Time and Place for the Celebration of Marriage, X-156 pp., 1942.

155. Donnellan, Rev. Thomas Andrew, A.B., J.C.D., The Obligation of the Missa pro Populo, VII-131 pp., 1942.

156. Eltz, Rev. Louis Anthony, A.B., J.C.L., Cooperation in Crime.

157. Gass, Rev. Sylvester Francis, M.A., J.C.D., Ecclesiastical Pensions, XI-206 pp., 1942.

158. Guiniven, Rev. John Joseph, C.SS.R., J.C.D. ,The Precept of Hearing Mass, XIV-188 pp., 1942.

159. Gulczynski, Rev. John Theophilus, J.C.D., The Desecration and Violation of Churches, X-126 pp., 1942.

160. Hammill, Rev. John Leo, M.A. J.C.D., The Obligations of the Traveler According to Canon 14, VIII-204 pp., 1942.

161. Haydt, Rev. John Joseph, A.B., J.C.D., Reserved Benefices, XI-148 pp., 1942.

162. Huser, Rev. Roger John, O.F.M., A.B., J.C.D., The Crime of Abortion in Canon Law, XII-187 pp., 1942.

163. KEARNEY, REV. FRANCIS PATRICK, A.B., S.T.L., J.C.L., The Principles of Canon 1127.

164. LINAHEN, REV. LEO JAMES, S.T.L., J.C.D., De Absolutione Complicis In Peccato Turpi, 114 pp., 1942.

165. MCCLOSKEY, REV. JOSEPH ALOYSIUS, A.B., J.C.D., The Subject of Ecclesiastical Law According to Canon 12, XVII-246 pp., 1942.

166. O'NEILL, REV. FRANCIS JOSEPH, C.SS.R., J.C.D., The Dismissal of Religious in Temporary Vows, XIII-220 pp., 1942.

167. PRINCE, REV. JOHN EDWARD, A.B., S.T.D., J.C.D., The Diocesan Chancellor, X-136 pp., 1942.

168. RIESNER, REV. ALBERT JOSEPH, C.SS.R., J.C.D., Apostates and Fugitives from Religious Institutes, IX-168 pp., 1942.

169. STENGER, REV. JOSEPH BERNARD, J.C.D., The Mortgaging of Church Property, 186 pp., 1942.

170. WALDRON, REV. JOSEPH FRANCIS, A.B., J.C.D., The Minister of Baptism, XII-197 pp., 1942.

171. WILLETT, REV. ROBERT ALBERT, J.C.D., The Probative Value of Documents in Ecclesiastical Trials, X-124 pp., 1942.

172. WOEBER, REV. EDWARD MARTIN, M.A., J.C.D., The Interpellations, XII-161 pp., 1942.

173. BENKO, REV. MATTHEW ALOYSIUS, O.S.B., M.A., J.C.L., The Abbot *Nullius.*

174. CHRIST, REV. JOSEPH JAMES, M.A., S.T.L., J.C.L., Dispensation from Vindicative Penalties.

175. CLANCY, REV. PATRICK M. J., O.P., A.B., S.T.Lr., J.C.D., The Local Religious Superior, X-299 pp., 1943.

176. CLARKE, REV. THOMAS JAMES, J.C.D., Parish Societies, XII-147 pp., 1943.

177. CONNOLLY, REV. JOHN PATRICK, S.T.L., J.C.D., Synodal Examiners and Parish Priest Consultors, X-223 pp., 1943.

178. DRUMM, REV. WILLIAM MARTIN, A.B., J.C.L., Hospital Chaplains.

179. FLANAGAN, REV. BERNARD JOSEPH, A.B., S.T.L., J.C.D., The Canonical Erection of Religious Houses, X-147 pp., 1943.

180. KELLEHER, REV. STEPHEN JOSEPH, A.B., S.T.B., J.C.D., Discussions with non-Catholics: Canonical Legislation, X-93 pp., 1943.

181. LEWIS, REV. GORDIAN, C.P., J.C.D., Chapters in Religious Institutes, XII-169 pp., 1943.

182. MARX, REV. ADOLPH, J.C.D., The Declaration of Nullity of Marriages Contracted Outside the Church, X-151 pp., 1943.

183. MATULENAS, REV. RAYMOND ANTHONY, O.S.B., A.B., J.C.L., Communication, a Source of Privileges.

184. O'LEARY, REV. CHARLES GERARD, C.SS.R., J.C.D., Religious Dismissed After Perpetual Profession, X-213 pp., 1943.

185. POWER, REV. CORNELIUS MICHAEL, J.C.L., The Blessing of Cemeteries.

186. SHUHLER, REV. RALPH VINCENT, O.S.A., J.C.D., Privileges of Regulars to Absolve and Dispense, XII-195 pp., 1943.

187. ZIOLKOWSKI, REV. THADDEUS STANISLAUS, A.B., J.C.D., The Consecration and Blessing of Churches, XII-151 pp., 1943.

188. HENEGHAN, REV. JOHN JOSEPH, S.T.D., J.C.L., The Marriages of Unworthy Catholics: Canons 1065 and 1066.

189. CARROLL, REV. COLEMAN FRANCIS, M.A., S.T.L., J.C.L., Charitable Institutions.

190. CIESLUK, REV. JOSEPH EDWARD, Ph.B., S.T.L., J.C.L., National Parishes in the United States.

191. COBURN, REV. VINCENT PAUL, A.B., J.C.L., Marriages of Conscience.

192. CONNORS, REV. CHARLES PAUL, C.S.Sp., A.B., J.C.L., Extra-Judicial Procurators in the Code of Canon Law.

193. COYLE, REV. PAUL RAYMOND, A.B., J.C.L., Judicial Exceptions.

194. FAIR, REV. BARTHOLOMEW FRANCIS, A.B., S.T.L., J.C.L., The Impediment of Abduction.

195. GALLAGHER, REV. THOMAS RAPHAEL, O.P., A.B., S.T.Lr., J.C.L., The Examination of the Qualities of the Ordinand.

196. GANNON, REV. JOHN MARK, S.T.L., J.C.L., The Interstices Required for the Promotion to Orders.

197. GOLDSMITH, REV. J. WILLIAM, B.C.S., S.T.L., J.C.L., The Competence of Church and State over Marriage—Disputed Points.

198. GOODWINE, REV. JOSEPH GERARD, A.B., S.T.B., J.C.L., The Reception of Converts.

199. KOWALSKI, REV. ROMUALD EUGENE, O.F.M., A.B., J.C.L., Sustenance of Religious Houses of Regulars.

200. MCCOY, REV. ALAN EDWARD, O.F.M., J.C.L., Force and Fear in Relation to Delictual Imputability and Penal Responsibility.

201. MCDEVITT, REV. VINCENT JOHN, Ph.B., S.T.L., J.C.L., Perjury.

202. MARTIN, REV. THOMAS OWEN, Ph.D., S.T.D., J.C.L., Adverse Possession, Prescription and Limitation of Actions: The Canonical "Praescriptio."

203. MIKLOSOVIC, REV. PAUL JOHN, A.B., J.C.L., Attempted Marriages and Their Consequent Juridic Effects.

204. MUNDY, REV. THOMAS MAURICE, A.B., S.T.L., J.C.L., The Union of Parishes.

205. O'DEA, REV. JOHN COYLE, A.B., J.C.L., The Matrimonial Impediment of Nonage.

206. OLALIA, REV. ALEXANDER AYSON, S.T.L., J.C.L., A Comparative Study of the Christian Constitution of States and the Constitution of the Philippine Commonwealth.

207. POISSON, REV. PIERRE-MARIE, C.S.C., A.B., Ph.L., Th.L., J.C.L., Droits Patrimoniaux des Maisons et des Eglises Religieuses.

208. STADALNIKAS, REV. CASIMIR JOSEPH, M.I.C., J.C.L., Reservation of Censures.

209. SULLIVAN, REV. EUGENE HENRY, S.T.L., J.C.L., Proof of the Reception of the Sacraments.

210. VAUGHAN, REV. WILLIAM EDWARD, J.C.L., Constitutions for Diocesan Courts.

211. PARO, REV. GINO, S.T.D., J.C.L., The Right of Apostolic Legation.

212. BALZER, REV. RALPH FRANCIS, C.P., J.C.L., The Computation of Time in a Canonical Novitiate.

213. DOUGHERTY, REV. JOHN WHELAN, A.B., S.T.L., J.C.L., De Inquisitione Speciali.

214. Dziob, Rev. Michael Walter, J.C.L., The Sacred Congregation for the Oriental Church.

215. Eidenschink, Rev. John Albert, O.S.B., B.A., J.C.L., The Election of Bishops in the Letters of Pope Gregory the Great.

216. Gill, Rev. Nicholas, C.P., J.C.L., The Spiritual Prefect in Clerical Religious Houses of Study.

217. Hynes, Rev. Harry Gerard, S.T.L., J.C.D., The Privileges of Cardinals, XII-183 pp., 1945.

218. McDevitt, Rev. Gerard Vincent, S.T.L., J.C.D., The Renunciation of an Ecclesiastical Office, XIV—179 pp., 1946.

219. Manning, Rev. Joseph Leroy, J.C.L., The Free Conferral of Offices.

220. Meyer, Rev. Louis G., O.S.B., A.B., S.T.B., J.C.D., Alms-Gathering by Religious, XII—163 pp., 1946.

221. O'Donnell, Rev. Cletus Francis, M.A., J.C.D., The Marriage of Minors, XII-268 pp., 1945.

222. Prunskis, Rev. Joseph, J.C.D., Comparative Law, Ecclesiastical and Civil, in Lithuanian Concordat, X-161 pp., 1945.

223. Sweeney, Rev. Francis Patrick, C.SS.R., J.C.D., The Reduction of Clerics to the Lay State, X-199 pp., 1945.

224. Vogelpohl, Rev. Henry John, J.C.D., The Simple Impediments to Holy Orders, XVI-190 pp., 1945.

225. Brockhaus, Rev. Thomas Aquinas, O.S.B., J.C.D., Religious Who Are Known as *Conversi*, X-127 pp., 1945.

226. Griese, Rev. N. Orville, S.T.D., J.C.D., The Marriage Contract and the Procreation of Offspring, XVI-224 pp., 1946.

227. Boudreaux, Rev. Warren Louis, J.C.D., The "*ab acatholicis nati*" of Canon 1099, § 2, XII-110 pp., 1946.

228. Bowe, Rev. Thomas Joseph, A.B., J.C.D., Religious Superioresses, VIII-206 pp., 1946.

229. Diederichs, Rev. Michael Ferdinand, S.C.J., J.C.D., The Jurisdiction of the Latin Ordinaries Over Their Oriental Subjects, XIV-153 pp., 1946.

230. Dingman, Rev. Maurice John, A.B., S.T.L. J.C.L., The Plaintiff in Contentious Trials.

231. Frison, Rev. Basil, C.M.F., M.Mus., J.C.D., The Retroactivity of Law, X-221 pp., 1946.

232. Galvin, Rev. William Anthony, M.A., J.C.D., The Administrative Tranfer of Pastors, XII-288 pp., 1946.

233. Goracy, Rev. Joseph C., J.C.L., The Diriment Matrimonial Impediment of Major Orders.

234. Hale, Rev. Joseph Francis, M.A., S.T.L., J.C.L., The Pastor of Burial.

235. Henry, Rev. Joseph Arthur, A.B., J.C.D., The Mass and Holy Communion: Inter-Ritual Law, XII-138 pp., 1946.

236. Linenberger, Rev. Herbert, C.PP.S., J.C.L., The False Denunciation of an Innocent Confessor.

237. Lowry, Rev. James Martin, A.B., J.C.D., Dispensation from Private Vows, XII-266 pp., 1946.

238. LYNCH, REV. GEORGE EDWARD, A.B., S.T.L., J.C.D., Coadjutors and Auxiliaries of Bishops, X-107 pp., 1947.

239. LYNCH, REV. TIMOTHY, M.S.SS.T., J.C.D., Contracts Between Bishops and Religious Congregations, XIV-232 pp., 1946.

240. MCCLUNN, REV. JUSTIN DAVID, A.B., S.T.L., J.C.D., Administrative Recourse, VII-142 pp., 1946.

241. LOHMULLER, REV. MARTIN NICHOLAS, A.B., J.C.D., The Promulgation of Law, XII-140 pp., 1947.

242. MCGRATH, REV. JAMES, A.B., J.C.D., The Privilege of the Canon, XII-156 pp., 1946.

243. MARBACH, REV. JOSEPH FRANCIS, A.B., J.C.D., Marriage Legislation for the Catholics of the Oriental Rites in the United States and Canada, XIV-314 pp., 1946.

244. SHIMKUS, REV. BERNARD ALOYSIUS, A.B., J.C.L., The Determination and Transfer of Rite.

245. SMITH, REV. VINCENT MICHAEL, A.B., S.T.L., J.C.L., Ignorance Affecting Matrimonial Consent.

246. WACHTELE, REV. PAUL ANTHONY, A.B., J.C.L., The Baptism of the Children of Non-Catholics.

247. CROTTY, REV. MATTHEW MICHAEL, J.C.D., The Recipient of First Holy Communion, X-142 pp., 1947.

248. EAGLETON, REV. GEORGE, J.C.L., The Quinquennial Faculties, Formula IV.

249. GIBBONS, REV. MARION LEO, C.M., LL.B., J.C.D., Domicile of the Wife Unlawfully Separated from Her Husband, XIV-171 pp., 1947.

250. KELLY, REV. BERNARD MATTHEW, S.T.L., J.C.D., The Functions Reserved to Pastors, XII-141 pp., 1947.

251. KILCULLEN, REV. THOMAS JOHN, LL.M., J.C.D., The Collegiate Moral Person as Party Litigant, X-150 pp., 1947.

252. LAFONTAINE, REV. GERMAIN JOSEPH, W.F., J.C.L., Relations Canoniques entre le Missionnaire et Ses Superieurs.

253. LANE, REV. LORAS THOMAS, A.B., S.T.L., J.C.L., Matrimonial Procedure in the Ordinary Court of Second Instance.

254. LOVER, REV. JAMES FRANCIS, C.SS.R., J.C.D., The Master of Novices, X-168 pp., 1947.

255. MCNICHOLAS, REV. TIMOTHY JOSEPH, J.C.L., The *Septimae Manus* Witness.

256. MAROSITZ, REV. JOSEPH JOHN, M.S.C., J.C.D., Obligations and Privileges of Religious Promoted to the Episcopal or Cardinalatial Dignities, XII-180 pp., 1947.

257. MURPHY, REV. FRANCIS JOSEPH, A.B., J.C.D., Legislative Powers of the Provincial Council, XII-158 pp., 1947.

258. O'BRIEN, REV. ROMAEUS WILLIAM, O.CARM., J.C.D., The Provincial Superior in Religious Orders of Men, X-294 pp., 1947.

259. PFALLER, REV. BENEDICT AUGUSTINE, O.S.B., J.C.L., The *Ipso Facto* Effected Dismissal of Religious.

260. POPEK, REV. ALPHONSE SYLVESTER, M.A., J.C.D., The Rights and Obligations of Metropolitans, XVIII-460 pp., 1947.

261. Ristuccia, Rev. Bernard Joseph, C.M., J.C.L., Quasi-Religious.
262. Sonntag, Rev. Nathaniel Louis, O.F.M.Cap., J.C.D., Censorship of Special Classes of Books, XII-147 pp., 1947.
263. Stadler, Rev. Joseph Nicholas, J.C.L., Frequent Holy Communion.
264. Szal, Rev. Ignatius Joseph, J.C.L., The Communication of Catholics with Schismatics.
265. Wagner, Rev. Urban Stanley, O.F.M.Conv., J.C.D., Parochial Substitute Vicars and Supplying Priests, X-126 pp., 1947.
266. Quinn, Rev. Joseph, M.A., J.C.L., Documents Required for the Reception of Orders.
267. Bennington, Rev. James Clement, A.B., J.C.L., The Recipient of Confirmation.
268. Blaher, Rev. Damian Joseph, O.F.M., A.B., J.C.L., The Ordinary Processes in Causes of Beatification and Canonization.
269. Clune, Rev. Robert Bell, B.A., J.C.L. Judicial Interrogation of the Parties.
270. Courtemanche, Rev. Basil F., B.A., J.C.L., The Total Simulation of Matrimonial Consent.
271. Dlouhy, Rev. Maur John, O.S.B. A,B., J.C.L., The Ordination of Exempt Religious.
272. Donovan, Rev. John Thomas, Ph.B., S.T.L., J.C.L., The Clerical Obligations of Canons 138 and 140.
273. Freking, Rev. Frederick W., A.B., S.T.B., J.C.L., The Canonical Installation of Pastors.
274. Fulton, Rev. Thomas B., J.C.L., Prenuptial Investigation.
275. Godley, Rev. James P., J.C.L. The Time and the Place for the Celebration of Mass.
276. Kane, Rev. Thomas A., A.B., B.S., J.C.L., Jurisdiction of Patriarchs until 1439.
277. Kennedy, Rev. Andrew A., J.C.L., The Annual Pastoral Report to the Local Ordinary.
278. Konrad, Rev. Joseph George, J.C.L., Transfer of Religious.
279. Kress, Rev. Alphonse, J.C.L., Contumacy in Ecclesiastical Trials.
280. McCartney, Rev. Marcellus Anthony, O.F.M., M.A., J.C.L., Faculties of Regular Confessors.
281. McCaslin, Rev. Edward Patrick, M.A., S.T.L., J.C.L., The Division of Parishes.
282. McElroy, Rev. Francis J., A.B., J.C.L., The Privileges of Bishops.
283. Quinn, Rev. Stephen, M.S.SS.T., J.C.L., Relation between the Local Ordinary and Religious of Diocesan Approval.
284. Schneider, Rev. Edelhard Louis, S.D.S., M.A., J.C.L., The Status of Secularized Ex-Religious Clerics.
285. Thompson, Rev. Chester J., A.B., J.C.L., The Simple Removal from Office.

www.ingramcontent.com/pod-product-compliance
Lightning Source LLC
LaVergne TN
LVHW050237080826
844660LV00012B/549
* 9 7 8 0 8 1 3 2 2 4 5 2 7 *